Manliness and morality

Middle-class masculinity
in Britain and America
1800–1940

J. A. MANGAN
and JAMES WALVIN *editors*

Manchester University Press

Published by MANCHESTER UNIVERSITY PRESS
Oxford Road, Manchester M13 9PL

British Library cataloguing in publication data
Manliness and morality: middle-class masculinity in Britain and America, 1800-1940.
1. Men — United States 2. Masculinity (Psychology)
3. Men — Great Britain
I. Mangan J. A. II. Walvin, James
305.3'1'0941   HQ11090

ISBN 0 7190 2240 1 *hardback*

Typeset in Galliard by Koinonia Ltd, Manchester

*Printed in Great Britain
at the Alden Press, Oxford*

Contents

Illustrations

Notes on contributors

Robert J. Higgs is Professor of English at East Tennessee State University, Johnson City, Tennessee. His publications include *The Sporting Spirit: Athletes in Literature and Life* (co-editor with Neil D. Isaacs, 1977), *Laurel and Thorn: The Athlete in American Literature* (1981) and *Sports: A Reference Guide* (1982).

John MacKenzie is Senior Lecturer in History at the University of Lancaster. He is the author of *Propaganda and Empire*, (1984) editor of *Imperialism and Popular Culture*, (1986) co-author of *The Railway Station, a Social History*, (1986) and general editor of the 'Studies in Imperialism' series (Manchester University Press).

J. A. Mangan is Head of Education at Jordanhill College, Glasgow. He is author of *Athleticism in the Victorian and Edwardian Public School: The emergence and consolidation of an educational ideology* (1981) and *The Games Ethic and Imperialism: Aspects of the Diffusion of an Ideal* (1986), editor of *Socialization, Education and Imperialism* (forthcoming) and *Pleasure, Profit and Proselytism: British culture and sport at home and abroad 1700–1914* (1987) and general editor of the 'International Studies in the Social History of Sport' series (Manchester University Press). He is also founder and general executive editor of *The International Journal of the History of Sport*.

Donald J. Mrozek is Professor of History at Kansas State University. He is the author of *Sport and American Mentality, 1880-1910* (1983) and has edited special issues of the *Journal of the West* on 'Sports and Recreation in the West' (1978) and 'Sports in the West' (1983). He has also researched and published extensively in American military history and strategic policy. He is co-editor of *A Guide to the Sources of U.S. Military History, Supplements I and II* (Hamden CT: 1981, 1986) and has published in journals such as *Military Affairs*.

Roberta J. Park is Professor of Physical Education at the University of California, Berkeley. She has published in *Research Quarterly for Exercise and Sport, Quest, The British Journal of Sports History* and other academic journals, and is co-editor of *Play, Games and Sports in Cultural Contexts* (1984).

Benjamin G. Rader is Professor of History at the University of Nebraska, Lincoln, Nebraska. Recent publications include *American Sports: From the Age of Folk Games to the Age of Spectators* (1983) and *In Its Own Image: How Television Has Transformed Sports* (1984)

Jeffrey Richards is Senior Lecturer in History at the University of Lancaster and author of *Age of the Dream Palace* (1984). He is co-author of *Britain Can Take It: British Cinema in the Second World War* (1986) and *The Railway Station: A Social History* (1986).

E. Anthony Rotundo is Instructor in History and Social Sciences at Phillips Academy, Andover, Massachusetts. He has published in the *Journal of Social History,* the *American Behavioural Scientist,* and other academic journals.

John Springhall is Lecturer in History in the Faculty of Humanities at the University of Ulster at Coleraine, Northern Ireland. He is the author of *Youth, Empire and Society: British Youth Movements, 1883-1940* (1977) and the editor of *Sure and Stedfast: A History of the Boys' Brigade, 1883-1983* (1983).

Peter N. Stearns is Heinz Professor of History at Carnegie-Mellon University, Pittsburgh, and editor of the *Journal of Social History.* Relevant publications include *Be a Man: Males in Modern Society* (1979) and *Anger: The Struggle for Emotional Control in America's History* (1986).

James Walvin is Reader in History at the University of York.

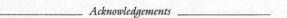

_____ *Acknowledgements* _____

First and foremost, we should like to thank the contributors to this volume for their involvement. Their enthusiasm for the idea has made its preparation a particular pleasure. We should like to express also our appreciation of the always courteous and constructive encouragement of John Banks of Manchester University Press. We are indebted to Doris Mangan for her efforts, as reader, grammarian and indexer, to save us from sins of both omission and commission. Finally, the usual acknowledgement is made with thanks to the Editor of *Stadion* for permission to reproduce J. A. Mangan's, 'Social Darwinism, Sport and English Upper Class Education' which first appeared in the journal in Vol. II, No. 1, Spring 1981. Photographs of the Scout Movement are by courtesy of the Scout Association.

J. A. M.
J. W.

J. A. MANGAN *and* JAMES WALVIN

Introduction

As Burnstyn's *Victorian Education and the Ideal of Womanhood* and Dyhouse's *Girls Growing up in late Victorian and Edwardian England* illustrate, there is considerable contemporary concern with the Victorian and Edwardian construction of female identity and the upper middle class conditioning which produced adherence to a narrow, restricted, inhibited concept of feminity. The nineteenth-century image of the male was a product of the same social forces, equally potent in their influence and similarly deserving of the attention of social and cultural historians. Both these significant concepts of the recent past have determined many of the reactions and reforms of the present.

Central to the evolution of the male image was the Victorian ideal of 'manliness'. It took a variety of forms, as Norman Vance has suggested in his *Sinews of the Spirit: the Ideal of Christian Manliness in Victorian Literature and Religious Thought,* but in general terms we find little to quarrel with in his summary of 'manliness' as embracing qualities of physical courage, chivalric ideals, virtuous fortitude with additional connotations of military and patriotic virtue. In the second half of the nineteenth century, as David Newsome has elegantly suggested, the concept underwent a metamorphosis. To the early Victorian it represented a concern with a successful transition from Christian immaturity to maturity, demonstrated by earnestness, selflessness and integrity; to the late Victorian it stood for neo-Spartan virility as exemplified by stoicism, hardiness and endurance – the pre-eminent qualities of the famous English public school system, without doubt one of the most influential education systems the world has witnessed.

In recent years the concept of manliness has attracted growing attention. This is a reflection of the appeal it has exercised over scholars from a range of intellectual disciplines: from sociology to history, from literary criticism to religious studies. This appeal has been partly inspired by critical reflection on those Victorian values and attitudes which have survived into the twentieth century, among which the shibboleths of the manliness creed have proved at one and the same time to be oddly pervasive yet curiously archaic. Current interest in ideas about Victorian masculinity, then, is an illustration of the way in which contemporary preoccupations shape and determine inquiries about the past.

Of those Victorian values which have survived into recent times, few have attracted a more sustained and comprehensive attack than those which have sought, directly or indirectly, to advance or sustain the dominance of the western male. In societies in which gender roles and the relationship between the sexes continue to be critically scrutinised, the previously unchallenged pre-eminence of the male and its associated ideological arguments have found themselves strongly challenged.

While patriarchy, in various forms, is an ancient phenomenon in western society, recent male dominance owes much to the ideal of manliness, shaped and nurtured as a Victorian moral construct by influential and often over-lapping groups of nineteenth century writers, educationists and activists in both the old and the new worlds.

Perhaps one of the most arresting features of Victorian manliness is the fact that it was a philosophy which, through the printed word and via prestigious and proliferating educational institutions, developed a swift and ubiquitous influence throughout the 'Anglo-Saxon' territories. Well before the Great War, on both sides of the Atlantic, proponents of the ideal had securely ensconced themselves in dominant positions in society, with the result that between approximately 1850 and 1940 the cult of manliness became a widely pervasive and inescapable feature of middle class existence in Britain and America: in literature, education and politics, the vocabulary of the ethic was forcefully promulgated. Nor was proselytism restricted to the properties and the privileged: through school textbooks, children's literature, philanthropic organisations and the churches both the image and associated symbolic activities of both Christian and Darwinian 'manliness' filtered down to the proletariat through an unrelenting and self-assured process of social osmosis.

In time, on both sides of the Atlantic, the cult became so potent that it formed, in effect, a distinctive and powerful moral code; it offered a set of values applicable to each and every facet of personal and collective life. There were, inevitably, differences of aspiration and realisation both within and between the two greatly differing societies, but the common concept of 'manliness' broadly bound together Briton and American in an attachment to a recognisably similar code of conduct. Its adherents were audacious in their aspirations and ambitions. Their task was teleological. To borrow Goldman's expression, they had a 'world vision'. 'Manliness' symbolised an attempt at a metaphysical comprehension of the universe. It represented an effort to achieve a *Weltanschauung* with an internal coherence and external validity which determined ideals, forged identity and defined reality.

After its inception in the mid and late nineteenth-century English public schools, a neo-Spartan ideal of masculinity was diffused throughout the English speaking world with the unreflecting and ethnocentric confidence of an imperial race. Its dissemination throughout the Empire has recently been considered in Mangan's *The Games Ethic and Imperialism: Aspects of the Diffusion of an Ideal,* yet despite the fact that the New World was equally susceptible to its appeal and both evolved its own separate and individual ethos and utilised, adapted and re-shaped a borrowed image for its own ends, this twin process of parallel evolution, emulation and adaption still awaits the attention of the historian.

Arguably the ideal was best articulated, represented and disseminated by products of the late Victorian English public school but it found powerful adherents and articulate advocates among the middle-class Yankees of the east coast of the United States. As this volume seeks to make clear, it would be wrong to imagine that manliness was a simple, single, coherent concept linked to a single locality. It was, in effect, a portmanteau term which embraced a variety of overlapping ideologies regionally interpreted, which changed over time and which, at specific moments, appear to be discrete, even conflicting, in emphasis.

Nevertheless, by the final quarter of the nineteenth century, at least in the rhetoric of idealists, manliness had evolved into the somewhat controversial and sometimes confusing phenomenon of 'muscular Christianity' which some came to impute to the works of Charles Kingsley, Thomas Hughes, Oliver Wendell Holmes and Thomas Wentworth Higginson. Muscular Christianity, certainly in the eyes of its critics, tended to exaggerate commitment to muscle at the expense of Christianity. Nonetheless the term was appropriate to the extent that it captured that excessive commitment to physical activity which was an unquestionable feature of middle class male society in Britain and the United States in the second half of the nineteenth century. This emphasis on physical manliness was given a sharper edge, wide prominence and broad based appeal through the creation of a minor literary genre – the school story. Of the genre, of course, no book was more popular, both in Britain and America, than *Tom Brown's Schooldays,* Thomas Hughes' idealised and distorted description of Arnold's Rugby, a paean to the virtues of the robust manliness in the making. *Tom Brown* inspired both British and American prose moralisers who defined a new ideal of boyhood perfected on playing fields rather than the chapel priedieu. Manliness now came to be gradually divorced, in fact if not in intent, from religion and found itself anchored securely in an obsessive love of games.

The concept of Victorian manliness, of course, ought not to be viewed in exclusion. It has its polar opposite in the period concept of femininity. This too was complex but in essence it demanded of women a docility, commitment to domesticity and subservience.

Both ideals were severely constrained by the overriding effects of social class and economic reality. The ideals of masculinity and femininity were unlikely to prove persuasive, even assuming they reached them, to the untold legions of urban poor who seemed forever beyond the reach (and understanding) of their social superiors. In both old and new worlds in the wake of industrialisation and urbanisation, just as there were regiments of middle-class men and women concerned with the nature of a proper masculinity and femininity, so there were armies of men and women committed to a life of arduous physical labour in factories, sweat shops, agriculture and domestic service who gave the issue little thought. For them, the ideals of masculinity and femininity were as remote as the advocates of these ideals. Nevertheless determined efforts were made to force those ideals through the barriers of social class. They were set before the proletariat by pedagogues and publishers and pressed on them by charitable organisations and philanthropic activists.

Such men and women were convinced of the importance of the ideals as a corrective to prevailing social problems. To a marked degree the encouragement given to manly pursuits among males of all social classes, therefore, was a function of the mounting concern felt about the physical, and later the psychological, condition of a highly urbanised plebian life where physical and social deprivation was widespread – the details of which were becoming ever more readily available. Those muscular patriots who encountered 'unknown England' for example – and many did as teachers, missionaries and philanthropists – were alarmed and felt that the consequences for the material and spiritual welfare of the nation were appalling. To encourage manliness among the poor and the deprived seemed to offer an antidote to a variety of human and social problems.

Thus the emphasis placed on manliness needs to be set both in the context of the chivalric ideals of Victorian romantics and a utilitarian concern about the social problems of the late nineteenth-century. In order to overcome those problems it was considered important to encourage a manliness with a broad social base; to move out from the private schools, elite universities and military academies – in both the USA and Britain – and to win over more humble disciples to the ideal.

With this ambition in mind, activists proliferated a host of organisations – scouts, missions, athletic organisations, brigades and more – which, in conjunction with similar efforts within the new compulsory elementary school system, sought to implant a broadly based attachment to manly ideals equally among both fortunate and less fortunate compatriots. However the drive to encourage working class commitment frequently stalled before the obstacles posed by hardship and poverty and the persuasiveness of both ideals tended to flounder on the rock of proletarian urban culture.

The successes of the ideal of manliness were many and undeniable but were neither automatic nor widespread. Among men from the propertied world, whose schools and teachers were the architects of the ideal, there developed a fierce attachment both to the ideal and to the world-view which it represented and this was as true on imperial frontiers as it was at home within Britain and the United States. It made important inroads, as we might expect, in middle-class schools, churches and homes but it is open to serious doubt whether the belief in manliness managed to take root and grow at the lower end of the social scale, where it encountered the antipathy of poor, ill-educated and aggressive urban youths who remained the perennial but hostile target of proponents of this middle-class ideal.

There is now a profusion of current British and American research on specific aspects of the ideal of manliness of the late nineteenth and early twentieth centuries, covering education, organisations, adolescence and literature. What this book seeks to do is to provide a focus for some of the more seminal themes and, more importantly, to give the debate a *transatlantic dimension* largely lacking up to the present. To date, it has been a topic mostly dominated by strictly national interpretations and preoccupations. The purpose is to bring together, in equal proportion, scholars from Britain and America to contribute to a study of the significant and hitherto strangely neglected issue of manliness in *both* the Old and New Worlds during the period 1800 to 1940.

Their essays are designed to fulfil a number of functions: to illustrate the diversity of the concept, to investigate its early, middle and late Victorian manifestations, to explore its familial, institutional and international influence and to establish the limitations of its appeal. It is tempting to be persuaded, by the sheer volume of contemporary literature committed to manly idealism, that the concept was universally pervasive and uniformly successful. Clearly this was not the case and the ideal seems to have been generally restricted in social appeal to the milieu whence it came and to the upper reaches of male working-class life. Elsewhere it was frequently rebuffed by the very forces it sought to overcome; the harsh realities of contemporary life. Notwithstanding such failures, the cult of manliness came to exercise a quite remarkable influence on both sides of the Atlantic. Within a generation of its conception as 'muscular Christianity', the ethos of manliness had managed to secure the attachment of a remarkable number of men and boys. It established itself as a powerful moral code and as a widespread social imperative. It was severely damaged by the holocaust of the Great War but the ideal proved remarkably resilient, surviving well into the twentieth century; into an age qualitatively different from the Victorian world which had been its inspiration and cradle. The strength of the cult of manliness can be gauged by the fact that, more than a century after its apogee, shadows of its former self continue to flicker across the largely unsympathetic and uncomprehending world of the 1980s.

Biological thought, athletics and the formation of a 'man of character': 1830–1900

In *The Healthy Body and Victorian Culture* Bruce Haley has argued persuasively that 'no topic more occupied the Victorian mind than Health – not religion, or politics, or Improvement, or Darwinism'.[1] By the 1860s, if not somewhat earlier, many of the concerns which formed part of the more general agitation about health were caught up in, and given expression through, the games-playing 'cult' that swept Victorian Britain.[2] 'To a nation preoccupied with health,' Haley asserted, 'the athlete was the new hero and the "human form divine"'. From a multitude of sources the new gentleman was proclaimed to be the man who was an 'aristocrat of character' not an aristocrat by birth.[3]

Nineteenth-century Americans also were intrigued by, if not obsessed with, the idea of 'health'. Their concerns took many forms, as James Whorton and Harvey Green have shown. Some, like Sylvester Graham, preached strict diet as the road to physical and spiritual salvation. Temperance had a particular appeal for women whose 'male kin' drank up wages and/or abused them, as well as for reformers like the theologian Henry Ward Beecher or the peripatetic Dioclesian Lewis, author of books on digestion and exercise, director of an early proprietary physical education training school, founder of the *Boston Journal of Physical Culture* and populariser of the 'New Gymnastics', a system of calisthenic exercises for men and women which attracted considerable interest in the decades between 1860 and 1890. Some advocated hydropathy – 'the water cure'; others, like George Windship, found salvation in strength training.[4]

In the 1870s, the Doctors George and Charles Taylor were leading exponents of 'the Swedish Movement Cure' which had first been brought to the attention of Americans in the 1850s through a Boston edition of Mathias Roth's *The Gymnastic Free Exercises of P. H. Ling, Arranged by H. Rothstein*.[5] The Women's Rights Movement of the 1850s stressed health and physical education as a means to bringing about the emancipation of women. Throughout the century, as Americans seeking relief from a variety of real and assumed ills dosed themselves with a wide assortment of patent medicines, many 'irregular' medical doctors emphasised exercise and hygiene rather than such heroic remedies as bloodletting, opium and arsenic – the standard medications in the pharmacopoeia of 'regular' physicians. Attention was given to improved home construction and sanitation. Those individuals who founded communitarian settlements like New Harmony and Oneida, or formed the loosely structured group which came to be known as the New England Transcendentalists, frequently devoted considerable attention to 'physical education' in their proposals for personal and collective regeneration.[6]

Much of the enthusiasm for health reform was grounded in the optimistic belief that it was within the capacity of men and women to improve themselves. Millennialism placed the responsibility for attaining perfection on the individual; therefore, as Harvey Green has cogently argued, physical degeneration was seen as a spiritual as well as a medical and physiological problem.[7] Many of those who urged their fellow Americans to attend to health and hygiene in the decades between 1820 and the Civil War (1861-5) made *exercise* and *physical education* a major component of their programmes.

In the 1820s American educators began to advocate physical education and a few attempted to organise some type of instruction. Although various efforts to provide exercises for school children continued, it was not until the last decades of the century that most schools and colleges instituted regular programmes. The establishment of the American Association for the Advancement of Physical Education (AAAPE) was instrumental in giving some focus to the theretofore disparate efforts. It was also during the last decades of the nineteenth century that games-playing – in the form of intercollegiate and interscholastic athletics – burst into prominence with such force that educators and concerned citizens were forced to acknowledge that these student-initiated and directed contests would have to be brought under the control of school authorities.[8]

Nineteenth century interest in exercise, physical education and athletics (particularly those conducted under the auspices of schools and colleges) was also influenced by developments in the 'life sciences'. The term *biology* first appeared in publications in 1800. During the ensuing decades, popular interpretations of, and debates about, the apparent discoveries of laboratory and field research filled the pages of a wide assortment of journals and periodicals, resulting in a bewildering collection of competing opinions and 'theories' about the nature of life and its processes. One result was the elevation of the body to a position of enormous, yet precarious, importance.

The extent to which biological thinking permeated Victorian society has been examined in works like Sally Shuttleworth's study of the novels of George Eliot and in Charles Webster's *Biology, Medicine, Society: 1840-1940*. In his aptly titled *Biology in the Nineteenth Century: Problems of Form, Function, and Transformation*, William Coleman has set forth the major outlines of the Victorian interest in studying the structures, the vital processes, and the origins and modes of development of living creatures. A salient feature of nineteenth-century studies regarding man was the presumption that he, too '. . . must soon become a proper object of scientific investigation'.[9] The concern with *form, function* and *development* found powerful expression in nineteenth century attitudes toward physical education and athletic sport.

By the end of the century, theories about health through exercise and character-development through sport – as well as a host of other ideas about the human body – were mixtures of traditional beliefs (many of which could be traced back to the Hippocratic and Galenic tradition) and various distillations of the findings of modern biological science. While some traditional beliefs fell rather quickly before the onslaught of science, others had a remarkable persistence. One of the most extended debates concerned the nature of 'mind' and its relationship to the body. It was widely held that mind was the seat of the 'will' and that 'will' performed a decisive role in the formation of 'character'. Moreover, because of the long-standing belief that mind and body were directly related in life, it was assumed that by strengthening the body one could also strengthen the will. Responsibility for the development of strength and character, like responsibility for the achievement of health, was largely an individual matter. However, since the individual was part of the social whole, the two were clearly linked. As the century progressed, greater emphasis was given to social units and by the 1890s more traditional attitudes about the private nature of improvement were challenged by competing ideologies which saw the future in bureaucratic terms.

The word 'action' permeated nineteenth century British, and only somewhat less so, American popular, educational, literary and scientific publications. The games-playing cult which emerged first in Britain and shortly thereafter in the United States gave concrete – and spectacular – attention to action through the medium of the male body, the ideal for which had changed from lean and lithe to mesomorphic by the 1890s. In Britain, concern about vigorous action was heightened by the demands of the Crimean War (1854-6) and the needs of a nation which was engaged in empire-building and intent upon expanding its commercial sphere of influence. In the United States, anxieties and dislocations created by the Civil War intensified much of the exisiting interest in health and exercise. By bringing men from different sections of the country together, the War also helped to foster the embryonic interest in sport. Of Victorian England at mid-century, Haley has observed: '. . . sports were no longer regarded as hindering moral development, they aided it'. Moral lessons of both battlefield and life, J. A. Mangan has shown, were taught in the Victorian and Edwardian public school through games-playing and the endless stream of poems, rhymes and songs which were rife with the language and metaphor of self-sacrifice and character developed in games-playing.[10] Analysing the effects of the Civil War on New England intellectuals, George Fredrickson has maintained that American college sports were embraced by Northerners of a patrician background as a means of reviving ideals of heroic struggle associated with the sectional conflict. Some three decades after its end, Henry Lee Higginson looked back upon the War and declared: 'Sports would make "full-grown, well developed men, able and ready to do good work of all kinds"'.[11] Such 'good work' as the nation needed could be accomplished best by men who had tested themselves and, having been found equal to the task, were prepared to be leaders.

On both sides of the Atlantic, by the 1880s anyone who wished to do so had ample opportunity to read about athletes as men of character. Moreover, a rapidly improving technology also made it increasingly possible to observe such men in action: champions like the cricketer W. G. Grace or Harvard University's star halfback Thomas 'Bum' McClung. Whereas earlier calisthenics, gymnastics or simple out-of-door pursuits provided the means by which the body – and morals – were to be developed, by the last decades of the century it was in the crucible of athletic competition that the male character was to be forged. The newer view, as Donald Mrozek has argued, gave particular prominence to the body as a dynamic organism '. . . whose nature was known in its actions and movement'.[12]

The nature of 'seeing' and interpreting – the 'gaze' – can be extremely important, as Michel Foucault's work has so powerfully shown.[13] A substantial literature in the social sciences maintains that the body may serve as a symbol – or *icon* – for communicating customs, role expectations, and perceived relationships to nature and even to the cosmos. Adorned with any number of a variety of coverings, in static or dynamic postures, alone or in configurations with others, the human body may symbolically convey deeply held cultural convictions and values. The contention that the human body can function as metaphor and icon for human values and concerns has been proposed by Mary Douglas, who holds that there are deep and persistent pressures to create consonance between the social and the physiological levels of existence.[14] Athletic events are, to use Victor Turner's phrase, a type of 'cultural performance' in which social dramas may be powerfully enacted. This is borne out by John MacAloon's penetrating study of the origins of the modern Olympic Games.[15] Athletic events also provide a powerful public arena for conveying beliefs about *physis* and *psyche*. It is probably significant that among the ancient Greeks, who were deeply concerned with anatomy, physiology and the natural world, and in the nineteenth and twentieth centuries, with their intense interest in biological science, athletics have received so much attention.

The extent of the changes in biology between 1800 and 1900 was immense. In 1897 *Harper's New Monthly Magazine* discussed discoveries which had already rendered many traditional beliefs regarding human life suspect by the time Darwin's *Origin of Species* (1859) was published.[16] By the 1840s the improved microscope had given physiologists a powerful instrument for opening up whole new lines of investigation. Around mid-century it was determined that the function of the red corpuscles was to carry oxygen to the cells and that the nucleus was the centre of cellular function. Claude Bernard discovered the glycogenic (carbohydrate) function of the liver and by the end of the century the importance of the glands in metabolic change had been established. Of particular importance, work on the nerves and the nervous system – at least for some commentators – had made 'mind' the object of biological rather than philosophical inquiry and provided a 'scientific' basis for explaining how 'character' was formed.

Early in the century, Charles Bell had discovered the sensory-motor division of the spinal roots. The English physician Marshall Hall established the spinal cord as the centre for the sensory-motor act in 1832. Galvani discovered that nerve cells produce electricity and Du Bois Reymond and Helmholtz experimented with the electrical signalling properties of nerve cells. These and other experiments later in the century helped to establish the physiological basis of 'mind'.[17] While David Ferrier and others who performed experiments on the brain and nervous system increasingly consigned human activity to the physical realm, Wilhelm Wundt endeavoured to limit experimental psychology to mental phenomena which were directly accessible to physical influences. Willing to admit that the individual '. . . brings with him into the world the germ of his future character', Wundt insisted the *psychical* states '. . . are never whole discoverable. . . we determine character from its effects. . .' and can only define it with reference to those effects. It was society which provided the source of 'determinants of volition'; hence, a substantial portion of the formation of character was to be found in the nature of interaction with other human beings.[18]

Although numerous Americans had studied under Wundt at Leipzig, it was William James who most influenced American thinking about psychology. Stimulated by Darwin's views of the effects of the environment, James saw life as a process of constant adjustment wherein repeated actions increased the 'plasticity of neural matter'. The senses were linked to muscular and glandular organs by 'nerve currents' flowing along the nervous system's 'reflex paths'. Repeated performances made it easier to perform an action on subsequent occasions and required less attention on the part of the individual. Such repetition developed proper 'habits'. Although James had never intended that habit be thought of as a substitute for moral autonomy, American social reformers seized on it as a means to foster desired behaviour and values, as Dominick Cavallo has claimed in his study of American attempts to inculcate morals through organised play.[19] For the majority of those American educators and social reformers who advocated organised play, physical education and athletics at the turn of the century, it was moral – or character – development which was the primary goal of their efforts. This is not to say that objectives like health and fitness were unimportant: these were absolutely necessary foundations for the higher goal of character formation.

In 1889 Edward Hartwell, one of the most scientifically prepared members of the AAAPE (PhD in biology from The Johns Hopkins University and MD from Cincinnati's Miami Medical College) drew upon the work of the German physiologist Du Bois-Reymond to claim that '. . . such bodily exercises as gymnastics, fencing, swimming, riding, dancing and skating [were] much more exercises of the central nervous system, of the brain and spinal marrow. . .' than they were of the muscular system. The most important effect of physical exercise was '. . . the functional improvement of the nervous mechanisms'. Although Hartwell did not directly equate 'brain power' with the will and morality, many of his contemporaries did. Opening the same 1889 Conference, US Commissioner of Education William Torrey Harris declared: 'I will define physical training as the conscious or voluntary training of the muscular side of our system, which is the special side under the control of the will'.[20]

It is one thing to isolate some physiological problem or system and examine it experimentally in a laboratory, but quite another thing to try to account for its actual role in the co-ordinated functioning of the integrated organism. If this is hard to manage for simple organisms, it is even more difficult in the case of human beings whose physiological functioning is embedded in a complex social, cultural, and ideological and religious matrix. Ill-prepared to deal with technical scientific discoveries, the majority of those who supported the character-forming potential of exercise and athletics advocated theories which mingled selected aspects of the newer discoveries of biological science with traditional beliefs.

In 1833 the *American Quarterly Review* published an article entitled 'Physical culture, the result of moral obligation' written by John Jeffries, a Boston physician. Drawing upon John Sinclair's *The Code of Health and Longevity* (1807) and, more extensively, from the Bible, Jeffries stated: 'The powers of the body should be cultivated, because of its connection with the mind'. Unable to explain the mechanisms by which this was achieved, Jeffries was content to observe: 'The nature of the union of the body and the soul, is one of those invisible and mysterious relations, which the Maker has been pleased to conceal from the utmost effort of investigation. But the fact is clearly seen in the mutual action of mind and matter. . .'[21] Relying upon reasoning by analogy, he informed his reader that the strength of the blacksmith, '. . . the strength and swiftness of the athlete, and the prodigious feats of the gymnasium, are all products of this law'.[22] Jeffries' article, illustrative of the majority of contemporary statements about mind, body and exercise, is retrospective, informed by seventeenth and eighteenth-century knowledge and ways of ordering ideas about the body. Nineteenth-century biology, albeit slowly and unevenly, would begin to alter such conceptions.

The Principles of Physiology Applied to the Preservation of Health and to the Improvement of Physical and Mental Education, published one year later, is informed by developments in the new biology. Its author was Andrew Combe, MD, Fellow of the Royal College of Physicians of Edinburgh and younger brother of the phrenologist George Combe. *The Principles of Physiology* (1834) was favourably reviewed in the December *American Annals of Education* and published in 1836 in the Harpers Family Library series. By 1854 this American edition had gone to a sixteenth printing and was considered one of the most authoritative and useful books available. Combe, who had studied medicine in Paris and Edinburgh, refers to the work of Beaumont, Cuvier, Bichat, Bell and other physiologists. His interest in the now discredited 'science' of phrenology does not seem to have impeded his ability to deal in a straighforward manner with new findings regarding the structures and functions of the body. Discussions of the muscular and circulatory systems are precise and those of motor and sensory nerves and the brain are informed by recent work. While he is emphatic that he does not consider '. . . mind and brain to be one and the same thing. . .', Combe insists that, because they are '. . , inseparably associated during life. . .', it is necessary to discover and apply the '. . . laws by which their healthy action is regulated. . .'. Significantly, he points out that because the brain is an organ, it is subject to the same laws of exercise as pertain to other organs of the body.[23]

Newer ways of looking at the body (especially Bell's work on the sensory-motor nerves and the 'reflex arc' described by Hall) gave support to the contention that muscle and mind were related in such a fashion that the action of one influenced the other. Science had begun to confirm – or at least give support to – the belief that muscle power became 'will' power. Precisely what the nature of this relationship was remained unclear, allowing conflicting theories to be advanced regarding the best method and amount of exercise. Combe stipulated that muscle and 'will' should be directed to the same end at the same time because divine wisdom had established a harmony between structure and function. The social and moral nature of active sports brought the 'nervous impulse' into especially full and harmonious operation and this, he maintained, accounted for their great superiority '. . . as a means of exercise over mere measured movements. . .' such as walking or routine calisthenics.[24]

The *American Annals of Education* in which the review of Combe's *Principles of Physiology* had appeared was successor to the *American Journal of Education,* established in 1826 by William Russell. In the first volume of Russell's journal the following statement had appeared: 'The time we hope is near when there will be no literary institution unprovided with the proper means of healthful exercise and innocent recreation, and when literary men shall cease to be distinguished by a pallid countenance and wasted body. . . the preservation of the animal system, must constitute the basis of every plan of education, which is capable of meliorating the condition of our race'.[25] This anxiety about 'pallid countenance' and 'wasted body' was one which would trouble middle-class Americans throughout the century.

While much of the information upon which Americans based their 'theories' of physical education was distilled from books published in Britain, they also drew upon German and Swedish sources. These were especially influential in providing forms or *systems* of exercise. In 1823 George Bancroft and Joseph Cogswell had founded the Round Hill School in Northampton, Massachusetts where a portion of each day was set aside for sports and gymnastics '. . . as the means of promoting firmness and vigour of mind. . .'.[26] In 1825 they engaged Charles Beck (one of several German émigrés who had settled in the Boston area) to institute a programme of gymnastics and out-door activities. A former gymnast at the Hasenheide Turnplatz, Beck translated (with numerous emendations) Jahn's *Die Deutsche Turnkunst* into English in 1828. His compatriot Charles Follen opened a gymnasium at Harvard College in 1825 and an open-air *Turnplatz* the following year in Boston. These were short-lived projects, however, and it was not until after 1848, when a new wave of German immigrant began founding *Turnvereine* and agitating for the inclusion of their form of exercises in the public schools, that German gymnastics became well-known in America. The indefatigable Turners established their own gymnastic training school in 1866 and for well over three decades the Normal College of the American Gymnastic Union provided most of the better-trained gymnastics teachers for the elementary and secondary schools.[27]

Although Americans had knowledge of Swedish gymnastics as early as 1830, it was the publication of Mathias Roth's *The Gymnastic Free Exercises of P. H. Ling, Arranged by H. Rothstein* that brought 'kinesipathy' – or the 'Swedish movement cure' – to the attention of numerous health reformers. Catharine Beecher referred to Ling (although it is not certain that she had much familiarily with his work) in her influential *Physiology and Calisthenics for Schools and Families* (1856). Dio Lewis taught his students at the Boston Normal School of Physical Education various exercises modified from the Swedish system in the 1860s. In 1880 Dr George Taylor published *Health by Exercise*, a manual comprised of exercises based on the Swedish system. Although it made brief references to Leibig, Helmholtz and Du Bois-Reymond, Taylor's popular book contained little which separated it from the ideas put forth by William Andus Alcott, who had died twenty years before *Health by Exercise* was published.[28]

A frequent contributor to Woodbridge's *American Annals of Education,* William A. Alcott, MD was a major figure of the pre-Civil War health reform movement. Through popular books such as *Young Man's Guide to Health* (1835) and numerous articles, he sought to instruct Ante-Bellum Americans about the nature of their bodies and urged them to attend to their health. The small didactic text *The House I Live In* (1837), intended for use by families and schools, discussed the body's structures in highly moralistic terms. 'House' is precisely what Alcott means. The skeletal structure is presented as frame, roof, doors, etc.; the internal organs as 'furniture'. Through pictures and text he repeatedly proclaimed that a beneficent Creator had established harmony of form and a unity of form with function.[29]

The Laws of Health (1839) a sequel to *The House I Live In,* offered a more detailed account of the structures and functions of the body. In the chapter 'Motion and Exercise: Why Exercise of the Body is Needful', Alcott upheld Christian ideology stating that '. . . order is heaven's first law; but one might. . . regard motion as before order'. God had *moved* to bring order out of chaos! Having specified that the defining characteristic of the animate world was *motion,* he then explained how muscles, ligaments and cartilage were put into action by the 'will': 'When we *will* motion, certain muscles contract to perform it. . . when in standing we lean a little in a certain direction, the mind, somehow conscious of it, *wills* it draw back from the point towards which the body is inclining. . .'. Running, dancing and other forms of locomotion were all performed in accordance with the same principle.[30] When one activated the motor system, one was also engaging the will.

Alcott also had something to say about which form of physical activity was best. Pleasure actively engages the mind; therefore, out-door activities like ball, running, leaping, jumping, fencing and swimming are more beneficial than are routine gymnastic exercises. This was a view shared by many of Alcott's contemporaries, including Ralph Waldo Emerson, chief spokesman for the New England 'Transcendentalists'. Convinced that American society was becoming too materialistic, Emerson, Henry David Thoreau, Margaret Fuller, Bronson Alcott and their like-minded associates sought to re-establish closer relations with nature; all were interested in out-door activities and physical education. For Emerson, *character* denoted '. . . habitual self-possession. . . a balance not. . . easily disturbed by outward events. . .'. Character involved 'self-reliance' or inner strength. Great men possessed exceptional character and were vital to society because they showed others the way. Character was developed in childhood and its proper formation could be powerfully influenced by boyish games: 'I like boys, the masters of the playground and the street,' Emerson wrote, 'Their elections at baseball or cricket are founded on merit, and are right. They don't pass for swimmers until they can swim, nor for stroke-oar until they can row'.[31]

By the 1890s, Emerson's 'self-reliance' and older notions of inner strength had been substantially replaced by the notion of the 'self-made man'. The 'self-made man' developed himself through his actions and his impact upon the world and others. Such men built financial empires and led. Anthony Rotundo has observed this shift in ideals of American middle-class manhood between 1770 and 1920 from a standard '. . . rooted in the life of the community and qualities of a man's soul to a standard based on individual achievement and the male body'.[32] Personal achievement, especially that defined by competitive success in business and athletics, became an increasingly important American value. So, too, did a preoccupation with the morphology of the male body. By the end of the century the dominant cultural value defined a man of 'character' as the man who made his *mark* on the world. Athletic sport provided a powerful arena where the making of marks — literally and figuratively — could be accomplished.

Although neither the newer values nor the modern forms of athletic sport would emerge with full force until around the time of the nation's centennial celebration (1876), the seeds were present before the Civil War. Catharine Beecher, perpetual labourer in the cause of female education and author of the extremely popular *Physiology and Calisthenics for Schools and Families* and other works on education and health, had noted as early as 1832 that because the normal play activities of children were too irregular, '. . . those gymnastic exercises which have been lately introduced into our country, might form, with some additions, a very useful substitute for the ordinary amusements of youth and childhood'.[33] By the early 1900s the contention that the play of children needed to be informed by 'scientific' theory, rationalised and controlled by specially trained adults would be repeatedly advanced by professional physical educators, play theorists, and organisations like the Playground Association of America and the Russell Sage Foundation. It was in this same period that football, baseball and other games were transformed into 'scientific' extravaganzas with highly codified playing rules, special training regimens, authoritarian coaches and other hallmarks of bureaucratised sport.

Even those who would come to criticise many of the values associated with late nineteenth-century sport, however, saw the importance of bringing modern science to bear on exercise and health. As early as 1861 Thomas Wentworth Higginson, for example, maintained that more attention should be directed to new developments in science. By the turn of the century American sport, like the American society, resembled the triptych described in Henry May's study in the years immediately preceding World War I. On the right, and smaller panel, were those who looked to an older, substantially Anglo-Saxon tradition for their values; men like Harvard's President Charles William Eliot who revered America but found it mortifying that in their games Americans were 'morally inferior' to the English. On the left, and larger panel, were the advocates of progress whose dispositions were embodied in men like Theodore Roosevelt; men who were building great steel companies, oil monopolies, and financial empires – who saw the United States replacing Great Britain as the world's industrial power and revelled in American victories at Henley and defeat of the London Athletic Club at the 1895 Penn Relays.[34]

In 1855 *The North American Review* had published a lengthy and laudatory commentary on Kingsley's *Westward Ho!* It also published an article entitled 'Gymnastics' in which the Unitarian clergyman A. A. Livermore praised Greek athletics and denounced mid-nineteenth century American attitudes toward health, exercise and vigorous manhood. Just as modern medicine directed its concerns to 'cure from without' rather than to prevention or 'cure from within', the author held, contemporary ethics devoted almost exclusive attention to '. . . special rules and principles of conduct. . .' rather than to the '. . . underlying conditions of the body and soul. . .'.[35] (This allegation anticipates a concern that would appear with considerable force and in several contexts at the end of the century. Critics of the burgeoning intercollegiate athletic programmes, for example, feared that the emergence of codified playing rules and referees now absolved the individual player of making ethical decisions.) Commenting with approval on German gymnastics, Swedish exercises and other programmes which had begun to attract popular interest, Livermore lamented the lack of vigour to be found among American men. In words which would have gladdened the heart of an English public school master, he called upon the colleges to devote due attention to physical education and athletic games:

O for a touch of the Olympic games rather than this pallid effiminacy! O for a return to the simple Persian elements of telling the truth, and hurling the javelin, instead of the bloodless cheeks, and lifeless limbs, and throbbing brains of our first scholars in Harvard, Yale or Princeton! . . . What bitter drops of gall have flowed from the pen of the dyspepsic! . . . how much more sound and beautiful would the masterpieces of literature have been, had they proceeded from hearty minds in healthy bodies, instead of being born, as has been the case, of gin and genius, of fancy and headache, of blindness and seraphic imagination, of angelic fancy and broken heart![36]

Warming to his topic, Livermore declared that whereas such hardy rural pursuits as hunting and woodcraft, and the French, Indian and Revolutionary Wars, had once been America's 'Olympic games' – the ramparts against disease and '. . . the effemination of a whole race of men' – with the growth of cities, a mercantile class had arisen and indulgence had set in. The result was a deterioration of both the body and the *character* of the native-born American male. In 1858 Oliver Wendell Holmes similarly warned his contemporaries of the dire consequences of inattention to the development of physical vigour: '. . . such a set of black-coated, paste-complexioned youth as we can boast in our Atlantic cities never before sprang from the loins of Anglo-Saxon lineage'.[37]

Three years later Holmes' young friend and fellow New Englander, Thomas Wentworth Higginson, urged the nation's common (public elementary) schools to develop an 'American' system of physical education which would be scientifically superior to those already existing in England and Germany. There is '. . . a melancholy loss of self-respect', Higginson declared, 'in buying cultivation for the brain by resigning the proper vigor of the body'.[38] Drawing upon the sanitary reform movement which was sweeping Britain and the anthropometric work of the Belgian mathematician Adolphe Quetelet, from height-weight-strength tables published in the *Journal of the London Statistical Society* and dynamometer tests of the strength of university students, Higginson concluded that the highest standard of civilisation, best physical condition, finest athletes and longest life were to be found among the Anglo-Saxon race. Reflecting mid-century notions of racial superiority and degeneracy, he asserted: 'It is undeniable that bodily strength goes with the highest civilisation. . . those races of Southern Europe which once ruled the Eastern and Western worlds by physical and mental power have lost in strength as they have paused in civilization. . .' He suggested that such technical innovations as the Fairbank's scale and the stopwatch be brought to bear on improving physical education and urged that more attention be directed to the study of the relation between mental and physical power. Too few physiologists, Higginson claimed, had been 'practical gymnasts'; hence the effects of exercise had not been adequately studied. What America needed was a programme of physical education uniquely designed for the American temperament; one that would develop '. . . such an harmonious mingling of refinement and vigor, that we may more than fulfill the world's expectation, and may become classic to ourselves'.[39] By the 1860s many Americans were becoming anxious to shape their exercise pro-grammes and their athletics – as well as their institutions – unhampered by the traditions of the Old World.

In 1869 W. W. Hall, MD had written in his *Guide-Board to Health, Peace and Competence, or the Road to Happy Old Age,* one of the many popular health guides, that 'mastery' meant temperance and moderation. By the 1880s and 1890s, however, 'mastery' more often than not might mean superiority and domination. Hall criticised those men who, like contem-porary boxing champions Tom Hyer and James 'Yankee' Sullivan, devoted all their energies to developing muscular strength. Drawing from conservation of energy concepts which influenced nineteenth-century biological thought, Hall contended that if vital force was used up in building muscle, the brain would suffer. What the proper balance between energy expenditure and energy conservation should be remained a dilemma throughout the century. So did efforts to deal with disloca-tions created by an urbanising society. In the *Guide-Board* the reader is confronted with drawings depicting such technological advances as the telegraph and railroads, as well as with the pastoral vistas of what many believed was a rapidly vanishing America.[40]

The oscillation between an idealised agrarian past and an optimistic but threatening urban-industrial future worried Americans and con-ditioned how they thought about their health, their exercise and their games. Walter Wells was concerned that, although America was becom-ing rich faster than any other nation, 'nervous diseases' were more frequent among the population. Dyspepsia, constipation, consumption and uterine difficulties took a fearful toll. 'The great social or industrial sin of our American people,' Wells declared, 'is that they habitually do too much. . . a general habit of amusement is unknown'. Americans even 'worked' young men and young women at their 'gymnastic duties'.[41]

H. C. Williston lamented that Americans had failed to develop a 'theory' of exercise. Their 'sporting literature' was confined to Dr R. T. Trall's *Family Gymnasium* (1857), some manuals on English sports, Lewis' 'light gymnastics' and Windship's 'heavy lifting'. The only 'professors (!)

of gymnastics' in the United States, he held, were pugilists. Therefore, gymnastics were '. . . indiscriminately and injudiciously applied either by patients or the brainless athletes who so frequently manage the gymnasiums'. Citing George Lewes' *Philosophy of the Common Life* (1867) as a type of book which should inform exercise enthusiasts, Williston maintained that more attention needed to be paid to the findings of physiologists when devising systems of exercise.[42] *The Galaxy* found Americans to be dissatisfied, restless and always '. . . seeking after a result'. When it asked in 1871: 'Are Americans Inferior to Europeans?' (which usually meant the English) it concluded that indeed they were, due to the frenetic pace of life and a lack of participation in vigorous sports among American males.[43]

Although organised sports had not been widespread in America before 1860, AAU President James E. Sullivan felt secure in boasting that by winning nearly all of the significant prizes at the 1900 Olympic Games, Americans had proven themselves to be foremost in international sport.[44] The emergence of organised sport in the United States had been swift. In 1859 *Harper's Weekly* had observed that all but four members of the American cricket team which had lost to a visiting English eleven were British immigrants. 'Men of thirty can remember well', the writer noted, 'that when they were in school, proficiency on the playground was regarded rather as a drawback than a merit'.[45] Ten years later, the *Nation* stated: The taste for athletic sports in America is not over fifteen years old'.[46] By 1869, the year of the transcontinental baseball tour of the Cincinnati Redstockings, many Americans were ready to extol the superiority of their 'National Game' (which could be played in a relatively short time) over slow-paced cricket. By 1876 the National League of Professional Baseball Clubs had been established and Harvard and Yale Universities had played each other in their first rugby football match. That same year George W. Green claimed, with some exaggeration, that athletic sports had been carried on in the colleges long enough to study their results on the men who had participated in them. (Green was familiar with Morgan's study of the men who had rowed in the Oxford/Cambridge race from 1829 to 1869). Both the skilful athlete and the man who aspired to the leadership of his class, Green held, were doing the same thing – striving for excellence and demonstrated success. However, although excellence in athletics was to be commended, athletic training tended to result in the over-development of one set of muscles and the neglect of others. Therefore, supplemental exercises were needed to ensure symmetrical development.[47]

The insistence on symmetrical development was influenced by biological thinking which posited an important relationship between form and function. Asymmetrical form was deemed inimical to health and possibly detrimental to the development of mind or character. Physical educators, in particular, gave extensive attention to anthropometry; so did a number of physicians as did the anthropologist Franz Boas. By the 1870s, both the form of the body and its active use in athletic sports had gained a prominent role in defining images of the male in America. Athletics were increasingly seen as a training ground for ensuring both personal success and the future of the nation: '. . . men who have begun by surpassing their comrades in manly activity. . .' Green held, were often those who achieved the greatest success in professional life or became '. . . the leaders of public opinion in the councils of State'.[48]

The college athlete was the conspicuous exemplar of the man who knew how to discipline himself and dedicate his efforts to the pursuit of excellence. On the playing fields, even more than in the gymnasium, young men learned lessons which they would need to succeed in life and lead their country to a position of world eminence. The athlete literally *embodied* power and prowess and provided the icon which could serve as a model for other young men – even those relegated to the role of spectator. The highly elaborated and intensely symbolic contests in which the athlete struggled for supremacy by intensifying these messages enabled the onlooker to partake of the whole.[49] Those who favoured increasingly extravagant intercollegiate athletics frequently maintained that the athlete provided a model worthy of emulation.[50]

In their influential book on the game which dominated the colleges by the 1890s, Lorin Deland and Yale's highly successful coach Walter Camp declared that '. . . advantages of a mental or ethical nature. . .' were even greater than the physical benefits of football. Football taught the player to think rapidly: 'He must train himself to meet emergencies. . . Early in his career there will be developed in him a degree of self-reliance which probably no other sport in the world would inculcate. . .'. However, this strength must be subjugated to the 'will'. Here was discipline and mastery of self; yet it could also be mastery over opponents. Moreover, the physical and moral courage learned on the football field were never wholly forgotten.[51] Eugene L. Richards, Director of Yale's gymnasium lauded football as '. . . the most manly and the most scientific game in existence. . .'. 'No one but a veteran can describe the fascination. . . which football possesses for its players. . . [The old player] lives his important matches over and over again in his dreams and before his fire; and he will see football come to harm with feelings akin to those of a lover at the loss of his mistress, and those of a patriot at the betrayal of his country'.[52] Discipline, courage, virility, domination, fascination which might verge on the erotic; these were all sentiments which supporters of the sport – and they were legion – echoed in their panegyrics to America's most masculine team game.

Football, it was believed, not only fostered courage and obedience; it also provided a means by which men (i.e. white Anglo-Saxon or perhaps northern European men) might avoid 'physical degeneration'.[53] Although football was the pre-eminent manly sport of the collegiate ranks, baseball, crew, and track were also held to be of value in 'building up the manhood' of the nation. The ability to survive the struggle with other nations was seen to be important to a country now intent upon fulfilling its destiny as a world leader; so was the ability to match the reproductive capacity of the tens of thousands of immigrants from Central and Southern Europe who began to arrive after 1870. Alarmed by falling birth-rates, middle-class Americans worried about 'race suicide', a rising tide of mental disease, crime and pauperism. Theodore Roosevelt warned his contemporaries that a race was '. . . worthless and contemptible if its men cease to be willing and able to work hard and, when needed, fight hard, and its its women cease to breed freely'.[54]

Another anxiety which was related to, but not identical with, racial degeneration and eugenics was *nervousness* or the loss of 'nerve force'. Although there had been concern about nervous diseases since the 1830s, it was in the last three decades of the century that 'neurasthenia' (nervous prostration resulting from excessive 'brain work') became a major American health complaint. It was assumed to be most prevalent among northern Europeans, whose cultures were the most advanced, and among men, whose brains were larger and intellectual capacities greater than those of women. Exercise programmes and athletics were advocated to restore energy which had been drained by intellectual pursuits and the pressures of the business world, as well as to enhance male potency. However, there was considerable disagreement regarding just when physical activity ceased to be a restorer and became a drain on a man's energy.[55] Numerous manuals and periodicals discussed these and other male problems. Eugene Sandow and Bernard Macfadden were two of the most successful entrepreneurs who built lucrative careers in the late nineteenth and early twentieth centuries by capitalising on these matters and the American interest in the mesomorphic male form. Even their popularity was eclipsed, however, by that of the man who would become the twenty-sixth

President of the United States.

Whereas many Americans objected to what they considered to be offensive, if not indecent, aspects of Macfadden's work, Theodore Roosevelt exemplified those manly qualities which appealed to the American middle class.[56] A tireless supporter of sport and the out-door life, Roosevelt praised the men who had served in his regiment during the short-lived Spanish American War (1898), giving particular credit to the fitness and bravery of those who had been athletes and 'the Western man'. In 'The strenuous life', 'The American boy', 'Manhood and State' and other essays he extolled rugged, ceaseless, vigorous activity: 'We need. . . the iron qualities that must go with true manhood. . . . If Washington and Lincoln had not had in them the whipcord fibre of moral and mental strength. . .' the nation would not have been founded and preserved.[57] There had been no room for cowards or weaklings among the frontiersmen and pioneers who settled in the wilderness and there could be no hesitation among men with expansionist aspirations. In 'Character and Success' he declared: 'Bodily vigour is good, and vigour of intellect is even better, but far above both is character'. He endorsed college sports for their ability to build body and character, but cautioned that if carried to excess they could be detrimental.[58] A loyal Harvard alumnus, Roosevelt clashed with President Eliot over athletics. As head of the nation's oldest and most respected university, Eliot's views regarding intercollegiate athletics were of no small consequence to those who, by the 1890s and early 1900s, wished to bring these programmes under institutional and education control. Eliot had been an oarsman while a student at Harvard in the 1850s and approved of what he considered to be 'gentlemanly' sport. However, he believed that college athletics had become so tainted by excesses that they lost their value in educating young men. Far from teaching moral values, they did just the opposite – they fostered immorality. Writing to the President of the University of California about that institution's conversion from American football to rugby in 1906, he declared that Harvard '. . . students in any keen competition would make it a rough and cheating game in fifteen minutes'. It was mortifying, Eliot contended, that in their games Americans were 'morally inferior' to the English.[59]

In the flood of discussion which filled the pages of newspapers, journals, magazines and student yearbooks, which occupied sessions at various educational gatherings and provided a basis for nostalgic sharing at alumni banquets, athletics were either 'good' or 'bad', character-building or a blight on the colleges, depending upon the values of the speaker.

Much depended, of course, on what one believed constituted proper manly character. Those who subscribed to a competitive, corporate, business ideology were usually inclined to favour the burgeoning inter-collegiate programs. Those who adhered to more traditional values tended to the belief that although in their 'pure' form athletics could be both physically and morally beneficial, they were being destroyed by commercialisation. Although this might be appropriate in professional sport, it was unacceptable when it came to athletics which were conducted under the auspices of educational institutions.

American educators had been interested in the contributions which 'physical education' might make to physical and moral development since at least the early 1800s. It had been in Henry Bernard's *American Journal of Education* that the classroom teacher was first introduced to Dio Lewis' 'new gymnastics'. The *New England Journal of Education*, founded in 1875, devoted a considerable amount of attention to physical training and its potential for both the maintenance of health and the formation of morality. By the 1890s it was also concerned with school athletics. Clark University's William Burnham called for a 'new physiology' which would '. . . show the sequence of the different stages of growth and their relation to the sensory and motor functions. Drawing upon recent experiments regarding the functions of various anatomical areas of the brain, T. M. Balliet, Superintendent of Schools for Springfield, Massachusetts, declared that the brian's '. . . motor cells can be exercised and developed only by making them contract the muscles'. This, it was held, established the absolute necessity of muscular exercise. Movements requiring fine co-ordination were considered to be '. . . more educational than those involving only crude adjustments'. Motor education, Balliet concluded, developed energy, courage and 'force of character' Spontaneous play and games were more valuable than gymnastics because the former called forth the acting out of the stages through which the race had passed.[60] This, of course, was the 'recapitulation theory' which received its most powerful expression in the work of the American psychologist G. Stanley Hall.

The importance of Hall's work for the emerging profession of physical education had been recognised in the late 1800s by his election to honorary membership in the AAAPE. Several physical educators sought to utilise the findings of modern science to give legitimacy and support to their field and those who had had training in biology and/or medicine had some limited success in bringing new knowledge to bear on the extremely complex and difficult questions with which the field presumed to be concerned. The majority of the men and women who became teachers of physical training, however, had very limited scientific preparation. Some had studied anthropometry and play theory and attended lectures on physiology and hygiene, but few had had any experimental laboratory work. (In this their training did not differ greatly from that of doctors before the 1890s.) Much of what the field advanced as arguments in support of the developmental functions of play, games and gymnastics, therefore, drew as much, if not more, from the older health reform paradigm than from the recent findings of science.[61]

One notable exception was Edward Mussey Hartwell (PhD in biology from The Johns Hopkins University and MD from Cincinati's Miami Medical College), President of the AAAPE from 1891-2 and 1895-9. In his address at the 1889 Boston Conference on Physical Training, and elsewhere, Hartwell endeavoured to provide his contemporaries with a scientific explanation of the physiological functions of exercise. Drawing upon the work of the German physiologist Du Bois-Reymond and others, he set forth the argument that bodily exercises were '. . . much more exercises of the central nervous system, of the brain and spinal marrow' than of the muscular system.[62] Ten years later he used the occasion of his AAAPE Presidential address to remind his colleagues that:

> Viewed in light of the modern doctrine of the human body, the office of the teacher of youth, be he a teacher of morals, of literature, or of gymnastics, possesses a new and heightened significance. . . The problems of education are mainly problems of evolution, problems concerning growth and development. The new education will be conceived and ordered as a biological science – as the quintessential biological science.[63]

Drawing upon Thomas Huxley's writings on 'man's place in nature', Hartwell discussed the physiology of oxygen consumption, the production of animal heat, embryology and growth and the relationship of the muscular, circulatory and nervous systems in relation to education. The integrated nature of the muscular, circulatory and nervous systems had been detailed in Michael Foster's *A Textbook of Physiology* (1877), unquestionably the most comprehensive work available in the English language up to the end of the century. But this and works like David Ferrier's *The Functions of the Brain* (published in 1876) were far too technical for all but the most informed reader. Other physiology texts were written for an intelligent lay readership. One of the most authoritative was *The Elements of Physiology and Hygiene: A Textbook for Educational Institutions* (a second and revised American edition published in 1881) by the eminent British biologist Thomas Huxley and the American physician William Jay Youmans. The last one hundred pages of *The Elements of Physiology* provided an extended discussion of hygiene, including the relationship of exercise to health of mind and body. According to the authors, because body, brain and mind are related '. . . the study of mental phenomena in their corporeal relations. . . becomes the business of the physiologist'. Whatever improves the physical qualities of the brain will improve the mind. The two have '. . . a common development [and] are equally increased in vigor, capacity, and power, by systematic and judicious exercise. . .'.[64]

Statements such as this were seized upon avidly by those who advocated the educational merits of play, games and gymnastics. Addressing his colleagues at the fifth annual meeting of the AAAPE, Luther Halsey Gulick, MD, Director of Physical Training at the Springfield YMCA Training School, proclaimed the importamce of the 'New Profession', stating:

> There are few scientific fields today which offer opportunities for the study of the problems of greater value to the human race. . . [Physical Education] is in line with the most thorough modern physiological psychology. . . [and] with our modern conception of evolution, as it works to develop a superior race. This profession offers to its students a large and broad field for intellectual activity, involving for its fullest appreciation a profound knowledge of man through physiology, anatomy, psychology, history and philosophy. . .[65]

In his epochal work *Adolescence* (1904), G. Stanley Hall declared play to be of inestimable educational value. To act vigorously gave the '. . . organism a sense of superiority, dignity, endurance, courage, confidence, enterprise, power, personal vitality, and virtue [manliness] in the etymological sense of that noble word'. Athletics (the mature form of play) provided opportunities where men's instincts towards struggle and warfare could be kept within bounds and controlled. Their combative nature offered a defence against weakening of the will, loss of honour and degeneration. Regrettably, Hall maintained, the growing tendency to 'codify sports', impose 'Draconian laws', study every athlete minutely and have '. . . every emergency legislated on and judged by an autocratic martinet' resulted in a pernicious specialism in games which excluded the majority of young men from participation.[66] Consequently, most boys and men were prevented from developing the vitality, endurance, courage and manliness which both they and their heirs needed. Ira N. Hollis, faculty athletic representative at Harvard University, criticised the growing professionalism in college sports but concluded that because of their potential to teach self-control, manliness and character they were worth keeping. Comparing English and American attitudes towards school and college sport, Ralph D. Paine acknowledged that although '. . . splendid qualities of manhood and discipline. . .' were bred '. . . in the ordeal of American football. . .', recruiting of athletes and special privileges for players had had an adverse influence on morals and ethics. Moreover, modern tendencies had eliminated most young men from participating and from any benefits and enjoyment the game might bring.[67] The athlete, then, was a man who stood apart from and above the mundane achievements of the average man.

The athlete was set aside not only by his achievements on the field, diamond, track or water, he was also to be known by his corporeal appearance. At the time that Hall was writing *Adolescence*, medical doctors like William T. Porter and Henry P. Bowditch (who established Harvard's physiology laboratory in 1871), the anthropologist Franz Boas and a very large number of physical educators were occupied with taking anthropometric measurements of children, young people and college undergraduates. Edward Hitchcock, MD had begun this type of work when he became Director of Physical Training at Amherst College in 1861. In 1888 Hitchcock proclaimed that the New England college student, not as previously the enlisted man or criminal, '. . . would now furnish an average, or mean to be used in the anthropometric study of the Anglo-Saxon race'.[68]

Dudley Allen Sargent established an extensive programme of anthropometric measurement after he became Director of Physical Training at Harvard in 1879. In the late 1880s Sargent published three articles in *Scribner's Magazine* on: the physical development of the 'typical man'; women, and male athletes. Only these few men who were chosen for the competitive teams, Sargent complained, benefited from the sporting craze which was sweeping the nation. The vast majority, discouraged that they could never attain the excellence needed to compete, settled for vicarious participation as spectators. This was inimical to their health and development. Even those few who excelled in their chosen sport were endangered because of the asymmetrical muscular development which athletics fostered. Invoking the argument that structure and function were intimately related, he declared: '. . . the size, shape, and structure of the body have a direct dynamic relation to all the vital organs, and appreciably influence the function of the brain and nervous system'.[69]

Late nineteenth-century physical educators designed programmes of exercises intended to foster symmetrical development and bring each individual as close as possible to an anthropometric 'ideal' – an *arithmetic mean* derived from the average scores of thousands of measurements. Significantly, *athletes* were classified according to 'ideal types' for various sports (e.g. track, baseball, crew and football) and even for specific position in these (e.g. half-back).[70] However, by 1901 Boas, who was measuring immigrant and other populations, and other scientists questioned the notion of 'one ideal type'. The psychologist Frederic Burke, for example, insisted that gymnasium work should give much more attention to *individual differences*. The YMCA's William Hastings reported that the assumption that '. . . symmetry of bone lengths and muscle girths was equivalent to physical perfection, the guarantee of normal function. . .' would need to be abandoned and more emphasis placed on tests of respiratory and vascular function.[71] In the popular mind, however, the visual form of the athletic male body continued to be associated with ideals of perfection and virtue.

Although much more attention was devoted to the individual after 1900, the mesomorphic male form continued to receive the adulation of large numbers of Americans. As Harvey Green and Donald Mrozek have contended, '. . . muscular bulk in men. . .' had become a highly prized cultural value. In part, it connoted the leisure time one had to *train* and, paradoxically, training conformed to notions of tireless action.[72] The well-ordered body also served as an icon for the well-ordered society at a time when many middle-class Americans were anxious about social changes they saw all around them. The domineering figures of football heroes in padded sweaters and canvas pants – the battle dress of their sport – conveyed rather unambiguously messages of power, vitality and prowess. Rhetoric about the athlete repeatedly declared that he was a man who possessed discipline, self-control, courage and virility.

Athletes were not men who assumed *static* poses, however; theirs were *dynamic* statements. *They* used their bodies for a clearly defined purpose – contest victory which was quantitatively determined. In his study of the American male, Peter Stearns has said: 'The athlete, as American football coaches have not tired of saying in over a century, was a man'.[73] The athlete personified new ideals of achievement and success. The athlete's body also united all that modern biology had separated into systems, tissues, cells and the like. His achievements – over himself and over an opponent – were demonstrable proof that man was not unduly fragile *and* that the social order would not necessarily come apart. Through their own actions such men could make an impression on the world and, perhaps, even control parts of it. Such were the new men of character!

Notes

1 Bruce Haley, *The Healthy Body and Victorian Culture,* Cambridge, MA, 1978, p. 3.

2 *Ibid.,* Part II. By now several important works have examined the emergence of this intense interest in athletics. See, for example, James A. Mangan, *Athleticism in the Victorian and Edwardian Public School: The Emergence and Consolidation of an Educational Ideology,* Cambridge, 1981; Malcom Tozer, *Physical Education at Thring's Uppingham,* Uppingham, 1975; David Newsome, *Godliness and Good Learning,* London, 1961; Richard Jenkyns, *The Victorians and Ancient Greece,* Cambridge, 1980, especially Ch. IX and X. Keith A. P. Sandiford, 'English cricket crowds during the Victorian Age' *Journal of Sport History,* IX, Winter 1982, pp. 5-22, reports that 377,449 spectators watched the Oxford-Cambridge match between 1871 and 1887 and another 244,000 watched the Eton-Harrow match in the same period.

3 Haley, *Healthy Body,* especially Ch. X. For a marvellous discussion of games and character-building in the context of the extension of the British Empire, see James A. Managan, *The Games Ethic and Imperialism: Aspects of the Diffusion of an Ideal,* Viking, 1986.

4 See James C. Whorton, *Crusaders for Fitness: The History of American Health Reformers,* Princeton, 1982. Also, Dioclesian Lewis, *The New Gymnastics,* Boston, 1868. In the first volume of his *Lewis' New Gymnastics for Ladies, Gentlemen and Children, and Boston Journal of Physical Culture,* Lewis reviewed Catharine Beecher's *Physiology and Callisthenics for Homes and Families,* included articles by Horace Mann and Henry Ward Beecher, discussed exercise clothing for women, heavy v. light gymnastics, gymnastics for the insane, the 'Movement Cure', physical culture in the schools and tobacco; and reported an exhibition of his system of gymnastics which had been given at a recent meeting of the American Institute of Instruction. See also, Joan Paul, 'The health reformers: George Windship and Boston's Strength Seekers', *Journal of Sport History,* X, 1983, pp. 41-57.

5 George H. Taylor, *Health by Exercise. What Exercises to Take and How to Take Them, to Remove Special Physical Weaknesses. Embracing an Account of the Swedish Method, and a Summary of the Principles of Hygiene,* New York, 1880; M[athias] Roth, *The Gymnastic Free Exercises of P. H. Ling, Arranged by H. Rothstein,* Boston, 1853; Roberta J. Park, 'Swedish gymnastics in the United States, 1830-1900: An analysis of its influence on educational and medical thought', in *Proceedings of the VIIIth International Congress for the History of Sport and Physical Education,* Uppsala, 1979.

6 Roberta J. Park, '"Embodied selves": The rise and development of concern for physical education, active games and recreation for American women, 1776-1865', *Journal of Sport History,* V, 1978, pp. 5-41; *idem.,* 'Harmony and cooperation: Attitudes toward physical education and recreation in utopian social thought and American communitarian experiments, 1825-1865', *Research Quarterly,* XLV, 1974, pp. 276-92; *idem.,* 'The attitudes of leading New England transcendentalists toward healthful exercise, active recreation and proper care of the body', *Journal of Sport History,* IV, 1977 pp. 34-50.

7 Harvey Green, *Fit for America: Health, Fitness, Sport and American Society,* New York, 1986, Ch. 1, *passim.*

8 A useful overview of the emergence of intercollegiate athletics may be found in John

A. Lucas and Ronald A. Smith, *Saga of American Sport,* Philadelphia, 1978. See also, Ronald A. Smith, 'Harvard and Columbia and a reconsideration of the 1905-06 football crisis', *Journal of Sport History,* VIII, 1981, pp. 5-19, and the references in Note 2 of this article.

9   Sally Shuttleworth, *George Eliot and Nineteenth Century Science: The Make-Believe of a Beginning,* Cambridge, 1984; Charles Webster (ed.), *Biology, Medicine, Society: 1840-1940,* Cambridge, 1981; William Coleman, *Biology in the Nineteenth Century: Problems of Form, Function, and Transformation,* Cambridge, 1977, p. 116 *passim.*

10   Haley, *Healthy Body;* Mangan, *Athleticism,* especially Ch. VIII.

11   George M. Fredrickson, *The Inner Civil War: Northern Intellectuals and the Crisis of the Union,* New York, 1965, especially Ch. XIV.

12   Donald J. Mrozek, *Sport and American Mentality: 1880-1910,* Knoxville, 1983, p. 190.

13   Michel Foucault, *The Order of Things: An Archaeology of the Human Sciences,* New York, 1970; *idem., The Birth of the Clinic: An Archaeology of Medical Perception,* New York, 1963.

14   Mary Douglas, *Natural Symbols: Explorations in Cosmology,* New York, 1982, pp. 65-71.

15   Victor Turner, 'Liminal to liminoid in play, flow and ritual: An essay in comparative symbology', In Edward Norbeck (ed.), *Rice University Studies: The Anthropological Study of Human Play,* 60, 1974, pp. 53-72; *idem., Dramas, Fields, and Metaphors: Symbolic Action in Human Society,* Cornell, 1974; *idem., The Ritual Process: Structure and Anti-Structure,* Chicago, 1969; John J. MacAloon, *This Great Symbol: Pierre de Coubertin and the Origins of the Modern Olympic Games,* Chicago, 1981; *idem.,* 'Olympic Games and the theory of spectacle in modern societies', In John J. MacAloon (ed.), *Rite, Drama, Festival, Spectacle: Rehearsals Toward a Theory of Cultural Performances,* Philadelphia, 1984, pp. 241-80.

16   Henry Smith Williams, 'The century's progress in anatomy and physiology', *Harper's New Monthly Magazine,* XCVI, 1898, pp. 621-32; *idem.,* 'The century's progress in scientific medicine', *ibid.,* XCIX, 1899, pp. 38-52.

17   Henry Smith Williams, 'The century's progress in experimental psychology', *Harper's New Monthly Magazine,* XCIX, 1899, pp. 513-27; Eric R. Kandel and James H. Schwartz (eds.), *Principles of Neural Science,* New York, 1985, Ch. 1.

18   Wilhelm Wundt, *Lectures on Human and Animal Psychology,* J. E. Creighton and E. B. Titchner, trans., New York, 1901, pp. 432-35. See also, L. S. Jacyna, 'The physiology of mind, the unity of nature, and the moral order in Victorian thought', *British Journal for the History of Science,* XIV, 1981, pp. 109-32.

19   Dominick Cavallo, *Muscles and Morals: Organized Playgrounds and Urban Reform,* 1880-1920, Philadelphia, 1981, pp. 70-1; William James, *Psychology,* New York, 1913, pp. 134-42.

20   Edward M. Hartwell, 'The nature of physical training, and the best means of securing its ends', in Isabel C. Barrows (ed.), *Physical Training: A Full Report of the Papers and Discussions on the Conference Held in Boston in November* 1889, Boston, 1899, pp. 5-22; William T. Harris, 'Physical Training', *ibid.,* pp. 1-4.

21   John Jeffries, 'Physical culture, the result of moral obligation', *American Quarterly Review,* I, 1833, p. 253.

22   *Ibid.,* pp. 259-60.

23   Andrew Combe, *The Principles of Physiology Applied to the Preservation of Health, and to the Improvement of Physical and Mental Education,* New York, 1836, pp. 208-9; 216 *passim.*

24   *Ibid.,* pp. 109-20.

25   'Physical Education', *American Journal of Education,* 1, 1826, pp. 19-23.

26   Fred E. Leonard, *A Guide to the History of Physical Education,* Philadelphia, 1947,

237-39; Bruce L. Bennet, 'The making of the Round Hill School', *Quest*, IV, 1965, pp. 53-63.

27 Leonard, *Guide*, pp. 294-314; Henry Metzner, *A Brief History of the American Turner-bund*, Theodore Stempfel, Jr, trans., Pittsburg, 1924.

28 Taylor, *Health by Exercise*, especially Ch. III.

29 William A. Alcott, *The House I Live In; Or the Human Body, For Use of Families and Schools*, Boston, 1837: A knowledge of anatomy and physiology may '. . . induce us to look "through Nature up to Nature's God"', p. viii.

30 William A. Alcott, *The Laws of Health: Or, Sequel to 'The House I Live In'*, Boston, 1857, pp. 23-7.

31 *Ibid.*, p. 40; Park, 'New England transcendentalists'; Ralph Waldo Emerson, *Works*, VI, Boston, 1904, pp. 53-64: *idem., Lectures and Biographical Sketches*, Boston, 1891, pp. 93-121. The essay first appeared in *Atlantic Monthly* in 1860.

32 E. Anthony Rotundo, 'Body and soul: Changing ideals of American middle class manhood, 1770-1920', *Journal of Social History*, XVI, 1983, pp. 23-38; John G. Cawelti, *Apostles of the Self-Made Man: Changing Concepts of Success in America*, Chicago, 1965.

33 C[atharine] E. Beecher, 'Physical education', *American Annals of Education*, II, 1832, pp. 463-66.

34 Henry F. May, *The End of American Innocence: A Study of the First Years of Our Time*, 1912-1917, New York, 1959; Roberta J. Park, 'Sport, gender and society in a transatlantic Victorian perspective', *British Journal of Sports History*, II, 1985, pp. 5-28.

35 [A. A. Livermore], 'Gymnastics', *North American Review*, CLXIX, 1855, p. 52; 'Westward Ho!', *ibid.*, pp. 289-324.

36 [Livermore], 'Gymnasics', pp. 65-66.

37 *Ibid.*, p. 67; Oliver Wendell Holmes, *The Autocrat of the Breakfast Table: Every Man His Own Boswell*, Boston, 1859, p. 197. These essays had appeared in *The Atlantic Monthly* in 1858. The poet and novelist Bayard Taylor expressed similar sentiments in *The Brawnville Papers: Being Memorials of the Brawnville Athletic Club*, Boston, 1869, based upon articles which he had prepared for *The Herald of Health* regarding his '. . . own Utopian Gymnasium. . .', p. iv.

38 Thomas Wentworth Higginson, 'Barbarism and civilisation', *Atlantic Monthly*, VII, 1861, pp. 51-61; *idem*, 'Gymnastics', *ibid.*, pp. 283-302.

39 Higginson, 'Barbarism', p. 61.

40 W. W. Hall, *Guide-Board to Health, Peace and Competence, or the Road to Happy Old Age*, Springfield, MA, 1869, pp. 9, 463. Like a number of these manuals, Hall's was only available through 'subscription'. John G. Gunn, the author of a similar work, boasted that his *New Family Physician; or Home Book of Health. . .*, New York, 1867, was in its one hundredth edition (!), the first having appeared in 1856. This 1200 page compendium offered the reader a great deal of health reform information, some superficial information about anatomy and physiology, and a small section devoted to 'exercise'.

41 Walter Wells, 'Strength and how to use it', *Lippincott's Magazine*, II, 1868, pp. 416-35.

42 H. C. Williston, 'Physical exercise considered as a preventive of disease and as a curative agent', *Knickerbocker Magazine*, LXII, 1863, pp. 1-9; R. T. Trall, MD, *The Illustrated Family Gymnasium; Containing the Most Improved Methods of Applying Gymnastic, Calisthenic, Kinesipathic, and Vocal Exercises to the Development of the Bodily Organs, the Invigoration of Their Functions, the Preservation of Health, and the Cure of Diseases and Deformities*, New York, 1857.

43 Julius Wilcox, 'Work and rest', *Galaxy*, I, 1868, pp. 514-18· S. G. Young, 'Are Americans less healthy than Europeans?' *Galaxy*, V, 1872, pp. 630-39.

44 James E. Sullivan, 'Athletics and the stadium', *Cosmopolitan*, XXXI, 1901, pp. 501-08.

45 'The cricket mania', *Harper's Weekly*, 15 October 1859, p. 658.

46 'The boat race', *The Nation*, IX, 1869, pp. 187-9.

47 Dee Brown, *The Year of the Century: 1876*, New York, 1966; John Garraty, *The New Commonwealth: 1877-1890*, New York, 1968; 'The philosophy of the national game', *The Nation*, IX, 1869, pp. 167-8; Robert K. Barney, 'Of rails and red stockings: Episodes in the expansion of the "national game" in the American West', *Journal of the West*, XVII, 1978, pp. 61-70; George W. Green, 'College athletics', *The New Englander*, XXXV, 1876, pp. 548-60.

48 Green, 'College athletics'.

49 The mechanisms by which spectators are made an integral part of the athletic contest has yet to receive sufficient attention. Building upon the work of Gregory Bateson and Erving Goffman concerning the 'framing' of experience, John MacAloon has provided one of the most useful studies to date for examining the symbolic (and perhaps metaphoric) nature of the extended athletic performance. See, MacAloon, *This Great Symbol; idem*, 'Olympic Games and the theory of spectacle'; See also, Roberta J. Park, 'Hermeneutics, semiotics, and the nineteenth century quest for a corporeal self', *Quest*, XXXVIII, 1986, pp. 33-49; Maragret C. Duncan, 'A hermeneutic of spectator sport: The 1976 and 1984 Olympic Games', *ibid.*, pp. 50-77.

50 See, Roberta J. Park, 'Morality embodied: the college athlete and American views of right action and success, 1870-1900', in *The University's Role in the Development of Sport, Past, Present, and Future*, Edmonton, 1983, pp. 328-41; *idem.*, 'From football to rugby – and back, 1906-1919: the University of California-Stanford University response to the "football crisis" of 1905', *Journal of Sport History*, XI, 1984, pp. 5-40.

51 Walter Camp and Lorin F. Deland, *Football*, Boston, 1896, pp. 193-204.

52 Eugene L. Richards, Jr, 'Foot-Ball in America', *Outing*, VI, 1885, pp. 62-6; Joseph H. Sears, 'Foot-Ball: Sport and training', *North American Review*, CCCXXI, 1891, pp. 750-53.

53 Works like those of Mark H. Haller, *Eugenics: Hereditarian Attitudes in American Thought*, New Brunswick, NJ, 1963, and Robert C. Bannister, *Social Darwinism: Science and Myth in Anglo-American Social Thought*, Philadelphia, 1979, point up the intense turn-of-the-century anxieties about racial degeneration.

54 Quoted in Haller, *Eugenics*, p. 79; also, Thomas G. Dyer, *Theodore Roosevelt and the Idea of Race*, Baton Rouge, 1980.

55 See, Green, *Fit for America*; Mrozek, *Sport and American Mentality*; Luther Gulick, 'Vitality and modern life', *Physical Education*, V, 1896, pp. 21-5; *ibid.*, pp. 33-5.

56 Stefan Lorant, *The Life and Times of Theodore Roosevelt*, New York, 1959; Edward Wagenknecht, *The Seven Worlds of Theodore Roosevelt*, New York, 1958.

57 Theodore Roosevelt, *The Strenuous Life*, New York, 1904, pp. 212-3.

58 *Ibid.*, pp. 98-106.

59 Quoted in Park, 'From football to rugby', p. 25.

60 For example, G. B. Emerson, 'Physical education', *New England Journal of Education*, I, 1875, p. 76; 'Exercise', *ibid.*; The 2 October 1875 issue reprinted President Chadbourne's remarks on 'The nature of play, and its importance as a means of education', pp. 147-8; William H. Burnham, 'Motor ability in children: development and training', *New England Journal of Education*, XL, 1894; T. M. Balliet, 'Value of motor education', *ibid.*, XLVIII, 1898.

61 Roberta J. Park, 'Science, service, and the professionalization of physical education, 1885-1905', *Research Quarterly for Exercise and Sport*, Centennial Issue, 1985, pp. 7-20.

62 Hartwell, 'Nature of physical training'; *idem.* 'On physical training', *Report of the Commissioner of Education for the Year* 1903, I, Washington, DC, 1905, pp. 721-57.

63   Edward M. Hartwell, 'President's address', *American Physical Education Review,* IV, 1899, 202-9. Hartwell delivered the address at the first 'national' convention of the AAAPE; previous conventions had been local or regional.

64   *Ibid.;* Thomas Huxley and William Jay Youmans, *The Elements of Physiology and Hygiene: A Textbook for Educational Institutions,* revised edition, New York, 1881, pp. 344-452.

65   Luther H. Gulick, 'Physical education: a new profession', in *Proceedings of the American Association for the Advancement of Physical Education, Cambridge and Boston,* 1890, Ithaca, NY, 1890, p. 65.

66   G. Stanley Hall, *Adolescence, Its Psychology and Its Relations to Physiology, Anthropology, Sociology, Sex, Crime, Religion and Education,* New York, 1908, I, pp. 202-5, 217-30.

67   Ralph D. Paine, 'The spirit of school and college sport: English and American football', *Century Magazine,* LXXI, 1905, pp. 99-116; *idem.,* 'The spirit of school and college sport: English and American rowing', *Century Magazine,* LXX, 1905, pp. 483-503; Ira N. Hollis, 'Intercollegiate athletics', *Atlantic Monthly,* XC, 1902, pp. 534-44.

68   Edward Hitchcock and H. H. Seelye, *An Anthropometric Manual, Giving the Average and Mean Physical Measurements and Tests of Male College Students, and Methods of Securing Them,* Amherst, 1889, p. 4. See also, B. J. Norton, 'The biometric defense of Darwinism', *Journal of the History of Biology,* VI, 1973, 290-3; Stephen Jay Gould, *The Mismeasure of Man,* New York, 1981; Charles Roberts, *A Manual of Anthropometry: Or a Guide to the Physical Examination and Measurement of the Human Body,* London, 1878, pp. 1-6.

69   D[udley] A. Sargent, 'The physical proportions of the typical man', *Scribner's Magazine,* II, 1887, pp. 3-17.

70   *Idem.,* 'The physical characteristics of the athlete', *ibid.,* pp. 541-61.

71   Frederic Burke, 'Growth of children in height and weight', *American Journal of Psychology,* IX, 1898, pp. 253-326; Franz Boas, 'Statistical Study of Anthropometry', *American Physical Education Review,* VI, 1901, pp. 174-80; William W. Hastings, *A Manual for Physical Measurement for Use in Normal Schools, Public and Preparatory Schools, Boys' Clubs, Girl's Clubs, and Young Men's Christian Associations, With Anthropometric Tables for Each Height of Each Age and Sex from Five to Twenty Years, and Vitality Coefficients,* Springfield, MA, 1902.

72   Green, *Fit for America,* especially Ch. IX; Mrozek, *Sport and American Mentality,* especially Ch. VII.

73   Peter Stearns, *Be a Man!: Males in Modern Society,* New York, 1979; see also, Elizabeth H. Pleck and Joseph H. Pleck, *The American Man,* Englewood Cliffs, NJ, 1980. Allen Guttmann, *From Ritual to Record: The Nature of Modern Sports,* New York, 1978, has provided a penetrating discussion of the tendency toward quantification.

Learning about manhood: gender ideals and the middle-class family in nineteenth-century America[1]

Nearly everything we know about human behaviour in the past concerns men and yet it is equally – and ironically – true that we know far more about womanhood and the female role than we know about masculinity or the man's role. The energetic work of women's historians over the past twenty years has shown the importance of gender as a system of power relations, a pattern of social relationships and a cultural construct of profound influence. But so far historians have learned more about gender by approaching it through woman's role than man's. To understand gender fully, we need to know more about the male role as well.

The purpose of this chapter is to fill a small part of that gap in our knowledge. In particular, the essay that follows will examine manhood as a cultural construct in nineteenth-century America, focusing first on a description of the ideals of manhood that were prevalent among northern middle-class men and then on the role of the family in passing on those cultural ideals to new generations. The correspondence and diaries of roughly one hundred middle-class men have provided the raw material out of which this chapter is shaped.[2]

Before moving on to explore this evidence though, some discussion of the term 'gender ideal' (or 'ideal of manhood') is in order. A gender ideal refers here to a *cluster* of traits, behaviour and values that the members of a society believe a person should have as a woman or a man. Seen in a wider perspective, the gender ideal is closely related to the broader values of the culture in which it develops – it represents a series of cultural choices out of the vast range of qualities possible for a man or a woman. For instance, emotional expression is part of an ideal of manhood in some cultures and not in others. A culture that includes this trait within an ideal of manhood is making a statement about what it values. To understand nineteenth-century middle-class gender ideals, then, is to understand an important aspect of American culture as well as a segment of gender history.

There were, in fact, three ideals of manhood held up to middle-class men in the nineteenth-century North. We will call them here the Masculine Achiever, the Christian Gentleman and the Masculine Primitive. The first two held sway throughout the nineteenth century. Historians not directly concerned with issues of manhood have analysed them.[3] And, indeed, their names come from Charles Rosenberg's article, 'Sexuality, Class and Role', which presented these ideals specifically as standards of male sexual behaviour.[4] The third, the Masculine Primitive, has been less frequently described. Unlike the others, it became a part of northern middle-class culture only gradually, emerging over the course of the century but taking a firm hold on the male imagination by the late 1800s.

Of these three ideals, the Masculine Achiever was linked most closely with the economic forms of the era. As commercial capitalism began to spread rapidly in the North at the end of the 1700s, a new ideal of manhood emerged – one that encouraged men to participate actively in the system and take advantage of its opportunities. The Masculine Achiever was an ideal that presented the male sex as naturally active and dynamic. As one lawyer put it: 'Man is made for action, and the bustling scenes of moving life, and not the poetry or romance of existence.'[5] Activity – strong, aggressive action – formed an important part of the ideal of the Masculine Achiever.

This emphasis on action has been a common feature of male ideals in many places and times. What made the ideal of the Masculine Achiever so distinctive to its own era was the way it focused on self-advancement as the primary goal for a man's active nature. In 1818 a New York father wrote to his son that there was a 'wide field' for young men to 'place themselves in pre-eminent situations'. 'Cultivate the talents which God has endowed you with', he advised, 'and you need not despair, of promotion in the fair Land of Independence'.[6] More than half a century later, the naturalist John Burroughs rephrased the credo of self-advancement in this way: 'We respect him less who is set up in business, with a fortune at his disposal, than he who, from humble beginnings, achieves his own success'.[7]

To reach such ambitious goals, a man had to work hard and with unfailing persistence. Thus, the ideal of the Masculine Achiever urged ceaseless effort.

One man, a salesman, resolved that he would 'improve' his time so that he could spend 'every hour to an advantage, either in acquiring, or getting wealth, or arising to some honourable station in life'.[8] Intense and enduring effort was a key virtue in the ideal of the Masculine Achiever.

However, a belief in hard work had been a revered Yankee value for generations. What made this aspect of the Masculine Achiever unique to its time was a tremendous faith in the effective power of simple dogged effort. Men believed that persevering industry was even more important than talent in determining how high a man could rise. As one lawyer wrote in 1846, a 'man of moderate abilities, by close application may rise above those of the brightest genius'.[9]

Hard work and persistence were not the only qualities needed for self-advancement, though. If a man wished to make his way in the world, he had to break free of the restraints of home and community and he could not rely on anyone else. Thus, the ideal of the Masculine Achiever encouraged men to be independent in their actions. Men expected themselves to be independent thinkers as well. As an ambitious college student, Rutherford B. Hayes wrote that 'artificial aids' to insight 'must be rejected'. Hayes believed that men who relied on the thoughts of others would 'finally fall below' those who were 'compelled to think and act for themselves'.[10]

For a man to rise above others in this competitive world, he needed more than independent thought and action; he also had to have freedom from emotional dependence on others, freedom to be clear-headed and rational. Thus, the ideal of the Masculine Achiever emphasised the restraint of tender or 'sentimental' feeling. A Massachusetts doctor, for instance, wrote in 1889 that grief was 'something to be ashamed of. . .'. He considered it 'morally. . . on a par with *fear* . . . (it) is a proof of weakness of spirit'. Accessible emotions could, in the long run, threaten a man's ability to think clearly and to act independently and, without the combination of independence and hard, persistent effort, self-advancement would be impossible. In sum, the ideal of the Masculine Achiever encouraged accomplishment, autonomy and aggression – all in the service of an intense competition for success in the market-place.

The ideal of the Christian Gentleman arose in opposition to the

Masculine Achiever and to the broader changes of which that ideal was a part. Viewed in one way, the Christian Gentleman was the product of an era of religious ferment and commercial enterprise, an evangelical response to the competitive impulse that was turned loose in the early nineteenth century. Viewed in another way, the Christian Gentleman was part of an effort to maintain moral order at a time when communal values had lost their force and individualism threatened to run unchecked. Both viewpoints explain the roots – and the functions – of the ideal of the Christian Gentleman.

From *either* perspective, this was a standard of manhood that opposed the values of the Masculine Achiever. The Christian Gentleman discouraged self-seeking and condemned the rewards offered to successful men by a commercial society. Young Daniel Webster's critique of wealth and fame was typical. He wrote that 'the seeker of wealth never accumulated to his desire' and added a harsher diatribe against fame. Anyone who sought public acclaim, said Webster, faced obstacles ranging from 'cold, arctic indifference' to 'the torrid heats of resentment, rivalry, emulation, and opposition'.[12] Webster was preaching against his own values, attacking the Masculine Achiever's quest for fame and fortune from the standpoint of the Christian Gentleman.

But the ideal of the Christian Gentleman was not just a set of negative values. The ideal stressed love, kindness and compassion. These were not only worthy *attitudes* for a man – they also formed the basis for right *actions* on his part. Such acts were called 'Christian benevolence' early in the nineteenth century and 'noble deeds' in later decades, but they amounted to the same things – philanthropy, church activities, self-sacrifice and a deep involvement in family life. Men who lived to serve themselves were condemned, however successful they might be. Thomas Wentworth Higginson wrote in 1891 of one energetic but arrogant man: 'We had too many officers like him in our war, with magnificent push and go, but otherwise ignoble, selfish, merciless'.[13] The ideal of the Christian Gentleman was in essence an ethic of compassion that directed a man's attention to the needs and concerns of others.

And yet, for all the opposition between the ideals of the Christian Gentleman and the Masculine Achiever, they could be combined in certain ways. Men who professed the virtues of the Christian Gentleman were not so much condemning a career in business as they were rejecting the greed, selfishness and dishonesty of the market-place. They accepted commerce as a part of their social order, but insisted that it be pursued in a spirit of Christian decency. One advocate of the ideal spoke out against the man who 'serves his God on Sunday, and cheats his neighbour on Monday. . . who prays with much feeling. . . and reads his Bible. . . but has not conscientious scruples when an opportunity presents itself during the week to defraud or lie a little. . .'. The good man has 'conscience every day in the week' and '[lived] a Christian life', refusing to 'exchange his soul for any pecuniary benefit'.[14] Success, in other words, clashed with the ideal only if it was gained in an unchristian manner.

If the ideal of the Christian Gentleman encouraged self-sacrifice in business, it demanded even more of it in personal conduct. The good man thought of the world beyond his doorstep as a place of 'a thousand allurements' – only he could prevent himself from giving in to them. These temptations were not only the vices of greed and cruelty but also the sins of the flesh. A man could not allow himself to become 'the devotee of sensual pleasure' or 'the votary of the wine cup'. One youth recited for his parents a chivalric creed that exhorted men: 'To lead sweet lives in purest chastity'.[15]

The ideal placed such a heavy emphasis on impulse control because pleasures of the flesh were sinful. But indulgences like sex and liquor were also condemned as habits that diverted men from lives of productive effort. In 1829, for instance, the friends of a young naval officer wrote to his parents to warn them of his reckless lifestyle. They feared that he would soon 'become confirmed in habits of debauchery' which would 'impair his constitution so as to render him forever here after incapable of making those exertions that are essential to happiness in [later] life'.[16] In other words, a man who failed to control his impulses was not only headed toward eternal damnation but to earthly failure as well. Here again, the ideal pointed toward an accommodation of sorts with the worldly goals of the Masculine Achiever.

Whatever its purposes, the ethic of self-mastery was not a doctrine of moderate restraint. The ideal of the Christian Gentleman maintained an absolute standard in controlling dangerous impulses. This goal of perfection was clearly implied in the concept of 'purity' that formed such a central part of middle-class morality. In his college diary, Rutherford B. Hayes preached this doctrine of extreme self-restraint: 'Everyone should bear in mind that when he yields to *any* passion, every repetition is giving it a power which may erelong bind with links stronger than steel and more galling than the cruel gyves of the galley slave'.[17] By calling for such total self-control, the ideal of the Christian Gentleman demanded a conquest of the inner environment much like the conquest of the outer environment for which the Masculine Achiever called. The two ideals converged in their heavy emphasis on mastery and conquest even as they differed on a wide range of other values and attitudes.

In sum, the ideals of the Masculine Achiever and the Christian Gentlemen were opposed but intimately related standards of manhood. To a great extent, each ideal thrived on its opposition to the other, but they did share important areas of agreement as well. In contrast, the third ideal of manhood that flourished within the nineteenth-century middle-class – the ideal of the Masculine Primitive – was not closely linked to the other two. Its dominant values and its pattern of development over time coincided very little with them.

The Masculine Primitive represented not only a different conception of manhood but a different conception of the human nature in which manliness had its roots. This ideal stressed the notion that civilised men – more than women – were primitives in many important ways. So habitual did this idea become that it affected men's view of themselves at moments of stress. A Union officer in the Civil War thought of himself in comparison with 'savages' – or even as a 'savage' himself. As he surveyed a deadly knoll that was being raked by Confederate gunfire, he thought of his reading in Cooper's novels and in *The Book of Indians*. He realised that he would have to be 'as cunning as a savage or a backwoodsman' in order to get across the knoll. In later years he recalled that his thoughts in that moment 'were perfectly sane and calm. . . ranging from an expectation of a ball through the spine to a recollection of Cooper's most celebrated Indians'.[18]

The comparison of middle-class men to 'savages' was not mere fancy. The ideal of the Masculine Primitive stressed the belief that all males – civilised or not – shared in the same primordial instincts for survival. One young man wrote: 'We have put reason in the place of instinct and are going to no good end'.[19] In the same vein, Theodore Roosevelt declared it a good thing to 'make the wolf rise in a man's heart'. Roosevelt elaborated by quoting a sermon on the subject: 'The history of the world shows that men are not to be counted by their numbers but by the fire and vigor of their passions'.[20] Suddenly, natural passions and impulses had become a valued part of a man's character.

Reliance on primordial instinct was only one part of the Masculine Primitive ideal. There was also a special respect – and concern – for a man's physical strength and energy. As the nineteenth century progressed, the measurement of growing bodies became a preoccupation of male middle-class youth. A graduate student wrote home from Germany to tell his parents the results of his self-imposed exercise programme. He listed his chest, stomach and hip measurements for them, exact to the quarter inch. A Massachusetts teenager traced his growth by inches in his diary. Male concern with physical development carried over into adulthood. A study of magazine heroes at the turn of the century found that men were admired far more for their strength, size and look of determination than they had been a century earlier.[21] Size and strength were not the only physical qualities by which males were judged. The vigour that a man brought to his tasks was an important aspect of manhood. He was expected to work 'with indomitable energy', to offer his community an 'energetic public spirit' and even to think with 'creative energy'. According to the popular view, it was 'a different world to those that (were) strong and vigorous'.[22]

The ideal of the Masculine Primitive honoured not only vigour and strength of body, but vigour and strength of personality as well. A man who lacked such power of personality was often judged deficient as a man. John Burroughs wrote scornfully that his ageing father's 'force and authority as a man were feeble'. More positively, Thomas Wentworth Higginson described an admired acquaintance as 'a man one part flesh and three parts fire'.[23] Clearly, this emphasis on personal force was related to other aspects of the Masculine Primitive ideal. Men especially associated a commanding personality with vigorous natural instincts.

There was, moreover, a distinct world-view implied in all of these Masculine Primitive traits – physical strength, powerful instincts, personal force. Life in the civilised world was seen as a wilderness struggle for survival. Men battled one another for mastery and success in the marketplace, the courthouse and the classroom. A young lawyer just starting his practice in Colorado wrote to a friend back east: 'Here is a vast field for workers. . . if I am only equal to the contest I shall win, if weak then some other and stronger one will carry off the spoils. I shall work and work to win'.[24] A college senior's description of a contest between debating societies shows the hostility and visceral excitement that could surface when men competed: 'The hope of crushing your opponents, the dignity of defending what we deem to be the truth, the consciousness of battling for the honour and prosperity of the (debating) society gives a wild elation, that one never feels in any other action'.[25] Even in the most civilised of settings, a bit of the wolf could rise as an impulse in a man's heart.

Men's instincts for battle surfaced more visibly and violently in other ways. It was a measure of the power of the Masculine Primitive ideal that, by the late nineteenth century, middle-class men sometimes approved of fist fights between boys, while the boys themselves boasted of their exploits in spontaneous fights. A gentle young art student, on learning that his brother had beaten some classmates in a schoolyard brawl, wrote to his parents: 'I should like to have seen Franklin lick the boys. Bully for him! Do it again every time – 'sic' him. I feel like doing something of the kind to a fellow in our class'.[26] Like the thousands of young men who played competitive sports in the late nineteenth century, these youths believed that they were preparing themselves for the savage struggles that lay ahead in the adult world of adult work.

The influence of the Masculine Primitive ideal was apparent in other well-known forms of male behaviour during the later years of the century. Some men left their civilised urban environment for the woods and the Western plains, hoping to cultivate their own 'natural' masculine strength and aggressiveness for life's battles. Others experienced their primitive instincts vicariously, thrilling to literary fantasies about cowboys, frontiersmen, jungle heroes and wild animals.[27] These new patterns of male behaviour came in response to the attitudes embedded in the Masculine Primitive ideal – the view of man as the master animal who could draw on primitive impulse when reason would not work, the evaluation of men according to their physical strength and energy, the popularity of the metaphor in which a man's life was a competitive jungle struggle and the pride in the physical combativeness of young men.

Clearly, this ideal lay far from the values and concerns of the Christian Gentleman ideal. Although it was compatible with the Masculine Achiever in its emphasis on aggression and competition, the ideal of the Masculine Primitive did not share in the intimately opposed, almost dialectical relationship that the other two ideals had with each other.

It should not be surprising, then, that the Masculine Primitive standard of manhood followed a different historical pattern in the timing of its origin and the growth of its influence. The evidence for the Masculine Achiever and Christian Gentleman ideals becomes readily visible in letters and diaries written at the beginning of the nineteenth century. The ideal of the Masculine Primitive does not begin to surface until the middle decades of the century. Cooper's *Leatherstocking Tales* and the popular literature on Davy Crockett first took hold of the public imagination in the 1830s. Theodore Weld presented himself to abolitionist audiences in the 1830s as a backwoodsman and found that the ploy drew a very positive response. Another development associated with the ideal of the Masculine Primitive – the rise of intercollegiate sports – began in the 1850s.[28] Taken together, this evidence suggests that there was no Masculine Primitive ideal until the middle third of the nineteenth century and it was only in the 1860s that this standard of manhood asserted its power in the private writings of the middle class.

Clearly, the ideal had a very different history from those of the Christian Gentleman and Masculine Achiever and there is no doubt that these ideals represented three distinctly different standards of manhood, even if they did have certain points of compatibility. Yet, for fifty years or more, the three ideals existed side by side and during that time each ideal seems to have had an influence on every individual studied here.

How did middle-class men learn such conflicting ideals? What people or institutions played a role in teaching ideals of manhood to middle-class males in the nineteenth century? There were a great many avenues of influence — ministers, teachers and physicians; prescriptive literature, popular fiction and schoolbooks; clubs, competitive sports and children's games; colleges, Sunday schools and lyceum lectures.[29] And the list could be extended much further. But of all the influences on a boy's developing ideals of manhood, the first one he encountered was the family. Any ideal which a boy confronted frequently at home must have had an important impact on him. Thus, an understanding of what a boy learned from his family about manhood is vital to an understanding of what attitudes and expectations he carried through life.

The role of the middle-class family in teaching its boys the ideals of the Masculine Achiever and the Christian Gentleman is readily evident from private documents. Indeed, one of the main topics in nineteenth-century correspondence between parents and sons was ideals of manhood. The teaching of the two ideals differed in one especially important way: women stressed the Christian Gentleman, while men tended to emphasise the Masculine Achiever. This gender-linked emphasis was not, as we shall see, exclusive. Men worried about the moral character of the boys in their families and women were concerned that their sons, brothers and nephews should be successful but family correspondence does reveal that the two sexes were relatively more concerned with teaching their boys different values.

This gender-linked pattern is most evident when comparing a son's correspondence with his mother to the correspondence he carried on with his father. A case in point is Allan Gay who, as a young artist, carried on an active correspondence with his parents in the 1830s and 40s. Allan's mother wrote him letters that focused on the virtues of the Christian Gentleman. When he first left home, Mary Gay warned him that the 'world is full of temptations to draw away the hearts of young men from the path of duty' and she urged him to shun the snares of an immoral world. She returned to that same theme again and again. Several years later Mary told Allan that she prayed he would 'return to us unsophisticated and uncontaminated by the world's vices and weaknesses, its follies and impurities' and Mary Gay was concerned with Allan's spiritual growth as much as his moral character. She hoped that Allan's experiences in the world would lift his 'young and innocent and affectionate heart to the (source) of all good – who will guide you by his council, and protect you with his power, and cheer you with his spirit'. Mary urged her son to read his Bible and discover 'God's mercy and kind care'.[30]

By contrast, Allan's father, Ebenezer Gay, used his letters to tutor his son in the values of the Masculine Achiever. Ebenezer wrote to Allan about the qualities that made a man successful: 'By perseverance, I am led to believe. . . you will succeed. Be not discouraged by occasional failure, but persevere, and concentrate the whole power of your mind to the attainment of your object and I shall feel confident of your ultimate success.[31] Ebenezer repeated his message many times. 'Bend the full force of your intellect to the object you have in view', he told Allan on one occasion 'and the result will perhaps be a greater degree of Success than you at present anticipate'. Allan appreciated which parent stood for what set of values. He wrote to his father in the language of the Masculine Achiever: 'It is not so much genius as untiring perseverance that determines to conquer every obstacle'. On the other hand, he replied to a letter of moral instruction from his mother by asking her to continue in that vein. 'I hope your letters will be long and full of good advice to me,' he said, 'Callous must be the heart that feels not the lasting impression the words of maternal tenderness must have on a young and pliant mind'.[32]

The letters that other middle-class sons wrote to their parents reveal the same sorts of differences that show up in the Gay correspondence. In 1852 a businessman and reformer named John Kirk wrote a letter to each of his parents. He reflected on their influence and thanked them for the helpful models they provided. Kirk offered gratitude to his 'kind and pious, and affectionate Mother' for the 'thousand blessings' she conferred upon him: 'How often have I been admonished by your godly prayers and your pious exhortations, when far from home and friends, how often when none but God, could see and hear (your) monitions followed me, and caused the tears of penitential sorrows and affection to flow from my weeping eyes. . .'.[33] The contrast between this letter and the letter Kirk wrote to his father could not be clearer. Kirk said in the second letter that he felt 'under ten thousand obligations' for his father's 'noble (example) of. . . untiring industry, that has so often passed before my mind, and has oftentimes, braced my drooping and flagging energies'.[34] In other words, Kirk learned key portions of the Masculine Achiever ideal from his father, while he absorbed from his mother the piety and moral fibre that underlay the ideal of the Christian Gentleman.

Although it was the mother's particular task to teach the virtues of the Christian Gentleman and the father's special duty to pass on the ideal of the Masculine Achiever, there was nothing exclusive about either one of these teaching roles. Women tended to supplement their husband's attempts to teach the values of achievement and success and men helped support their wives' efforts to teach morality and Christian piety. We have already noted Mary Gay's efforts to tutor her sons in the values of religion and purity. However, she also encouraged her boys' attempts at worldly success. When her son Martin needed a large sum of money to open a medical practice in Boston, she wrote to one potential creditor: 'To see my eldest son, in whom I have placed the best founded hopes of a mother's heart fail for want of. . . aid. . . will I verily believe send me to my grave' and when her son Charles jumped ship and fled a naval officer's commission that his family had worked hard to obtain, Mary Gay hired a carriage and driver and pursued Charles half way across New England – all in hopes of convincing him to return.[35]

At the same time, middle-class fathers often supplemented their wives' work in teaching the ideal. There was, in fact, one aspect of moral instruction for which men held primary responsibility – the ethics of business and property. When an Ohio boy named William Whittlesey began a clerkship in a small-town store, his father Elisha wrote him a letter explaining proper conduct in his new setting. He stressed the 'many temptations before you when intrusted alone in the store. . . my duty as a parent, requires me to say to you, be careful never to take an article clandestinely however small it may be'.[36] Another father lectured his son sternly on the subject of the Eighth Commandment after the boy was caught stealing apples from a neighbour's orchard. The lecture humbled the boy, as he remembered years later: 'I cried and begged pardon, repeated a prayer, went to bed and resolved I would never be guilty of so foul a deed again – which resolution I do not recollect to have broken since'.[37]

Aside from this specific responsibility as moral tutor, fathers supported the ideal of the Christian Gentleman in a broader way as well. The importance of coupling hard work with moral fibre was a refrain that ran through father–son correspondence. One advised his son that 'attention in business' combined with 'integrity' would ensure him a respectable place in the world. Another told his boy that in America lofty positions were open to 'young men of talents, and character' who were willing to work hard.[38] Evidently, men were concerned that their sons develop strong moral character even as they set out in aggressive pursuit of success.

In summary, *each* parent in middle-class families generally supported *both* the ideal of the Masculine Achiever *and* the ideal of the Christian Gentleman for their sons. But each parent emphasised one ideal far more heavily than the other. These differing emphases were clearly consistent with the doctrine of the spheres. Mothers focused their lessons in manhood on the ideal of the Christian Gentleman which stressed the pious moral values associated with womanhood and the domestic sphere. Fathers, on the other hand, emphasised the ideal of the Masculine Achiever which encouraged the drive for success and accomplishment that people connected with men and their 'proper' sphere – the world.

There was one important way in which fathers and mothers resembled each other in this business of teaching the Masculine Achiever and Christian Gentleman ideals – they were both teaching these standards of manhood *intentionally*. Parents may not have had a systematic plan or a fully-developed course of instruction, but they believed strongly in the values of the Masculine Achiever and the Christian Gentleman and urged them upon their sons when they felt that the opportunity was appropriate.

The same statement about intentional teaching, however, can *not* be made about the ideal of the Masculine Primitive. One searches in vain for a middle-class family that taught its boys the values and beliefs of the Masculine Primitive at any time before the 1880s and yet that set of values and beliefs was clearly an important influence in middle-class male culture a quarter of a century earlier than that. How could that be? How did boys absorb the values of the Masculine Primitive?

The language of the Masculine Primitive and the metaphors that dominated it – man as master animal, the world as a harsh wilderness, life as a competitive struggle for survival – all reflect the impact of Darwinian thought as it filtered through to middle-class men. But Darwin's influence cannot account for Civil War soldiers who, when in danger, instinctively thought of themselves as wily Indians – there was not time to read *Origins of Species,* absorb it and have it change one's outlook on life. After all, it was published in 1859, a few short years before the Civil War. More certainly, Darwin's ideas cannot explain why a young man of such civilised background as Francis Parkman should have developed his profound obsession with Indians and the wilderness during the 1840s.[39]

What experiences, then, *did* generate the ideal of the Masculine Primitive? A complete and detailed answer to that elusive question lies beyond us here. But perhaps a few threads of fact and circumstance can be offered – threads out of which a strong explanation might ultimately be woven. One such strand is the emergence of the human body as a focus of special attention in the early nineteenth century. This new focus of interest coincided with the rise of individualism and the growing belief in empirical, scientific explanation as well as the technological solutions that followed from them.[40] This increased attention to the body may have had a specific impact on men's ideals through the genre of early nineteenth-century child-rearing literature that placed heavy emphasis on a mother's responsibility for her children's physical development. Letters and diaries from the period offer some evidence that mothers heeded this advice and concerned themselves deeply with the physical well-being of their children. As growing boys found that their mothers were especially attentive to their bodies, they may have developed particular awareness of themselves as physical beings.[41] This would not in itself explain the existence of the Masculine Primitive ideal but it would help to account for the equation of manhood with the body which lay at the core of the ideal.

There was another way in which the middle-class family of the early nineteenth century may have played an unintentional role in developing the ideal of the Masculine Primitive. Given the frequent absence of middle-class fathers from the home and the new expectation that mothers would turn their sons into generations of virtuous Christians and republican heroes, it fell to women to teach sons many of their important lessons in manhood. Social scientists of recent decades have noted that, where the sexual division of labour forced women to do much of the teaching about manhood, boys were likely to grow up with the idealised or exaggerated notions of manhood.[42] Certainly, much of the language and imagery attached to the Masculine Primitive ideal – 'master animal', 'superior instincts' and so forth – greatly exaggerated real circumstances.

Another factor in middle-class life that may have bred this ideal of manhood during the early nineteenth century was the great migration from farms to cities. Men who grew up in the country and then spent their lives in offices, counting houses and formal parlours may have cast a fond eye back at the rural way of life. Comparing the satisfactions of hard physical labour to the frustrations of restrained, sedentary work in the city, these men might well have idealised the strong, hardy aspects of manhood. The movement from country to city no doubt affected the sons of migrants too. Tales of exciting physical adventure in the parents' childhoods may have seemed heroic to impressionable middle-class boys. Visits to country relatives could have brought some of this experience to life. A hunting expedition with an uncle or a day in the woods with a cousin could stir a sense of excitement and adventure.[43]

Fantasies of frontier adventure and memories of country childhoods may have given romantic appeal to the backwoodsman pose that Theodore Weld struck so effectively. And they could easily have whetted the appetites of middle-class men and boys for Cooper's novels, for tales about Davy Crockett and for the Indian lore that became popular in the decades before the Civil War. These novels and tales, in turn, became part of the process by which boys developed a sense of what was good and worthy in a man.

A further stimulus to the growth of a middle-class ideal of the Masculine Primitive was the rise of intercollegiate sports, starting in the 1850s. Where college students had once channelled their competitive urges into fierce debates between literary societies and their physical aggression into brawls with townspeople, the competitive urge and the physical drive now came together in an organised arena of sport. Competitive sports provided a testing ground for manhood, an experience in which qualities like endurance, will, and decisiveness met the challenge of basic physical hardship.[44]

Thus by the late 1860s, when Darwin's ideas became well-known in America, a variety of experiences were already teaching middle-class boys a new ideal of manhood. Popular fiction, sports, unintended consequences of child-rearing and of migration to the city and then the veneration of Civil War heroes – all of these experiences taught boys that their bodies mattered profoundly, that their most basic and visceral instincts were of great value, that competition and physical challenge were important tests of manhood. Darwin's ideas – as they were popularly understood – provided a governing metaphor for these beliefs about manhood and also produced a broader ideology into which the new ideal of manhood fitted. Families did begin to preach Darwinism intentionally during the last two decades of the nineteenth century, but that was years after the concept of the Masculine Primitive had taken hold.

What does this chapter tell us about the role of the family in teaching ideals of gender? Unfortunately, it does not suggest any laws or hard-and-fast rules. If anything, this exploration in gender history should be a warning against any such broad, simple generalities. The family's role in transmitting gender ideals can be intentional *and* unintentional. The burden of teaching an ideal – where the teaching is intentional – can be divided among family members in different ways. And some ideals are picked up and taught within the family almost as they come into existence, while other ideals seep into the family's teaching process very gradually.

In short, the role of the family in transmitting gender ideals is an elusive one that seems to defy a simple descriptive statement. Perhaps it is enough to remind ourselves that ideas about gender are cultural constructs – and that the family, while it is a pre-eminent institution of culture, does not have exclusive influence in transmitting even the most personal of values. History as yet has a great deal more to teach us about that process of transmission.

Notes

1　An earlier version of this essay was presented at the Smith-Smithsonian Conference on the Conventions of Gender, Smith College, Northampton, Mass., 16 February 1984.

2　The broader study that underlies this paper is E. Anthony Rotundo, 'Manhood in America: The northern middle class, 1770-1920', unpublished Ph.D. dissertation, Brandeis University, 1982. The subjects of the study were white, Anglo-Saxon and Protestant. All of these men came from east of the Mississippi River and north of the Mason-Dixon line. They were primarily of Yankee stock. In modern terminology, these were mostly men of the upper-middle class. Applying such a label to individuals often presents difficulties and some of the men in this study might be placed more accurately in the lower-middle or upper classes.

3　See John G. Cawelti, *Apostles of the Self-Made Man,* Chicago: University of Chicago Press, 1965, pp. 39-73; Bernard Wishy, *The Child and the Republic: The Dawn of Modern American Child Nurture,* Philadelphia: Univsersity of Pennsylvania Press, 1968, pp. 3-78.

4　Charles Rosenberg, 'Sexuality, class and role in 19th-Century America,' in Elizabeth Pleck and Joseph H. Pleck, eds., *The American Man,* Englewood Cliffs, N.J.: Prentice-Hall, 1980, pp. 219-54.

5　Charles Theodore Russell to Charles Russell, 30 May 1838, Charles Russell Papers, Massachusetts Historical Society; see also 'Diary of George Younglove Cutler' in Emily Vanderpol, *Chronicles of A Pioneer School: Being the History of Miss Sarah Pierce and Her Litchfield School,* Cambridge, Mass.: University Press, 1903, p. 206.

6　Aquila Giles to Henry Giles, 25 May 1818, Aquila Giles Papers, New York Historical Society.

7　*The Heart of John Burroughs Journal,* ed. by Clara Barrus, Boston: Houghton Mifflin, 1928, p. 99.

8　John Kirk to 'Brother Calvin,' 9 March 1853, Kirk Letterbooks, I, Chicago Historical Society; see also Timothy Ives to Ralph Leete, 20 March 1846, Ralph Leete Papers, Container 1, Western Reserve Historical Society.

9　Horace Leete to Ralph Leete, 20 March 1846, Ralph Leete Papers, Container 1.

10　*Diary and Letters of Rutherford Birchard Hayes, Nineteenth President of the United States,* ed. by Charles Richard Williams, Columbus, Ohio: Ohio State Archaeological and Historical Society, 1922, I, pp. 93-4.

11　Richard Cabot to Ella Lyman, 12 September 1889, Ella Lyman Cabot Papers,

Schlesinger Library, Radcliffe College; see also Elisha Wittlesey to William Whittlesey, 23 January 1836, William W. Whittlesey Papers, Container 1, Western Reserve Historical Society.

12 Daniel Webster to Mr Merrill, 16 March 1804, *The Writings and Speeches of Daniel Webster*, National ed., Boston: Little Brown, 1903, XVII, p. 184.

13 Thomas Wentworth Higginson to Mrs Elliot, January 1891, *Letters and Journals of Thomas Wentworth Higginson, 1846-1906*, ed. by Mary Thacher Higginson, Boston: Houghton Mifflin, 1921.

14 James Barnard Blake diary, 12 October 1851, American Antiquarian Society; 'Testimonial resolution', Edward D. Eaton Papers, Box 6, Wisconsin State Historical Society; *Diary and Letters. . . Hayes*, I, p. 57.

15 Charles Russell to C. Theodore Russell, 27 September 1834; James Barnard Blake diary, 12 October 1851; Sergeant Kendall to Frank and Elizabeth Kendall, 20 January 1889, Kendall Papers, New York Historical Society; Charles M. Baldwin diary, 24 September 1866, New York State Library Archives.

16 Quoted in Mary A. O. Gay to William Otis, 20 October 1829, Gay-Otis Manuscript Collection, Columbia University Library.

17 *Diary and Letters. . . Hayes*, I, p. 72.

18 John William deForest, *A Volunteer's Adventures: A Union Captain's Record of the Civil War*, New Haven: Yale University Press, 1946, pp. 130-1.

19 James Cattell to William and Elizabeth Cattell, 28 May 1885.

20 Roosevelt's wolf statement is quoted in Kathleen Dalton, 'Theodore Roosevelt and the idea of war', *The Theodore Roosevelt Association Journal*, VII, Fall 1981, p. 7. Roosevelt himself quoted the minister Sydney Smith in *The Strenuous Life: Essays and Addresses*, New York, Century, 1902, p. 275.

21 James Cattell to William and Elizabeth Cattell, 1 December 1884; *Diaries and Letters of Francis Minot Weld, MD. . .*, ed. by Sarah Swan Weld Blake, Boston: priv. print, 1925, p. 14; Theodore Greene, *America's Heroes: The Changing Models of Success in American Magazines*, New York: Oxford University Press, 1970, pp. 127-31.

22 Charles Van Hise to Alice Ring, 29 November 1877, Charles Van Hise Papers, Box 1, Wisconsin State Historical Society; Barrus, *Burroughs Journal*, p. 101; Elizabeth Cattell to James Cattell, 17 August 1884; L. E. Holden to Edward Eaton, 30 July 1892; Samuel Eaton to Edward and Martha Eaton, 1 August 1892.

23 Barrus, *Burroughs Journal*, p. 107; *Letters and Journals. . . Higginson*, p. 271.

24 Morton S. Bailey to James Cattell, 18 November 1880.

25 Charles Van Hise to Alice Ring, 24 November 1878.

26 Sergeant Kendall to Frank and Elizabeth Kendall, 10 January 1887; Frank P. Fetherston diary, 30 October 1887, 9, 16 and 18 February 1888 and 12 May 1888, New York Historical Society.

27 Roderick Nash, ed., *The Call of the Wild, 1900-16*, New York: Braziller, 1970, pp. 1-5; Peter Filene, *Him/Her/Self: Sex Roles in Modern America*, New York: New American Library, 1975, pp. 94-5; Jeffrey Hantover, 'The Boy Scouts and the validation of masculinity' in Pleck and Pleck eds., *The American Man*, pp. 285-301; Joe Dubbert, *A Man's Place: Masculinity in Transition*, Englewood Cliffs, N.J.: Prentice-Hall, 1979, pp. 122-5, 148-53; Richard Cabot to Ella Lyman, Summer 1889.

28 On Crockett as a male hero, see Carroll Smith-Rosenberg, 'Sex as symbol in Victorian purity: An ethnohistorical analysis of Jacksonian America', in John Demos and Sarane Spence Boocock, eds., *Turning Points: Historical and Sociological Essays on the Family*, Chicago: University of Chicago Press, 1978, pp. 5239-40; Robert Abzug, *Passionate*

Liberator: Theodore Dwight Weld and the Dilemma of Reform, New York: Oxford University Press, 1980, pp. 1-2, 146-7; John R. Betts, *America's Sporting Heritage, 1850-1950,* Reading, Mass.: Addison-Wesley, 1974.

29   Among the important works that have studied the effect of these 'avenues of influence' on ideals of manhood, see Ronald P. Byars, 'The making of the self-made man: the development of masculine roles and images in antebellum America', unpublished Ph.D. dissertation, Michigan State University, 1979; Jeffrey P. Hantover, 'Sex roles, sexuality, and social status: the early years of the Boy Scouts in America', unpublished Ph.D. dissertation, University of Chicago, 1976; G. J. Barker-Benfield, *The Horrors of the Half-Known Life: Male Attitudes toward Women and Sexuality in Nineteenth-Century America,* New York: Harper & Row, 1976.

30   Mary A. O. Gay to W. Allan Gay, 15 February 1840, 12 and 31 December 1840, 2 September 1847 and 17 February 1850.

31   Ebenezer Gay to W. Allan Gay, 26 February 1839.

32   Ebenezer Gay to W. Allan Gay, 20 March 1840; W. Allan Gay to Ebenezer Gay, 13 February 1839; W. Allan Gay to Mary A. O. Gay, 3 March 1840.

33   John Kirk to his mother, 18 December 1852.

34   John Kirk to his father, 18 December 1852. For two other examples of fathers and mothers teaching different ideals of manhood to their sons, see Frank Kendall to Sergeant Kendall, 6 January 1890; Elizabeth Kendall to Sergeant Kendall, 7 January 1890 and James Cattell to William and Elizabeth Cattell, 15 January 1885.

35   Mary A. O. Gay to William Otis, 4 April 1833 and 10 June 1827.

36   Elisha Whittlesey to William Whittlesey, 16 December 1830.

37   John Doane Barnard, 'Journal of his life, 1801-1858', pp. 3-4, Essex Institute, Salem, Massachusetts.

38   Elisha Whittlesey to Comfort Whittlesey, 20 January 1840; Aquila Giles to Henry Giles, 25 May 1818.

39   Richard Hofstadter, *Social Darwinism in American Thought,* rev. ed., Boston: Beacon Press, 1955, pp. 13-30; James Truslow Adams, 'Francis Parkman' *Dictionary of Americam Biography,* New York: Charles Scribner's Sons, 1943, XIV, pp. 247-50.

40   E. Anthony Rotundo, 'Body and soul: changing ideals of American middle-class manhood,' *Journal of Social History,* XVI, 1983, pp. 23-38.

41   Regina Markell Morantz, 'Making women modern: middle-class women and health reform in nineteenth-century America', *Journal of Social History,* X, 1977, pp. 493-497; Nancy F. Cott, 'Notes toward an interpretation of antebellum child-rearing', *Psychohistory Review,* VI, 1978, pp. 6-7; Betsy Salisbury to Stephen Salisbury, Jr, 21 February 1814, and 20 April 1814, Box 16, 7 January 1821, Box 20, and Stephen Salisbury, Jr to Stephen Salisbury Sr 2 July and 9 July 1800, Box 14; Elizabeth Cattell to James Cattell, 17 August 1884, 22 January 1885 and 11 May 1885.

42   See especially Erik Erikson, *Childhood & Society,* New York: W. W. Norton, 1963, 2nd ed., pp. 295-6; Erik Erikson, *Identity: Youth and Crisis,* New York: W. W. Norton, 1968, pp. 117-20.

43   Francis Parkman was heavily influenced by just such a set of experiences. See Adams, 'Francis Parkman', p. 247.

44   George Fredrickson, *The Inner Civil War: Northern Intellectuals and the Crisis of the Union,* New York: Harper and Row, 1965, pp. 222-4.

Building character in the British boy: the attempt to extend Christian manliness to working-class adolescents, 1880-1914 [1]

'Christian manliness is a wonderful thing', enthused the Bishop of Down, Connor and Dromore, addressing a Boys' Brigade rally at the Queen's Hall, London, on 3 May 1895, 'the objection which a Boy had to religion is removed by it'. This contribution sets out to investigate whether or not there is any historical evidence to support the Bishop's sanguine judgement, with particular reference not to the upper middle and middle-class English public schoolboy most often associated with training in manliness but to the ordinary working class adolescent the speaker most probably had in mind. Thus, in what follows, an assessment will be made of how successfully the English, middle-class, Anglican ideal of Christian manliness – associated as 'muscular Christianity' with Charles Kingsley, Thomas Hughes and the cult of games in the public schools – was communicated through such channels as the Boys' Brigade to the less privileged, board school-educated, working-class boys in the nation's large urban centres. Boys' papers, such as the pre-eminent *Boy's Own Paper,* and writers for boys, such as George Alfred Henty, will also be touched on here in relation to the manly ideal and the popularisation of the public school ethos among a readership far more extensive than that of the schools themselves.[2]

The Boys' Brigade, founded in late Victorian Glasgow, is crucial for any understanding of the topic under consideration because it had – and still has – for its object, 'the advancement of Christ's Kingdom among Boys and the promotion of habits of Obedience, Reverence, Discipline, Self-Respect *and all that tends towards a true Christian Manliness*' The Brigade must, therefore, be seen as one of the primary instruments for the transmission of Christian manliness to the non-public school-boy and today as almost the only surviving embodiment of the Victorian religious idealism of Kingsley and Hughes. Other youth organisations also shared, or paid obeisance to, the idea that they were in the business of encouraging manliness among their membership. Scouting, for example, was much publicised by Baden-Powell before 1914 as a form of training to reverse decadence in the coming generation by restoring manliness and character to the adolescent male. Nonetheless, propagating Christian manliness was not in the forefront of the objectives of the Boy Scout and other adult-sponsored organisations directed at the young in the same way that it was for the Boys' Brigade. Hence the last sentence of Norman Vance's recent study of the ideal of Christian manliness in Victorian literature and religious thought, *The Sinews of the Spirit* (1985), is devoted to the centenary of the latter movement, with its reminder that there are still men and boys pledged, like their Victorian ancestors, to strive for this particular goal. Manliness at least has staying power.[3]

The Boys' Brigade and Christian manliness

In the autumn of 1872 a young Glasgow businessman, William Alexander Smith, later to become known as the founder of the Boys's Brigade, joined one of the 180 branches of the Young Men's Christian Association (YMCA) in the city, where it was over seven thousand strong. Two years later, under the influence of Dwight Moody and Ira Sankey's revivalist campaign in Glasgow, Smith formed a Young Man's Society, closely modelled on the YMCA, at the College Free Church he attended in the West End of the city. (When the Free Church had broken away from the established Church of Scotland in 1843, it had taken with it the most dynamic, Calvinist forces in the Presbyterian Church.) The YMCA, started in 1844 by George Williams, a former apprentice draper and evangelical Sunday School teacher, was essentially an attempt to bring Christianity down to the level of the average Victorian by showing him that religion was not really about what was perceived as 'feminine' piety and incense but was instead a robust and manly affair in the Kingsley mould. As the century wore on, the YMCA became progressively more secular and more of a vehicle by which manliness was to reach the aspiring lower middle class, especially clerical and office workers in the large cities. In the 1880s the movement had a total membership of over 80,000 but, although it had started out with the aim to 'influence religious young men to spread the Redeemer's Kingdom amongst those by whom they are surrounded', the YMCA came gradually – under the influence of 'muscular Christianity' – not to represent anything in particular, except an emphasis on the all-round spiritual and physical development of young men.[4]

It is problematic why Smith, who did not himself receive a public school education, should have chosen to adopt a 'manly' form of religion as the basis of his new movement for boys. Roger Peacock, a close associate until Smith's death in 1914, depicts the founder of the Boys' Brigade in his biography as following Kingsley and Arnold and as a firm believer in the merits of 'muscular Christianity' but he provides no evidence to support this claim and Smith himself left little behind in the way of autobiographical writing from which a judgement could be made. Smith, in all likelihood, acquired his taste for a more 'manly' form of religion from the YMCA in that, like them, he set out to demonstrate that boys or adolescents could – without fear of ridicule – be both manly and Christian. In 1874 Smith had enlisted in the (1st Lanarkshire Rifle) Volunteers – a British part-time military force replaced in 1908 by the Territorials and immensely popular with the Glasgow mercantile class. Military training certainly imbued Smith – by 1881 he had become a Lieutenant in the Volunteers – with ideas of duty and discipline which he imported into the Brigade, many of whose early officers were drawn from a Volunteer background. A manly religion also served to differentiate his Protestant-based youth movement from the 'effeminate', 'morbidly introspective' and antipathetic kind of religion constantly referred to in early Brigade literature and which, in the context of the sectarian divisions of late Victorian Glasgow, readers will have had little trouble in identifying with Catholicism. On the other hand, manliness may have equally well been a reaction against the 'effeminate' influence of rather unworldly Scottish evangelicism and pious Protestant Bible-reading. What such speculations tend to overlook is that Sunday School teachers like Smith worried just as much about finding a method to control rowdy, working-class boys in their mission classes as they did about fostering a particular concept of masculinity. Someone suggested to Smith that he use the military organisation and drill of the Volunteers to improve Sunday School discipline and to maintain order. This is just what he did by starting the first company of the Boys' Brigade at the North Woodside Mission Hall of the wealthy Free Church in nearby Hillhead on 4

October 1883 where, after three nights allowed for recruiting, fifty nine boys were registered by Smith in the company enrolment book.[5]

The basic short-term intention behind the formation of the Boys' Brigade was to bridge the gap between the ages of thirteen or fourteen, when most boys left Sunday School to correspond with the age they left their state schools, and the age at which they could join the ···· at seventeen. As one of the original members of the first Boys's Brigade company put it in a 1954 interview: 'When we reached thirteen most of us felt we were too big for the Sunday School, and there was a gap of a few years until we were able to join the ···· at seventeen. To fill this gap, Captain Smith formed the Boys' Brigade. During that gap period, many working class boys ran wild, became hooligans and street-corner loafers. What else was there for them, in those days, to do?' Some contemporary youth workers, although certainly not Smith himself, considered the influence of Sunday Schools on boys to be detrimental, since many of the teachers were women, the classes were too sedentary and they failed to hold teenage boys who left once their state school attendance was over. By the end of 1884, however, Smith had started the first Boys' Brigade Bible Class, allowing him to draw on a wider range of recruits than attended Sunday School, as well as to assert a semi-autonomous status within the Presbyterian Church.[6]

'There is undoubtedly among Boys an impression that to be a Christian means to be a "molly-coddle" and in order to disabuse their minds of this idea we sought to construct our organisation on a model which would appeal to all their sentiments of manliness and honour', Smith declared at an 1891 Brigade public meeting in Liverpool. Thus the message put across in the Brigade's earliest promotional literature was that the aspect of Christianity which could be made to appeal most strongly to a boy's nature was that of manliness: 'All a boy's aspirations are towards *manliness,* however mistaken his ideas may sometimes be as to what that manliness means. Our boys are full of earnest desire to be brave true *men;* and if we want to make them brave, true *Christian* men, we must direct this desire into the right channel. . . We must show them the *manliness* of Christianity'. The hell-fire Congregationalist preacher C. H. Spurgeon, in a posthumous book of sermons for young men and women, echoed the same sentiments but from a more calculating perspective tailored to suit his audience: 'There has got abroad a notion, somehow, that if you become a Christian, you must sink your manliness and turn milksop. . . Young men, to you I would honestly say that I should be ashamed to speak to you of a religion that would make you soft, cowardly, effeminate, spiritless, so that you would be mere naturals in business, having no souls of your own, the prey of every designing knave'. It would obviously never do for late Victorian Nonconformists to turn out impractical businessmen who could be outwitted by their more worldly competitors. 'By associating Christianity with all that was most noble and manly in a Boy's sight, we would be going a long way to disabuse his mind of the idea that there was anything effeminate or weak about Christianity', Smith explained, 'an idea that is far too widespread among Boys, as no one who has anything to do with them can have failed to see'. If so few adolescent boys were practising Christians, reasond Smith, the solution was to show them the manliness of Christianity and to play down its softer, more 'feminine' tendencies of compassion and turning the other cheek.[7]

Manliness, like military drill and discipline, was a means to the end of Christian teaching for the Brigade. It was, that is, a necessary part of godliness. Boys' Brigade officers themselves appear to have had little difficulty in defining what they meant by manliness. To be manly meant to be a man, to act in every way worthy of one's manhood – 'watch ye, stand fast in the faith, quit ye like men, be strong'. (Paul, 1 Corinthians, XVI, 13). The Brigade was lauded by Lt Col Seton Churchill, founder in 1892 of the Universities Camps for Public Schoolboys movement, for having recognised a basic sexual division of labour: 'that Boys are especially interested in soldiers, in drill, in discipline, and things of that kind; and I think every one of us must also be willing to add the word *games*. Wherever you find Boys, there you will find – that is to say if they are developing naturally – you will find them playing games'. Seton Churchill was convinced that 'nature' had so provided that boys would 'naturally' take an interest in tin soldiers and drums, while girls, with their maternal instinct, would also quite 'naturally' be more interested in dolls. When the boys grew up they would become defenders of the hearth and home, while the girls would become the mothers of the future. Not surprisingly, Smith and his fellow 'muscular Christians' in the Brigade thought it possible that too many clergy had made the mistake of projecting Christianity to boys largely by showing the same side of it as would recommend it to the gentler nature of the girl.[8]

Hence William Smith viewed healthy outdoor sports as a 'splendid field' for the moral and spiritual, as well as the physical, training of boys, an idea previously restricted to the playing fields of the fee-paying public schools. The Brigade merits congratulation, perhaps, for being among the first voluntary youth organisations to introduce working-class boys to codified sports and games, extending what had hitherto been public school *esprit de corps* to a much wider social spectrum. The highly organised structure of competitive Brigade league football led to many boys working their way through company and battalion Boys' Brigade teams to enter the junior and senior professional ranks of the game. Smith endorsed the 'muscular Christianity' message to the hilt in 1891 with the unlikely image of boys discussing religion on the playing field: 'Here is the whole idea of The Boys' Brigade in a nutshell. Boys talking to each other in the most perfectly natural way about their Company Bible-Class before all their comrades on the football field! That is of the very essence of the The Boys' Brigade, for it aims at taking up everything that should enter into healthy Boy-life, and consecrating it all to the service of Christ'. Curiously, only two years earlier, the *Boys' Brigade Gazette,* which Smith edited, had warned boys against that 'absorbing devotion to sports' seen among the spectators at a professional football match. Actual participation in a 'manly' game of cricket or football would, of course, have been seen as a much healthier form of leisure or recreation for the growing boy.[9]

So what success did the Boys' Brigade actually have in extending Christian manliness beyond the narrow social base of the English public school system? It is obviously impossible to provide statistical evidence to confirm or deny the effectiveness of the Boys' Brigade in propagating its Christian message, since membership cannot strictly be identified with acceptance of the movement's religious object and could, instead, be simply instrumental; that is, for a boy to gain access to the Boys' Brigade's sporting or other leisure activities. In any case, even at its pre-First World War peak in 1910, there were only 61,660 boys in the movement throughout Britain, while there were about three and a half million boys in the ten to nineteen age group in England and Wales alone. Information about the proportion of Boys' Brigade members who were or became regular church-goers is also difficult to obtain, simply because after 1896 the Brigade only published collective figures for boys attending church, Sunday School or other religious meetings in addition to meetings of their company. The actual proportion of Boys' Brigade 'Old Boys' becoming church members at a later date, after their Boys' Brigade careers were over, is a different question and has never been formally investigated by the movement. It is interesting to note, however, that whereas in 1887-8 almost eighty per cent of Boys' Brigade members were regular church-goers, by 1895-6 this had fallen to below sixty per cent, probably reflecting wider recruitment outside of Sunday school circles. If it is difficult to obtain evidence for the success rate of the Boys's Brigade in converting boys to a more manly Christianity, countervailing evidence can be produced of their failure to penetrate the lowest social strata and also of the hostility which they encountered from among the most deprived, 'hooligan' elements of working class youth.[10]

The testimony of the 12th Earl of Meath, the Honorary President of the Dublin Battalion of the Brigade and the President of the Lads' Drill Association, to the Royal Commission on Physical Training for Scotland on 17 June 1902, may be taken as representative of the sceptical approach to the Boys' Brigade's more exaggerated claims. In his judgement, the Boys' Brigade and the Church Lads' Brigade – since 1891 the Anglican equivalent of the Boys' Brigade – could 'never hope to obtain the rough lads from the great mass of the population'. The majority of working-class adolescents were, he claimed, excessively shy of any connection with a religious organisation, whereas the 'better-behaved lads, those who have already a desire for something better, a tendency towards religious organisations, those are the lads who join these bodies'. It is only fair to report that on 1 October 1902 the Royal Commission interviewed the Brigade Treasurer, Thomas Cuthbertson, who hotly denied that The Boys' Brigade got only the 'better' boys, the sons of small shopkeepers and artisans. Cuthbertson claimed that in Glasgow, at least, the Boys' Brigade also included in its ranks the sons of ordinary eighteen s a week unskilled labourers, such as in the Broomielaw district where the sons of quay labourers were prominent in his own company; 'men of very irregular occupation and very irregular habits'. The Boys' Brigade was the only method, he claimed, that 'seems to bring into the life of that class of boy the same sort of *esprit de corps* as is got in the best class of boy in the great English public schools'.[11]

A sample of twenty-four boys enrolled in the second session – 1884-5, of the original 1st Glasgow company gives fourteen boys with skilled and only three with unskilled fathers, three as while collar and four dead at the time of the census return. Of the eleven boys who had started work at the date of enrolment, three were joiners' apprentices and the others were: a cabinet maker, a lithographer, a sewing needle groover, a blacksmith, an engine fitter, a warehouseman, a clerk and a ticket writer. A further sample of fifty three boys taken from company enrolment books extant for 1890-5 gives a total of thirty six or seventy two per cent from skilled manual homes (sons of joiners, cabinet makers, engine fitters, shoemakers, masons), while fourteen came from lower middle class homes (sons of salesmen, clerks, travellers, insurance agents, drapers,

grocers) and only three from unskilled homes (labourers and a commiss-
ionaire). Boys in this company came overwhelmingly from among the
sons of the skilled, 'respectable' artisan and white collar families living in
the North Woodside district of Glasgow's West End, an area which contained tenements much superior to those of the overcrowded city centre.
The early companies were, in the main, set up by prosperous churches
with missions in adjoining working-class areas and could draw upon a
Sunday School catchment which the 'respectability' of the above samples
confirms but as the movement expanded it was able to take on boys from
a broader social range, as for example in the East End of Glasgow. In the
small towns and rural districts of England and Scotland a much wider
social intake, at both boy and officer levels, was more apparent from the
outset. The strong hold which the Brigade developed in the north of
England, particularly in Liverpool and Sheffield, gave it a wider cross-
section of membership which went far beyond the 'respectable' Sunday
School or church congregation. 'I was much impressed with the fact that
with your sixpence or shilling entrance fee and two shilling uniform, you
are reaching the street arab, the "scape", as we would call him, or the
"hooligan", as you have it', observed an American visitor, the Rev Joseph
H. Cudlipp of Lancaster, Pennsylvania, in 1905. 'I am aware that many
companies are formed of the better and more fortunate class of Boys, but
on the whole you reach more factory hands, message boys and. . . boy
bread-winners. This is well. Here and there we (in America) are reaching
the street boy, but as a rule we are more apt to get the schoolboy and
those of the better classes'.[12]

What about the boys who did *not* join one of the many uniformed
youth movements springing up during the late Victorian and Edwardian
periods in Britain? How was the message of Christian manliness and *esprit
de corps* received by those young men on the streets accustomed to a different culture of working class masculinity? There is a great deal of anecdotal
evidence to suggest that a substantial number of those 'rough lads' who
did not join a youth organisation – in particular the 'hooligans' Cudlipp
refers to – could make themselves a considerable nuisance to those of
their peers who did volunteer to wear a uniform and carry a dummy rifle.
'Many a company in those ancient days was conscious of a highly
organised underground movement whose purpose was to conduct a con-
tinuous guerilla campaign against the Boys' Brigade', wrote Roger
Peacock only partly tongue-in-cheek, 'often was a drill parade conducted
under a fusillade of stones and bricks hailing upon the roof, and sometimes hurtling through the windows'. Dr R. Leslie Ridge, the Captain of

the 1st Enfield Boys' Brigade Company in North London, looking back in 1948 to the 'heroic struggle' of sixty years earlier, recalled that, 'few drills went by without attacks from hooligans and the "discontents", even officers in uniform were pelted with bottles and other missiles as they went to drill, and the boys had to defend their uniform often with their fists'. On 22 April 1891 there was a 'free fight' occasioned by a row outside the 3rd Enfield drill hall, when an officer in the Brigade knocked out one of the 'hooligans' who had been making a nuisance of himself! The perse-cution of roving bands of 'hooligans' in this part of North London led to the local Boys' Brigade companies banding together for survival to cope with such a hostile environment, for 'it was a long time before Drill and other gatherings could be held without the risk of interruption from row-dies outside'. The evidence from local records of the Brigade, in this par-ticular instance, would seem to contradict the more bland pronounce-ments of Headquarters that the movement was making progress among all sections of the adolescent population.[13]

If gangs of 'hooligans' were waiting outside drill halls to ambush the boys inside wearing their 'pill box' hats, white satchels and belts over their everyday clothes, it is not difficult to imagine the following dis-respectful ditty being chanted:

> 'Ere comes the Boys' Brigade,
> All smovered in marmalade,
> A tuppeny 'apenny pill box,
> An' 'alf a yard of braid.

The boys who joined the dockland-based Catholic Boys' Brigade in Ber-mondsey, South London, after 1896 were, not surprisingly, none too keen to be seen wearing their uniforms in public so they came along to the boys' club where the Brigade met bringing their uniforms wrapped up in brown paper and changed on arrival. Even after 1914 Boys' Brigade parades and marches very often met with ribald jeers, derisive songs and occasional stone-throwing by youths, not just in slum neighbourhoods but also in 'respectable' working-class districts. Stephen Humphries asserts in *Hooligans Or Rebels?* (1981), an oral history of working-class childhood and youth from 1889 to 1939, that scurrilous songs, such as the above, expressed sardonic insight and detachment, forming part of a con-tinuous tradition of resistance to middle class control stretching from the Boys' Brigade to army recruitment. Sport, the brass band and the annual camp were the activities that most attracted the members, he surmises.

Bible Class, drill and military exercises were usually regarded as tiresome concessions to authority to be avoided wherever possible. 'The grand pretentions of group leaders and the public school ethos of manliness that permeated these movements were often received with cynical detachment', he argues. On the other hand, transcripts of interviews with former Brigade members, conducted for this book and held in the Avon County Reference Library, Bristol, suggest a slightly less detached working-class attitude and, in one particular case, a positive enthusiasm for the physical training classes the Boys' Brigade offered ('Oh I loved it. Oh they (the officers) was lovely. Yes.'). It is one of the temptations of oral history, as of any other kind of history, to make selective use of evidence to corroborate a particular interpretation, but where the historian is himself, through taped interviews, engaged in creating raw data as well as in making sense of it, the temptation that has to be resisted is all that much greater.[14]

Juvenile literature and manliness

Popular juvenile literature, embracing magazines and novels, exemplifies – even more clearly than the history of organised youth movements – a basic shift in the concept of manliness during the second half of the nineteenth century and after, moving away from the strenuous moral earnestness and religion of Dr Thomas Arnold, headmaster of Rugby from 1827-1839, to a much greater emphasis on athleticism and patriotism. Hence the tradition of 'sturdy' English manliness, which George Alfred Henty (1832-1902) disseminated through such juvenile novels as *With Kitchener in the Soudan* (1903) and *Held Fast for England* (1893), was, to some extent, a reaction against an earlier literary tradition of moral and spiritual manliness in writing for boys. Henty referred to himself as carrying out a similar task to that of the Boys' Brigade, of which he was an Honorary Vice-President, animating the readers of his books with 'a spirit of manliness, of steadfastness, and of courage'. He thought that the discipline provided by the Boys' Brigade was 'an excellent thing for boys, and would stop a great deal of the rowdyism and bad language of the streets'. Henty, who went to Westminster School and Cambridge before embarking on a long career as a war correspondent, started writing juvenile fiction by following the current conventions but by his regular output of two or three books a year, dictated to an amanuensis, he probably gave them wider circulation than most of his contemporaries. His boys' novels, largely written to make money on his retirement from war reporting, reflected many of the prejudices of a middle-class, late Victorian 'strong old-fashioned Tory' and at least a quarter of his output contained as a hero a manly public schoolboy who wins his spurs fighting in some far-off British colonial war. Henty dominated the boys' book market from about 1885 to the beginning of the First World War and it has been estimated that each edition of his novels sold about 150,000 copies in Britain alone, so that, given the enormous number of reprints, his total sales run into millions. Henty set out to encourage 'manly and straight living and feeling among boys', using the public schoolboy hero as the medium through which this message was put across, shorthand for the characteristics which the late Victorians and Edwardians most admired in the national character. Henty's mid-nineteenth-century predecessors in the expanding field of juvenile literature were much more fond of preaching to their boy readers and often cast their heroes in a pious mould that Henty would have abhorred.[15]

R. M. Ballantyne, author of *Coral Island* (1857), was a Scottish Free Church evangelical, like William Smith, whose fictional heroes often turned to God and Mother in their hour of peril. Here his hero Ralph Rover contemplates death when faced with a tricky situation:

> My heart sank within me; but at that moment my thoughts turned to my beloved Mother, and I remembered these words, which were among the last that she said to me: 'Ralph, my dearest child, always remember in the hour of danger to look to your Lord and Saviour Jesus Christ. He alone is both able and willing to save your body and your soul'. So I felt much comforted when I thought thereon.

In this kind of dilemma a Henty hero was far less likely to offer up a prayer and more inclined to seek some practical assistance, usually in the shape of his faithful native servant, to extricate himself from imminent danger. Henty, although a warm upholder of the Anglican Church, was careful to avoid accusations of preaching in his boys' books, being well aware that his heroes could be manly and brave without being at all priggish. Ballantyne did, nonetheless, hold to a mid-Victorian concept of manly behaviour and in his slaughter-house of a boys' book *The Gorilla Hunters* (1861), opposes this ideal type to that of the 'muff', a boy who is mild, diffident, gentle, timid and unenthusiastic – a contrast that is also featured in Hughes' *Tom Brown's Schooldays* (1856). Henty's heroes were in a similar fictional mould to Ballantyne's but by the 1880s and 1890s patriotism had replaced religion in their catalogue of manly virtues; they were more British, more conscious of the might of the British Empire which they served and which, to a certain extent, replaced the Kingdom of Heaven in their emotions. Tom Brown was, ultimately, still their model but not the 'muscular Christian' who knelt down to say his prayer in a hostile boys' dormitory to win the respect of Dr Arnold, more the manly hero of the cricket and football fields.[16]

The brief character sketches which Henty supplied for his boy heroes make it abundantly clear that the moral and spiritual manliness of the Ballantyne hero had been replaced in the last quarter of the nineteenth century by a different 'ideal type' in juvenile fiction. These stereotyped characters, as *The Times* put it in 1932, all possessed that 'nameless air of command which distinguishes most young men who have passed through the upper forms of a great public school'. Charlie Marryat, who had the good fortune to travel *With Clive to India* (1884), personified the prevailing trend in juvenile fiction towards a more sportsmanlike and athletic manliness:

> (He was) slight in build, but his school-fellows knew that Charlie Marryat's muscles were as firm as those of any boy in the school. In all sports requiring activity and endurance rather than weight and strength he was always conspicuous. No-one in the school could compete with him in long-distance running, and when he was one of the hares there was little chance for the hounds. He was a capital swimmer and one of the best boxers in the school. He had a reputation for being a leader in every mischievous prank; but he was honourable and manly, would scorn to shelter himself under the semblance of a lie, and was a prime favourite with his masters as well as his school-fellows.

The claims of athleticism which are personified by Charlie Marryat eventually became so deeply engrained in the public school system and mentality that it is difficult to realise how relatively novel they were in the late Victorian period. The gradual introduction of compulsory games playing into the English public schools between 1860 and 1880, which the above passage celebrates, must be seen as a significant development which was to have important repercussions on the concept of manliness.[17]

Henty's heroes, with their sporting prowess and character as manly Englishmen abroad, represented in a diluted form the robust, muscular Christian ideals which Charles Kingsley and Thomas Hughes had been so influential in popularising among an earlier generatiom. Henty, who wrote nearly eighty historical adventure stories for boys, a dozen three-decker adult novels, edited two boys' periodicals and contributed to a number of other boys' journals, such as the *Boy's Own Paper,* was typically Victorian in his prodigious output and, it must be said, in his apparent unconcern for the highest literary standards. Henty did not usually bother even with sketching out a plot before he started a book. Like his now more respected contemporary H. Rider Haggard, he let the story develop itself without very much idea of what was coming next. It would be surprising if at least part of this massive output did not filter down to the ordinary working-class boy, although only middle-class parents would be able to afford the necessary shillings to purchase the latest Henty novel as a Christmas present for their sons. Sunday School Unions, for example, bought them in bulk to give away to boys who excelled in scripture reading and the shelves of many boys' club libraries would have been well stocked with Hentys. A record of three days' book withdrawals in September 1907 from the Heyrod Street Lads' Club in Manchester indicates that eight out of forty five books borrowed were written by Henty. Membership of both Sunday Schools and boys' clubs was, however, largely confined to the upwardly-aspiring, respectable working-class boy – only about one third of the employed members of the Heyrod Street boys' club were in unskilled or semi-skilled jobs. The ordinary errand boy or schoolboy would be far more likely to spend his earnings or pocket money on the kind of 'penny dreadful' that was extremely unlikely to contain Henty stories. Changing tastes and values among the post-First World War generation of young readers led to a reaction against the 'manly' hero, boys deeming him too bovine and stupid as the manly young gentlemen of Henty's era had deemed Ballantyne's over-zealous heroes too pious. Sadly, if Henty's 'campaign' novels survive at all today, it is not in their capacity as readable fiction but for their usefulness as historical documents which can give some insight into the popular mentality during the period of colonial warfare associated with late Victorian British imperialism.[18]

In 1884 a survey of juvenile reading habits conducted by Edward Salmon for *The Fortnightly Review* calculated that out of a sample of six hundred schoolboys about two thirds read the *Boy's Own Paper* as their favourite weekly. 'The *Boy's Own Paper* has had greater success than any other boys' paper of a high class published in England, and the healthy vigour and excellence of its stories, to say nothing of the instructiveness of its articles, are a model of what a boys' periodical ought to be', Salmon enthused. The *Boy's Own Paper* was originally an outcome of clerical disapproval towards the 'penny dreadful' which led the Religious Tract Society, rather reluctantly, to launch their own boys' paper in 1879 that

would rival the former's circulation without imitating their sen-
sationalism or absence of moral restraint. The launching of the *Boy's Own
Paper* also represented the attempt of the Religious Tract Society to come
to terms with the currently popular juvenile demand for a wide sports
coverage and for adventure tales set against an imperial backcloth. Under
its first and greatest editor, George Andrew Hutchinson (1842-1913), the
Boy's Own Paper quickly became the most important and influential
juvenile periodical ever published, despite its firmly moral and Christian
tone. By the mid-1880s, the magazine, with its clutch of successful boys'
writers, like Talbot Baines Reed, W. H. G. Kingston, Jules Verne, R. M.
Ballantyne and, of course, G. A. Henty, had exceeded the circulation of
its nearest rivals, such as Edwin J. Brett's 'penny dreadful' weekly journal
The Boys of England, and was printing over half a million weekly copies
which, if an average of two or three boys read each issue, suggests an
actual readership of at least one and a quarter million. From the start each
issue of the *Boy's Own Paper* had a variety of material on hobbies, sports,
nature rambles, interviews with the famous, 'Health Hints for Growing
Boys' and a long-running adventure serial. The success of the *Boys' Own
Paper* inspired the Religious Tract Society to launch a similar paper for
girls and in 1880 the *Girl's Own Paper* made its first appearance.[19]

In the pages of the *Boy's Own Paper,* manly, intrepid lads wandered
around the world, proving their character as plucky Englishmen and,
eventually, finding fame and fortune. The portrayal of manliness became
the most essential staple of the *Boy's Own Paper,* so much so that it has
been called by Patrick Dunae the 'unofficial organ' of the 'muscular Christianity' movement. Manliness was held, in its pages, to be the highest
virtue to which a British schoolboy could aspire. 'There is probably no
feeling so deeply rooted in a public school, none so common alike to the
highest and lowest form, as the wish to be accounted manly', the *Boy's
Own Paper* declared in 1894. 'Nothing that sends the glow of satisfaction
tingling through your veins so much as the thought that your companions, or those who are near you, think you conspicuous for manliness'.
When the paper first appeared, the ideas of Kingsley and Hughes were
still in circulation and in the 1880s and 1890s there was even to be a revival
of Christian Socialism among Anglicans and others, hence doctrines of
manliness were a part of the cultural climate and soon found their way
into the *Boy's Own Paper.* Yet the Religious Tract Society was an intensely
conservative, evangelical organisation, founded to restore piety among
the people and in 1866 one of their publications for young men on *Christian Manliness* had even attacked the 'folly of so-called "muscular Christ-

ianity"', for 'a man is not the less strong for being gentle'. So there is a certain irony in the Religious Tract Society in subsequent decades becoming, through the agency of a successful boys' paper that subsidised their overseas missionary work, such an ardent populariser of the fashionable manly ethos. Manliness became, in effect, an essential staple of the *Boy's Own Paper* and was used to add a moral tone to many of the more secular features of the magazine, to justify articles on athletics or the accounts of various colonial military campaigns and to give an added emphasis to the countless school stories the magazine carried. Sermons and articles in the *Boy's Own Paper* on 'The Manliness of Christ', also the title of a collection of talks published in 1870 by Thomas Hughes, identified Jesus as a physically strong individual, a carpenter, a courageous and manly leader of men, almost as a glorified public school House Captain. In the 1890s there was even a regular *Boy's Own Paper* feature called 'Some Manly Words for Boys by Manly Men' and an article in 1890 on Bishop James Fraser of Manchester, whose biography Hughes had published in the previous year, was headed 'A Manly Bishop' and described him as some kind of episcopal Tom Brown.[20]

In the public schools, playing games and athletics came increasingly to be looked upon as an intrinsic part of manliness and were in themselves justified as character building. Hence the very first issue of the *Boy's Own Paper,* on 17 January 1879, contained a story by the editor's friend, Talbot Baines Reed ('An Old Boy'), titled 'My First Football Match'. Once the public schools came to be regarded as hothouses for breeding manliness and as playing games came to be a unique aspect of the British public school system, then it was natural that games and manliness would become synonymous. Hence the propagation of athletics and games became a staple feature in boys' papers, such as *Chums* (1892), *The Captain* (1899) and the *Boy's Own Paper,* which not only romanticised sport in their idealised school stories but paid lip service to it in articles and editorials. Juvenile literature in general revered athletics and significantly rated rowing, cricket and football as more 'manly' sports than horse-racing, boxing and shooting, the latter associated by *Chums* in 1900 with cheating, 'blackguardism' and trickery. Above all, team sports were identified as the most important experience of character building as a process, comprising an ethos of loyalty, team spirit, patriotism, pluck and manliness. ('Pluck' was fast becoming a term which was interchangeable with manliness in the 1890s but there was some uncertainty as to what it actually meant.) Games and physical exercises supposedly built up the national character and thereby contributed to the Empire's greatness, hence the link between sports and the perpetuation of the imperial mission was constantly made in the *Boy's Own Paper*. The public schools were regarded by the middle-class public as character building institutions and the manly characters which they shaped on the playing field and elsewhere were popularly believed to account for Britain's ability to administer and defend an ever-expanding Empire. 'One thing is certain, and may as well be at once admitted, that as long as England wishes to maintain her supremacy and reputation as a great nation, our boys must be trained in those games which develop physical strength, endurance, skill and courage', as a contributor to the *Boy's Own Paper* explained in 1892. Surprisingly, there is less evidence that G. A. Henty subscribed to the conventional viewpoint that team games were allied to character building and the growth of the Empire. Skinner, the house football captain in *The Dash for Khartoum* (1892) is, in fact, drawn as a caricature of the football devotee with no thought in his head except winning the next game, even under the Egyptian sun in the proximity of the Dervishes![21]

It is improbable, however, that a great many ordinary working class boys would have received the manly ethos through the pages of the *Boy's Own Paper* since 'it was a great social step from a halfpenny to a penny (the price of the *Boy's Own Paper*). Between that section of society which had a penny to burn and that which had only a halfpence was a very distinct barrier'. Frederick Willis, writing this in his 1948 memoir, recalled that Alfred Harmsworth's cheaper halfpenny publications, such as *The Union Jack* and *The Halfpenny Marvel,* were more popular with working boys from the mid-1890s, even if 'anathema to the older generation who dismissed them contemptuously as "ha'penny bloods"'. Thousands of early issues of the *Boy's Own Paper* were distributed free in London board schools by the Religious Tract Society to help ensure a more popular readership but, in most cases, the price would have been prohibitive except to those from a 'respectable' family background. Thus adolescents who would have subscriptions to the *Boy's Own Paper* (and some readers' letters suggest an even older age group), beyond the ranks of the solid middle classes, would be found among the sons of skilled artisans, small shopowners, white collar office workers and, in general, the kind of boy most likely to join a uniformed youth movement. Richard Church, the poet and novelist, who wrote a prize-winning autobiography *Over the Bridge* (1955), was a great admirer of Henty and the other adventure story writers found in the *Boy's Own Paper*. His father was a sorter in the South London Post Office and his socially ambitious mother was a teacher working for the London School Board, while Church himself, who lived with his family in Battersea, entered the Civil Service in 1909, when he was sixteen, doing clerical work in a government laboratory. He remembers that his parents went to considerable expense in having the monthly parts of the *Boy's Own Paper* bound in firm boards, with red leather backs and corners. A boy from this kind of home background, straddling the upper working class and the lower middle class, might be seen as a more representative *Boy's Own Paper* reader than, say, the son of a poor labourer who left school at thirteen or fourteen for an unskilled, errand boy or factory job.[22]

A watered-down version of the manliness ethos did, eventually, reach a more popular mass audience through the public school stories, written by the prolific Charles Hamilton, found in the Harmsworth weeklies *The Gem* (1907) and *The Magnet* (1908). In his recent autobiography, the stage and screen actor Peter Cushing accords the role of major influence in his early life to the fictional Tom Merry who, along with his school-friends at St Jim's, was a stalwart of the 'Martin Clifford' stories in *The Gem*. 'Tom Merry was my hero, and I tried to mould my way of life according to his tenets', Cushing told a reporter. Robert Roberts, writing of the importance of these stories for his own childhood in the slums of Edwardian Salford, also suggests their pervasive influence among working class boys:

> Even before the First World War many youngsters in the working class had developed an addiction for Frank Richards' (Hamilton pseudonym) school stories. The standards of conduct observed by Harry Wharton and his friends at Greyfriars set social norms to which schoolboys and some young teenagers strove spasmodically to conform. . . Over the years these simple tales conditioned the thought of a whole generation of boys. The public school ethos, distorted into myth and sold among us weekly in penny numbers, for good or ill, set ideals and standards. This our own tutors, religious and secular, had signally failed to do. In the final estimate, it may well be found that Frank Richards during the first quarter of the twentieth century had more influence on the mind and outlook of young working class England than any other single person, not excluding Baden-Powell.[23]

Lest the above statement be taken to represent the normal working-class response on reading such literature – as it invariably has been by social historians – and as evidence for the extension of gentlemanly public school ideals to a wider audience via popular culture, the chastening fate of another schoolboy who lived according to the Greyfriars code of conduct is worth recalling. The Irish writer Frank O'Connor grew up in

Cork just before the First World War, his father a drunken ex-soldier, his mother a charwoman, and like Robert Roberts he also devoured *The Gem* and *The Magnet:*

> I played cricket with a raggy ball and an old board hacked into shape for a bat before a wicket chalked on some dead wall. I kept in training by shadow boxing before the mirror in the kitchen, and practised the deadly straight left with which the hero knocked out the bully of the school. I even adopted the public-school code for my own, and did not tell lies, or inform on other boys, or yell when I was beaten. It wasn't easy, because the other fellows did tell lies, and told on one another in the most shameless way, and, when they were beaten, yelled that their wrists were broken, and even boasted of their own cleverness and when I behaved in the simple, manly way recommended in the school stories, they said I was mad or that I was 'shaping' (swanking), and even the teacher seemed to regard it as an impertinence.

Greyfriars, that is, may have provided one model of behaviour but the streets and working class life provided another. If impressionable Robert Roberts, Peter Cushing, Frank O'Connor and a few of their like-minded school friends adopted some of the weird public school slang or the manly code of behaviour found in the stories, working-class adolescents living in over-crowded urban areas and attending substandard state schools read them, in general, more for their escapist fantasy than to find role models to imitate. Imaginative, talented boys, like those cited above, were the exception rather than the norm in seeking to absorb the manly ethos of Greyfriars or St. Jim's in such a literal fashion. Thus when Frank O'Connor took what he read at face value, he was rewarded by his peers with ostracism for imitating public school norms of behaviour which were – even before the slaughter of the First World War – largely confined to Charles Hamilton's prolific imagination.[24]

It thus becomes untenable to argue, if this analysis is correct, that the gentlemanly standards of the public school culture – and manliness in particular – successfully percolated down to the working-class young via the historical agencies of school stories, sport, youth movements and popular culture in general, thereby maintaining the *status quo* and containing the forces of the 'violent undermass' awaiting their opportunity to be unleashed. We have seen how the Christian manliness promoted by the Boys' Brigade was not well received by those adolescents, grouped together indiscriminately as 'hooligans', who were accustomed to an alternative cultural ethos of working class masculinity which placed a heavy emphasis on drinking and fighting. 'Hooligans' broke up Boys' Brigade meetings and assaulted their officers well before the advent of what Jeffrey Richards has labelled a 'hooligan culture' among modern-day football supporters. One reason for the failure of Christian manliness to penetrate the 'lumpenproletariat' of late Victorian and Edwardian cities was that the majority of working class youth shared a different concept of manliness from that embodied in the Boys' Brigade or the *Boy's Own Paper*. Manliness, as understood in this environment, was often identified by the middle class as synonymous with 'hooliganism' – an elongated 'rite of passage' in which the manly was to be reached through swaggering, brawling and the oblivion induced by either alcohol or violence.[25]

Those agencies which attempted to channel public school manliness from above (and nothing has been said here, for reasons of space, about cadet corps, settlement houses, boys' clubs and Boy Scouts) were, in general, much more attractive to the upwardly-aspiring upper-working-class or lower-middle-class parent than to the families of the non-respectable, 'rough' working class who supplied the bulk of the 'hooligan' element in towns and cities. On grounds of financial cost alone, aside from any cultural or ideological differences, the channels for Christian manliness discussed here were often beyond the purses of the poorest working-class families. (Albeit the Boys' Brigade, with its minimal uniform, was a lot cheaper to join in 1883 than the expensively-accoutred Boy Scouts when they appeared twenty five years later.) The boys or adolescents that the Boys' Brigade, the *Boy's Own Paper,* Boy Scouts and boys' clubs appealed to, in other words, were not those whom much of their propaganda so constantly claimed that they were trying to reach: for example, the 'street corner' boys so often targeted for recruitment to the uniformed youth movements. Christian manliness may have extended beyond the narrow social base of the English public schools but, for the most part, it was a message that was only received by those working-class children and adolescents who were already well predisposed – through parental encouragement, church attendance or the ethos of 'respectability' in which they were raised – to receive it.[26]

Notes

1 I should like to acknowledge the receipt of a grant from the British Academy which allowed me to carry out research for this essay in London and Cambridge. .

2 Boys' Brigade addresses, *Boys' Brigade Gazette*, III, 10, 5 June 1895, p. 257; Norman Vance, 'The ideal of manliness', eds. Brian Simon and Ian Bradley, *The Victorian Public School*, Dublin, 1978, pp. 115-28.

3 John Springhall (ed.), Brian Fraser and Michael Hoare, *Sure and Stedfast: A History of the Boys' Brigade, 1883 to 1983*, London, 1983; Norman Vance, *The Sinews of the Spirit: The Ideal of Christian Manliness in Victorian Literature and Religious Thought*, Cambridge, 1985, p. 206.

4 John Springhall (ed.), *Sure and Steadfast, op. cit.*, pp. 30-9; Clyde Binfield, *George Williams and the YMCA: A Study in Victorian Social Attitudes*, London, 1973, *passim*.

5 Roger S. Peacock, *Pioneer of Boyhood: The Story of Sir William A. Smith*, London, 1961 edn., p. 92. I am indebted to Brian Fraser of Glasgow University for some of the more sensible ideas about the origins of Smith's Christian manliness employed here.

6 Cited: Rushworth Fogg, 'A Scotsman started it all – in 1883', *The Scotsman*, October, 1954, p. 24.

7 Address by Smith, 'The Boys' Brigade: its organisation and methods', *The Boys' Brigade Gazette*, I, No. 10, 2 February 1891, pp. 168-9; William Smith, *The Story of the Boys' Brigade*, Glasgow, 1888, pp. 8-9; C. H. Spurgeon, *A Good Start: A Book For Young Men and Women*, London, 1898, pp. 16, 24.

8 Address of Seton Churchill, 'Drill, discipline and games, as aids to the spiritual life of boys', *The Boys' Brigade Gazette*, IV, No. 5, 1 June 1896, p. 111.

9 Address of Smith, *op. cit.*, p. 168; Anon., 'Athletics and the Boys' Brigade', *The Boys' Brigade Gazette*, I, No. 3, 2 September 1889, p. 43.

10 John Springhall (ed.), *Sure and Stedfast, op. cit.*, pp. 248-9.

11 Minutes of Evidence, *Royal Commission on Physical Training* (Scotland), Cd. 1508, 1902, XXX, pp. 341, 562.

12 John Springhall (ed.), *Sure and Stedfast, op. cit.*, p. 40; idem., *Youth, Empire and Society: British Youth Movements, 1883 to 1940*, London, 1977, p. 25; J. H. Cudlipp, 'Impressions of an American officer', *The Boys' Brigade Gazette*, 1, December 1905, p. 84.

13 Roger Peacock, *Pioneer of Boyhood, op. cit.*, p. 63; Leslie Ridge, '1st Enfield B.B. Co.', *The Enfield Battalion Souvenir Handbook, 1888-1948*, Enfield, 1948, p. 2; F. J. Ridge to R. L. Ridge, 17 February 1943; A. J. Ridge, 'Early history of the 1st Enfield', Ms. in possession of E. J. Berkelmans, South Woodford, London.

14 John Springhall, *Youth, Empire and Society, op. cit.*, p. 51, n. 43; Stephen Humphries, *Hooligans or Rebels? An Oral History of Working Class Childhood and Youth, 1889-1939*, Oxford, 1981, pp. 134-5; Bristol People's Oral History Project, transcript RO15, County of Avon Central Library, Bristol.

15 Henty Boys' Brigade Address, *The Boys' Brigade Gazette*, 5 June 1895, p. 255; *Chums*, 26 June 1895; Will Allan, 'G. A. Henty', *The Cornhill Magazine*, 181, No. 1082, 1974, pp. 71-100; Guy Arnold, *Held Fast for England: G. A. Henty, Imperialist Boys' Writer*, London 1980.

16 Ballantyne cited: Gilian Avery with Angela Bull, *Nineteenth Century Children: Heroes and Heroines in English Children's Stories, 1780-1900*, London, 1965, p. 144; Eric Quayle, *Ballantyne the Brave: A Victorian Children's Writer and His Family*, London, 1967, p. 149;

(*Top left*) Tom's visit to Dr Arnold's tomb: Arthur Hughes' illustration for *Tom Brown's Schooldays*

(*Top right*) 'Lionel flashed the warning words, "Rebels are here", and the brave lad's last hour was come' (from G. A. Henty, *In Times of Peril*)

'A very gallant gentleman' (from the painting for the Cavalry Club by J. C. Dollman)

Raymond Blathwayt, 'How boys' books are written: a talk with Mr. G. A. Henty', *Great Thoughts From Master Minds,* II (5th series), No. 497, October, 1902, pp. 8-10.

17 'A school for heroes', *The Times,* 3 December 1932; G. A. Henty, *With Clive To India or, The Beginnings of an Empire,* London, 1884, p. 11; see also Yorke Harberton, the 'typical public schoolboy' in: *idem, With Roberts to Pretoria: A Tale of the South African War,* London, 1902, p. 16.

18 C. E. B. Russell and L. M. Rigby, *Working Lads' Clubs,* London, 1908 ed., pp. 190-1. *The Henty Society Bulletin* can be obtained by members from the Society's Honorary Secretary, Terry Corrigan, 6 Darracott Road, Bournemouth, England.

19 Edward Salmon, 'What boys read', *The Fortnightly Review,* XLV, 1 February 1886, p. 256; Patrick Dunae, 'Boy's Own Paper: origins and editorial policies', *The Private Library,* 2nd series, IX, No. 4, Winter 1976, pp. 123-58.

20 *Boy's Own Paper* cited: Patrick Dunae, 'British juvenile literature in an age of Empire, 1880-1914', Ph.D., 1975, Manchester University, p. 239; Peter D'A. Jones, *The Christian Socialist Revival: Religion, Class and Social Conscience in Late Victorian England,* Princeton, 1968; Anon., *Christian Manliness: A Book of Examples and Principles for Young Men,* London, Religious Tract Society, 1866, p. 146; Rev Dr Cuyler, 'A manly word to young men', *Boy's Own Paper,* XIII, No. 649, 20 June 1891, pp. 606-7; 'A manly bishop', *ibid,* XII, No. 586, 5 April 1890.

21 Bruce Haley, *The Healthy Body and Victorian Culture,* Harvard, 1978, p. 168; 'The editor to his chums', *Chums,* VIII, No. 393, 21 March 1900; 'What " British Pluck" means', *Chums,* VIII, No. 376, 22 November 1899, p. 213; *Boy's Own Paper,* cited: Patrick Dunae, 'British juvenile literature', *op. cit.,* p. 279; G. A. Henty, *The Dash for Khartoum,* London, 1892, pp. 246-7; J. A. Mangan, *The Games Ethic and Imperialism: Aspects of the Diffusion of an Ideal,* New York, 1986, *passim.*

22 Frederick Willis, *101 Jubilee Road: A Book of London Yesterdays,* London, 1948, p. 109; Richard Church, *Over The Bridge: An Essay in Autobiography,* London, 1955, p. 163; see also: Eds. Faith Sharp with Heather Tanner, *A Corsham Boyhood: The Diary of Herbert Spackman,* 1877-1891, Chippenham, 1981, p. 19.

23 Quintin Falk, 'Boy's Own hero who became master of horror', *The Gardian,* 22 March 1986, p. 13; Robert Roberts, *The Classic Slum: Salford Life in the First Quarter of the Twentieth Century,* London, Penguin edn., pp. 160-1.

24 Frank O'Connor, *An Only Child,* 1961, cited: Gilian Avery, *Childhood's Pattern: A Study of the Heroes and Heroines of Children's Fiction,* 1770-1950, London, 1975, pp. 189-90.

25 Jeffrey Richards, 'The hooligan culture', *Encounter,* LXV, No. 4, November, 1985, pp. 15-23; 'The violent froth precipitated by a complex social brew', Letters, *The Guardian,* 4 June 1985; Geoffrey Pearson, *Hooligan: A History of Respectable Fears,* London, 1983, *passim.*

26 For financial costs see: John Springhall, 'The Boy Scouts, class and militarism in relation to British youth movements, 1908-1930', *International Review of Social History,* XVI, 1971, pt. 2, p. 140; one Scoutmaster admitted that it had 'proved difficult to bring the poorest class of boy into touch with Scouting, owing in great part to the expense of the uniform'. Jerrold W. Law, 'Scouting and the workhouse boy', *The Headquarters Gazette,* 14 November 1911, p. 23.

chapter four PETER N. STEARNS

Men, boys and anger in American society, 1860-1940

The history of male emotionality has been inconsistently explored amid the growing attention to changes in emotional standards, and possibly emotional experiences as well, in modern time. The neglect is not surprising, of course, insofar as historians have followed nineteenth-century experts in viewing women as more 'naturally' emotional than men. Thus we know a good deal about women's emotional ideals, interests and anxieties, as women became gatekeepers to what was supposed to be an emotional haven for both genders: the home. We know something about women's emotional attachments in friendship but nothing systemtic after the seventeenth century about men's,[1] we know a good bit about changing assumptions of maternal love but little about the emotional involvements and tensions of fathers, at least after the eighteenth century.[2] On a slightly different tack, we know a great deal about the emotional tensions which the commitment of adult women to work outside the home has entailed. Indeed, bookstore shelves are still filled with literature on emotional conflicts and emotional styles embraced in the work trends of the past three decades but we have no explicit exploration of men's emotional reactions to a somewhat analogous development as work took them out of the family orbit during the early decades of industrialisation.

The reasons for neglecting this aspect of men's history are not obscure. The whole subject of emotionality as a historical topic is relatively new, though it was evoked some decades ago by Lucien Febvre and other French social history pioneers.[3] Assumptions about women and emotion, and also about the home as centre for emotional interactions, have tended, though without warrant, to exclude men as if men did not face changing emotional expections even as they were increasingly removed from the domestic orbit. Yet in failing to deal with men and emotion as an historical subject, we risk a needlessly unbalanced picture, both of emotional change and of changes in the masculine experience. We risk, indeed, seeing men as emotional constants – wooden throughout time – just as we have sometimes seen them as sexual constants, whose ever-ready lust only awaits opportunity, which depends in turn on changes on the female side.

Ironically, some ingredients of an historical framework for male emotionality already exist, though they have not been pursued systematically in the modern period. It seems probable that, at least in Protestant areas, men were encouraged to raise their emotional investment in family (and possibly lower that in their male friends) in the seventeenth and eighteenth centuries.[4] Certainly all the work on changing familial emotional styles in the eighteenth century emphasises a male as well as female involvement. Men, thus, took new interest in children, even among the British aristocracy being present at childbirth. They, along with women, sought new romantic love in courtship and marriage and were beginning to consider divorce when these goals were not met.[5] Additionally, as changes heightened the emotional intensity of child-rearing, boys as well as girls were affected, leading to another, and reasonably consistent, shift in emotional context as children learned more clearly that love could be expected. There is much, to be sure, that remains to be done on these shifts in personal and familial goals, even within the upper and middle classes where they have been most studied. It remains unclear how much really changed and how much was simply newly articulated, but it does seem clear that some change in standards and expectations was brewing.

This change feeds into some of what we know about the emotional standards of home and feminine ideals in the nineteenth century. However, for men, the inquiry seems to end at that point, apart from a few valuable but quite specific treatments of courtship romance.[6] We know that in the United States an imagery developed of the tough-guy hero for whom romantic love was an irrelevant distraction[7] and we certainly know how, in the contemporary feminist era, women and liberated men alike have criticised a constricted male emotional style that, if accurate, presumably had its origins somewhere.[8] However, about actual male emotional styles and their evolution in the past two centuries we know, again, too little.

This essay deals with one aspect of emotional change that begins at least to relate the subject to more familiar issues of evolving masculinity. The subject is anger, most particularly the standards applied to anger in men but, to some measurable extent, the actual experience of anger as well. The focus is on a particular period of male anger standards: the late nineteenth and early twentieth centuries when a distinctive American effort to blend family emotional goals with more specifically masculine goals emerged, and with some demonstrable effect. However, to grasp this period's importance, both preceding and succeeding approaches must also be considered.

The background: a distaste for anger

Beginning in the eighteenth century, a new concern developed about anger control on both sides of the Atlantic. One key symptom was a vocabulary change. The word tantrum, previously unknown save for a seventeenth century Welsh aberration, crept into the language, initially as a disapproving term for adult displays of high temper. The word temper itself began to take on unfavourable connotations, requiring use of the term temperament in its stead. Personal letters and diaries denoted a new level of anxiety about anger control which, though previously theoretically an ingredient of a good Christian life, had not commanded great concern.[9]

Efforts at anger control were uneven of course. The American South long maintained a culture in which, among males, hot temper seemed a positive asset.[10] Even among Northern Protestants, interest in the issue varied, with the evangelical strain insisting officially on control but amid such tension that anger remained ready to burst forth against religious or political enemies.[11] Nevertheless, the new interest was noteworthy.

The concern for anger control had several sources, including the religious influence of what Philip Greven has termed moderate Protestantism. In a broad sense, the new interest in self-control was part of the general movement toward more civilised manners, described some time ago for Western society by Norbert Elias.[12] Temper control also fits into a society where community supervision was beginning to dissolve somewhat and where familial insistence on obedience was also beginning to flag. Temper control became a personalised substitute for the more traditional social controls which had focused however on overt behaviour, not on its emotional base.

Interest in anger control followed most precisely, of course, from the new emphasis on familial affection. Anger and love were seen to be antitheses in an early version of the 'make love, not war' slogan that in fact maintained what has become a fairly general Western emotional ideal. Some family historians have indeed claimed to find evidence of measurable declines in familial anger as measurably increased emphasis on the importance of affection developed.[13] John Demos, indeed, sees even in seventeenth century New England a desire to keep the family free from anger, though not because anger was yet seen as generally unfortunate but rather because the family, in the American context, was too important to threaten with this kind of display. Anger was, as a result, turned against neighbours and rank outsiders.[14] Certainly the search for alternatives to previous will-breaking methods of child-rearing, designed both to curb parental anger and to avoid the provocation of later anger in children themselves, resulted in part from the new concern for emotional control. By the eighteenth century, when positive disapproval of anger became more articulate, advice manuals directed at families consistently seized on the importance of mastering one's temper – a motif new to the genre since about 1700. It was also noteworthy that a concern to limit expressions of anger against animals began to surface at the same time, ultimately forming an unusual Western feature in the repression of anger.[15]

This theme continued in the more widespread and increasingly secular advice literature of the early nineteenth century. By this point, the increasing separation of family from a more hostile 'outside world' situated anger control as a key emotional ingredient of the haven-home. In contrast to the eighteenth century approach, when anger control was seen as part of general character development, applicable to non-family as well as family, the early nineteenth century literature particularly emphasised avoidance of anger in dealing with spouse and children.

This advice, furthermore, was not specific to either gender; both male and female had equal obligations and boys and girls should be raised with the same emotional goals in mind. During the eighteenth century both men and women had shared new anger control goals, as with Jonathan Edwards who resolved when young to 'strive most to feel and act good-naturedly' when he was 'most conscious of provocations of ill-nature and anger', or Hannah Heaton who wrote 'I am ashamed to have what I said in anger. . . brought into judgement at the great day'.[16] Early nineteenth century manuals similarly emphasised identical goals for both men and women: 'I say to any father or mother, are you irritable, petulant? If so, begin this moment the work of subjugating your temper'.[17] The general theme was of childish innocence; if parents could curb their own anger in dealing with children, the latter would grow, as they should, to be anger-free. Thus, with Horace Bushnell: 'Fretfulness and ill temper in the parents are provocations'.[18] Characteristic children's stories in this period also emphasised the need for anger control. In Louise Chandler Morton's 'Coals of fire' (1868), a hot-tempered boy promises his mother never to fight. The mother lacks a husband's help in instilling self-control, hence her special insistence. The boy fears being labelled cowardly but when he rescues a girl without a fight he demonstrates true self-mastery, illustrating the ideal of a Christian gentleman. Catherine Sedgwick drove home the same point in her best-seller. A child describes his mastery over temper in avoiding fights at school. 'But I did not, father, I did not, I had to bite my lips though so that the blood ran'. 'God bless you, my son'. To cap the examples of control, moralists cited George Washington's dominance of his temper – his worst personal fault – as his greatest victory.[19]

As these latter examples suggest, early nineteenth century orthodoxy did implicitly focus somewhat more on boys than on girls when urging temper control. Similarly, advice about parental control frequently turned out to rely on some special maternal sweetness. In discussing marriage itself, authorities sometimes suggested a male-female differentiation similar to that undertaken for sexuality; women were naturally free from anger, while men had to struggle to achieve the same goals. This differentiation, though not consistently offered, did help prepare the next approach to problems of anger, where a specifically masculine style was much more clearly recognised; but it is vital to insist that in this period, before the 1860s, the demands on both genders were identical – men were allowed no more legitimate outlets for anger than women were. Indeed, in raising children no distinction was made at all as boys had to fit into what was in many ways, in terms of early Victorian standards, a rather feminine mode of emotional expression by loving parents.[20] This followed from an intense desire for emotional consistency within the household, newly seen as a separate refuge from the harsher outside world, but oddly it made no allowance for those people – men – who admittedly had to deal with this world as well.

The domestic standards for anger control so widely trumpeted in the early nineteenth century were of course ideals, translations to the new family imagery of goals somewhat more generally sought during the previous century. They were middle-class in bias and indeed served as yet another vantage-point from which working-class family styles might be criticised, particularly in noting angry treatment of children. How widely the standards were recognised, how if at all they affected actual emotional bahaviour (or regrets at behaviour when inconsistent with ideals) cannot as yet be determined. Scattered evidence suggests that, as in the eighteenth century among moderate Protestants, the goals were taken seriously at least in principle, with corresponding guilt when anger did in fact flare toward children or spouse. Concern about angry treatment of children, not only at home but also in schools, reflects the spread of the standards. But the standards were still rather new in an area of behaviour – personal and familial styles – where change comes slowly. Even aside from evidence of distinctive social class and regional standards, it seems safe to hypothesise that the internalisation of the rigorous norms of anger control was only beginning, even among the northern middle class. It was for this reason, as well as because of the powerful domestic imagery, that the lack of distinction between genders raised no particular comment.

This situation was to change after the 1860s for a variety of reasons but partly because authorities now recognised separate roles for men and women that required separate anger standards as well. The result was not an abandonment of control standards for men but rather a more complex statement that would more realistically cover the male experience, preserving the home anger-free but encompassing the workplace and public life as well.

The American ambivalence: the late nineteenth century

Replications of the mid-century approach to anger in child-rearing continued into the twentieth century, particularly in explicitly Christian manuals. Parents had thus a 'sacred duty' to instill control, by forming habits early, through their own example. By the twentieth century, however, there was somewhat more anxiety about the possibility of violence: 'The same temper that smashes a toy in anger may, when the child is grown, kill a man'.[21]

On the whole, however, the mid-century approach did not survive intact. New scientific information about children and some related changes in assumptions about childish innocence brought modifications and, of course, older will-breaking views, undoubtedly more widespread in practice than in the published literature, would inevitably have complicated the picture. More important, however, was the production during the later nineteenth century of the kind of American ambivalence concerning anger that could still be discerned in the 1950s.

For, in men, anger could now be good as well as bad. Not in raw form; no one pulled back from disapproval of literal displays of personal temper. But, properly channelled, anger was a useful spur. Indeed, its absence was to be lamented.

Some of the new tensions about anger emerged in separate works, particularly during the 1860s and 1870s. Thus while hand-books on the Christian gentlemen stressed control of anger, concomitant literature in the Horatio Alger school urged the importance of aggressive, competitive behaviour in which values such as anger were instrumental in personal advancement. Anger, in this literature, was by itself of no concern for it could easily shift to spur achievement. Children's literature similarly provided examples of pacificsm cheek-by-jowl with the more sensational stories of the post-Civil War era, which praised brawling and manly strength.[22]

But by the end of the nineteenth century, and recurrently to the present day, the new tensions produced near-contradictions in individual discussions. G. Stanley Hall blasts anger as destructive, damaging to health and the sign of a weak will and decaying intellectual power but 'a certain choleric vein gives zest and force to all acts' and, in an effort to reconcile, in the tension between anger and control, 'the best work of the world is done'. The American Institute of Child Life states: 'Anger is not lovely'; children's rages, though inevitable to a point because of the fighting instinct, create such ugly physical symptoms that the person seems 'a child no longer, but a creature under demoniacal possession'. However, while childish anger warrants some 'counsel and punishment, an atmosphere of grief and disapproval', as well as efforts to prevent or distract and while the aggression that leads to 'wars, rapine and misery' is unquestionably bad, anger cannot and should not be entirely eliminated. It has many good qualities and should be 'a great and diffused power in life, making it strenuous, giving zest to the stuggle for power and rising to righteous indignation'.

The same theme, though less tied to muscular Christianity, continued for several decades into the twentieth century. Dorothy Canfield Fisher considers that one should 'never permit a child to gain anything by showing anger, for children must learn to solve problems by other means'. However, anger can spur useful energy. A Watsonian of the 1930s was of the opinion that 'parents can easily teach children not to throw tantrums by ignoring it, and indeed while some anger is unavoidable, since children must be restrained, it is a learned emotion and can largely be omitted from a child's emotional lexicon'. Anger is nonetheless valuable to individuals and to society: 'If he is stirred, if he reacts powerfully, out of that very stirring may come achievements and performance of a high level'. A more permissive approach from the 1940s stresses that civilisation depends on rational control of anger and that a well-adjusted person is not angry but, some pages later, considers that anger is a great thing, from childhood onward, in calling attention to individual rights.[23]

Benjamin Spock, in his first edition, replicated the common tension. Although possibly pioneering in urging smooth peer relations and other changes away from inner-directed personality, Spock stressed the import-ance of anger in a baby's quest for independence. Children must of course learn to control their aggression but this is a natural process that need not usually evoke special parental concern and contol should never be carried too far; people need aggressive instincts in the world, as in business com-petition, so let children enjoy violence as part of the complex process of channelling aggressive instincts.[24]

The idea of contradiction should not be pushed too far. Many authorities carefully distinguished between tantrums and other displays of uncontrolled rage and the moderate anger that could impel effective action. They talked of curbing anger in children without destroying it. Above all, the manuals argued, child-rearing must produce a distinction between personal anger and socially useful values such as competition and righteous indignation.[25] The key was channelling as part of character building. Thus a turn-of-the-century manual urged a balance between encouraging and discouraging anger as the fighting instinct. Too much combativeness is obviously bad but a boy with no tendency to fight would be an unnatural nonentity. Consequently, fighting should never be encouraged but no parent should ever say 'never fight'. For adulthood, competition 'is a form of fighting that is very prominent all through life'. The founder of the National Congress of Mothers considered that, while girls should be trained to prepare a tranquil home and face problems 'cheefully', boys should simply be trained in righteous indignation. The process was to be highly rational. Children could be taught to look at the results of ungoverned temper and then urged on the proper targets as in this uplifting conversation between mother and son on a dirty street; '"I'm sure, my little one, when you are a man, and serve in the City Coun-cil, you will see that the laws are enforced and that we have a clean town". See the flash of righteous indignation in the boyish eyes. . . the active brain has received an indelible impression, the emotional nature has found a legitimate vent'. Even a violent temper, with such training, can be a 'splendid force', providing 'royal service'.[26]

Thus, the tension about the uses of anger, though it did produce some contradictory or confusing statements, was not fundamentally illogical. It did pull away from the simpler disapproval of anger that had developed by the mid-nineteenth century without returning to the lack of explicit concern characteristic of will-breaking. To this extent, the tension was more complex. Even when not illogical in theory, it could add new worries to the process of parenting. Thus parents should be concerned when children were insufficiently angry, unduly passive, as well as when the more familiar problems of ungovernable temper described the child.[27] Furthermore, the new, limited value found in anger did not remove the parental obligations of self-control. Children must be allowed some anger but adults should have learned that anger was inappropriate in the home. Both competition and righteous indignation were for external use only. Thus the translation of the new tension into practice, while it may have been constructive, raised several potential difficulties.

Gender differentiation was crucial in easing the problem of putting the new ambivalence about anger into effect. Parents could and did disagree. A number of studies, from the 1920s onwards, showed greater tolerance by fathers of aggressive children than by mothers. Differences in the treatment of boys and girls, though surely not new, helped feed the heightened complexity of emotional goals. Repression of anger in girls fulfilled the older impulse to combat anger, while efforts to channel anger could be confined to boys.

The new ambivalence about anger in boys stemmed from several sources, from the 1860s onwards. Emphasis on business competition was an obvious ingredient. The first decades of American industrialisation had not spurred an effort to develop competitive children but by the 1860s the interest was in full swing. Darwinian interest in anger, or the fighting instinct, as a survival mechanism also contributed. Darwinian studies of expressions of anger in young children helped modify the mid-nineteenth century view of childish innocence; children clearly had some angry emotions that could not be ignored, though they were not judged fundamentally bad as a result. The social Darwinian gloss on these findings, which spread much more widely in the United States than in Europe, helped convert childish temper, properly trained, into a competitive asset. The new approach also had the potential merit of translating into more realistic parental tactics than had the reliance on gentle role models and childish innocence of mid-century. Anger was a force to contend with in children, though not an overpowering one. Discipline might be needed, as Hall among others recommended, but the onerous task of complete repression (at least in boys) need not, indeed should not, be attempted.

Changes in ideology, including relevant science, and in the business climate thus most obviously account for the new approach to anger. It is also possible that mothers, increasingly responsible for actual upbringing but increasingly excluded from productive labour, may have demonstrated their lack of confidence, particularly in the treatment of boys, by reducing their effort to combat all expressions of childish aggression. Certainly mid-twentieth century comparative studies rated American mothers along with other non-working mothers (notably in India) as manifesting a low level of self-confidence in repressing childish aggression and attributed this trait to correspondingly low levels of economic power.

More surely, the new approach to anger paralleled, and was fed by, growing interest in competitive sports and the Progressive esteem for moral indignation in the cause of reform as part of masculine culture. The new approach to anger thus touched base with several larger trends in American history and the evolving standards of masculinity. Male rituals directly stemmed from the new approach to anger. G. Stanley Hall, for example, recommended boxing as a perfect means of training adolescent males in anger control for it channelled the emotion away from unwarranted targets without quelling it. Boxing became not merely a sport of growing spectator interest but also a symbolic part of middle-class boyhood as, until the 1940s, most boys received a growing-up gift of boxing gloves.[28] Attention to distinct male anger standards also meshed with the turn-of-the-century concern about the 'Sissification' of boys by female-dominated schools. In a period when the raising of boys was in fact increasingly in women's hands, the assertion of separate emotional goals helped preserve a gender identity still seen as essential to later distinctions in family and social roles. In meeting these needs in defining masculinity, the new approach to anger also proved surprisingly durable, surviving a variety of shifts in child-rearing fads from the 1860s to the 1940s.

And because of its durability, its immunity to a century's worth of fads and fashions, the tension over anger produced measurable impact on American child-rearing in fact. It lies at the base of the special inconsistency, the absence of overall rules on aggression, which several comparative studies have found in this aspect of American child-rearing. Specifically, the ambiguity about anger found the following translation in American practice: during the first half of the twentieth century Americans were rated severe in punishments of anger directed against parents but unusually tolerant of angry behaviour, particularly retaliation, toward peers, where a boy's ability to stand up for himself – the talisman of later competitiveness – could safely be tested. There were thus no overall rules on anger but an effort to channel it toward approved outlets from quite an early age. This approach contrasted not only with several non-Western cultures (some more permissive, some less permissive on expressions of anger overall) but also with Western Europe. Thus the American prompting to do battle with peers, at least when provoked, finds no echo in French or German child-rearing culture. Here, children are encouraged to turn to adults to right the wrongs done to them. It is the adult supervisor who will step in when a child's toy is taken away and the child himself is punished if he takes direct action.

Thus late nineteenth century, early twentieth century American child-rearing culture seems to have moved away from otherwise common Western patterns, despite the parallel evolution toward anger in Western society in the eighteenth and early nineteenth centuries. Elements of the American duality may go back to the colonial period, in the separation that Demos had noted between anger against neighbours and harmony within the all-important nuclear family. Protecting the family against childish anger may simply have been more important in a land of comparative strangers, protection of neighbours less so but the duality was unquestionably deepened and legitimised by the child-rearing approach that took shape in the later nineteenth century. The particular appeal of social Darwinism in the United States was an element in the unique American style toward childish anger. More basically the American middle class, free from concern about irrational effects of aristocratic temper (a concern evident in Western Europe in the ongoing debates over duelling), may also have been freer to shape a child-rearing style that seemed moulded to the emotional context of business competitiveness. American indulgence toward children, noted by travellers far earlier, may also have encouraged an approach that allowed legitimate outlets for childish emotion, rather than a stricter discipline when it turned out that children were not angelic. Whatever the combination of causes, American experts, while sharing in interests such as competitive sports that developed more widely in Western middle-class culture, forged an ambivalence about anger whose effects would be visible for many decades.

American anger standards, translated into actual child-rearing, must thus be considered as an ingredient in explaining certain other distinctive features of American masculinity, including perhaps specific sports preferences (American football as more symbolically anger-channelling than soccer). The standards also invite exploration in the area of American gender relations. For here too, there is no question that differentiation in advice literature reflected and furthered distinctions made in practice. Girls were indeed taught not to show anger, while boys gained greater latitude. The result, according to various studies extending to recent decades, was not necessarily a clear differentiation in adulthood, for women did learn to be angry and ultimately have been seen as distinctive only in a tendency to cry when confronted with anger. However, girls and boys did differ, so that while adult styles could be predicted from boys' behaviour, it could not be predicted from girls! As boys and girls interacted, in dating and other occasions, this aspect of their emotional socialisation, as well as more familiar issues of romantic intensity, warrants further consideration.[29]

The complex approach to anger introduced for American males adds to the impression of the tremendous tensions involved in growing up male in the turn-of-the-century decades, a point already evoked by Peter Filene.[30] For, though male anger standards had a beautiful logic relating to home-work distinctions as well as male-female divisions and though they were accompanied by special devices, such as sports, to help them work, they did raise real problems for boys actually growing up – problems of balancing being angry enough not to be a sissy (an ongoing concern of fathers) with not being too angry (a great concern of mothers and particularly teachers): 'Big boys do not get angry about that' but 'every big boy should be angry when smaller children are fought by bigger ones'.[31] Lloyd Warner noted the same tension, more academically, when he wrote in the 1950s that anger constituted one of the two greatest tensions in American child-rearing standards, along with sex.[32] These tensions were not simply abstract. They bothered parents trying to raise boys and they bothered boys. Living up to father-encouraged expressions of anger might frequently result in confusions at school as a pronounced gap opened, from the 1920s to mid-century, between parental and teacher perceptions of the problems posed by expressions of anger. Home and peer culture presented a different emotional context for boys from that offered by schools and the result, at least for a time, could be disorienting.[33] Boys' lives, though less emotionally repressed in this area than girls', involved more dilemmas of choice and more adjustments according to environment – a set of subtleties not easy to learn.

The end of channelling

The masculine style toward anger summed up in the channelling approach began to lose favour after the 1940s. New popular and social-science-expert fears about aggressiveness made anger seem less attractive. Indeed, in the child-rearing manuals aggression replaced the more neutral anger as an index term. New workplace controls, particularly appropriate in an increasingly white-collar labour force, began to translate anger repression efforts to the job site, which made differentiation between public and domestic emotional styles less relevant.[34] The same Dr Spock who in 1943 urged channelled anger as a spur to business success wrote in later editions of the need to curb aggression to promote the virtues of the salesman and manager[35] (as well as to discourage wars). References to anger as a useful goad for competitiveness or moral indignation dropped out of American child-rearing manuals after the mid-1940s to be replaced by anxious efforts to talk out any childish anger that might develop lest it fester into a permanent character trait. Anger now had no good purpose and though it could not be entirely avoided – mid-twentieth century children were not, after all, total innocents – it should be reduced to the greatest extent possible: 'Feelings can be changed, with changed behaviour intelligently following' and anger should be replaced with other emotions 'more socially useful and personally comfortable'.[36] Thus, in a period of American history in which people, and particularly men, were increasingly urged to be open about feelings, even 'let them all hang out', the attempt to repress anger, though through novel mechanisms, in fact tightened.

And with this shift the interest in differentiating emotional goals between men and women also disappeared. There was no distinction, concerning anger, in the ways children should be raised. Feminist and male-liberationist attacks on stereotypic masculine aggressiveness, though coming after the essential shift in styles and greatly oversimplifying previous male ambivalence, simply built on the decline in gender-specific emotional goals and again, this change in socially approved norms had its echo in male reality. Attempts to restrain anger at work did increase. Boxing gloves disappeared from the Christmas lists. Americans shifted in the comparative rankings on anger, becoming the people most likely to attempt to conceal anger – ambivalent still, perhaps, but in a different way from that of the early twentieth century. American character, and particularly male character, began to shift. Not accidentally, a variety of observers began to note new problems in confronting anger and also a decline in the moral indignation that had previously fuelled certain kinds of social movements.

This shift highlights the special flavour of the standards applied to masculine anger, in ideal and to some extent at least in actual fact, during the decades around 1900. Emotional standards and their relation to gender change in modern history according to prevaling ideology, occupational structure and home-work balance. While actual emotional experience and judgements on one's own emotional reactions surely do not change as rapidly or completely, they too show signs of evolution. It is both desirable and possible to build this emotional-historical component into our understanding of the male, and female, experience.

The particular quality of male anger standards between 1860-1940 also raises some fascinating issues of evaluation. Unlike some aspects of male-female differentiation in this period, which seem increasingly archaic, the masculine emotional ideals have some undeniably attractive features. To be sure, they did separate men from women, or at least boys from girls. Their ongoing impact may still complicate male-female relations though even the earlier ideals insisted in principle on anger control in marriage for both sexes. Channelled anger, even if directed toward other men, could be abusive: anger often expresses social hierarchies and the anger styles of the late nineteenth century are no exception. In moving away from the ambivalence expressed in the idea of channelling, American men have moved towards an emotional basis for greater equality, away from emotional individualism. They may also have gained, or be in the process of gaining, greater emotional consistency, for a more thoroughgoing attempt to repress anger may simplify certain aspects of emotional life. Yet, for all the potential for abuse, when a society sought an emotional basis for righteous indignation, when certain men could even taste the pleasure in outrage – like the Homeric Greeks, who knew that anger was 'sweeter than honey' – there may have been a certain richness now being lost. Lamenting lost masculine virtues has emerged as an interesting recent pastime, if still a slightly surreptitious one. In the case of changes in anger, gains as well as losses can be suggested in the current movement away from turn-of-the-century values. According to one recent study, the only modern American men who admit to enjoying anger are athletes under the influence of amphetamines – another way, perhaps, in which athletics continues to serve symbolic purposes in recalling worlds we have lost.

Notes

1 Benjamin Nelson, *The Idea of Usury,* Chicago, 1969; Carroll Smith-Rosenberg, 'The female world of love and ritual: relations between women in nineteenth-century America', *Signs: Journal of Women in Culture and Society I,* 1975, pp. 1-29; George L. Mosse, *Nationalism and Sexuality: Respectability and Abnormal Sexuality in Modern Europe,* New York, 1985.

2 Elizabeth Badinter, *L'Amour en plus: histoire de L'amour maternel* (17e-20e siècles), Paris, 1980; Elizabeth Pleck and Joseph Pleck, *The American Man,* Englewood Cliffs, NJ, 1980; see also Caroline Hallett, *Fathers and Children,* London 1909.

3 Lucien Fabvre, *A New Kind of History,* Peter Burke, ed., F. Folca, tr., New York, 1973, pp. 13-26; Peter N. Stearns with Carol Z. Stearns, 'Emotionology: clarifying the history of emotions and emotional standards', *American Historical Review,* 90, 1985, pp. 813-36.

4 Edmund Leites, 'The duty to desire: love, friendship, and sexuality in some Puritan theories of marriage', *Journal of Social History* 15, 1982, pp. 383-408.

5 Randolph Trumbach, *The Rise of the Egalitarian Family: Aristocratic Kinship and Domestic Relations in 18th Century England,* New York, 1978, see also Lawrence Stone, *The Family, Sex and Marriage in England* 1550-1800, New York, 1977.

6 Ellen Rothman, 'Sex and self-control: middle-class courtship in America, 1770-1870', *Journal of Social History* 15, 1982, pp. 409-26.

7 Rupert Wilkinson, *American Tough: The Tough Guy Tradition and American Character,* Westport, CT, 1984.

8 Marc Fasteau, *The Male Machine,* New York, 1974.

9 Carol Z. Stearns and Peter N. Stearns, *Anger: The Struggle for Emotional Control in America's History,* Chicago, 1986.

10 Rhys Isaac, *The Transformation of Virginia,* 1740-1790, Chapel Hill, 1982; Elliott J. Gorn, '"Gouge and bite, pull hair and scratch": the social significance of fighting in the southern backcountry', *American Historical Review* 90, 1985, pp 18-43.

11 Philip J. Greven, Jr, *The Protestant Temperament: Patterns of Child-Rearing, Religious Experience and the Self in Early America,* New York, 1977.

12 Norbert Elias, *The Civilizing Process: The History of Manners,* E. Jephcott, tr., New York, 1978.

13 Trumbach, *Egalitarian Family;* Stone, *Family, Sex and Marriage.*

14 John Demos, *A Little Commonwealth: Family Life in Plymouth Colony,* New York, 1970.

15 Jean-Louis Flandrin, *Families in Former Times: Kinship, Household and Sexuality,* R. Southern, tr., Cambridge, Eng., 1979; Philip J. Greven, ed., *Childrearing Concepts,* 1628-1861, Itasca, IL, 1973; Keith Thomas, *Man and the Natural World: A History of the Modern Sensibility,* New York, 1983.

16 Quoted in Greven, *Protestant Temperament,* pp. 111, 113.

17 Martha Jane Jewsbury, *Letters Addressed to Her Young Friends,* Boston, 1829; John Angell James, *The Family Monitor, or a Help to Domestic Happiness,* Concord, N.H., 1829; L. Hoare, *Hints for the Improvement of Early Education and Nursery Discipline,* Salem, MA, 1920.

18 Horace Bushnell, *Views of Christian Nurture,* Hartford, 1847; see also Greven, *Childrearing,* p. 142. On the ongoing Calvinist theme, see Robert Sumleh, 'Early nineteenth-century American literature on child-rearing', in Margaret Meade and Martha Wolfenstein,

eds., *Childhood in Contemporary Cultures*, Chicago, 1955, pp. 150-67; and Anne L. Kuhn, *The Mother's Role in Childhood Education: New England Concepts 1830-1860*, New Haven, 1947, p. 000. Catherine Beecher devoted a whole chapter to 'Cheerfulness' in her *Domestic Economy*, Boston, 1841. In much of the advice literature of this period, temper is discussed obliquely for men, on the assumption it can be successfully disciplined in childhood, but not explicitly at all for girls or women. Thus Catherine Sedgwick notes that business cares may legitimately ruffle a man's temper, but 'His wife was of a happier temperament. Her equal, sunny temper soon rectified the disturbed balance of his'. Catherine Sedgwick, *Home*, Boston, 1841, p. 15.

19 R. Gordon Kelly, *Mother Was a Lady: Self and Society in Selected American Children's Periodicals* Westport, CT, 1974, pp. 74-5; Bernard Wisby, *The Child and the Republic* Philadelphia, 1968, pp. 43ff; Sedgwick, *Home, pp.* 20ff.

20 This theme of feminisation is more fully developed in Stearns and Stearns, *Anger,* Ch. 3.

21 Flora H. Williams, *You and Your Children,* Nashville, 1946, pp. 40, 43.

22 Kelly, *Mother Was a Lady;* Abigail J. Stewart, David G. Winter & H. David Jones, in 'Coding categories for the study of child-rearing from historical sources', *Journal of Interdisciplinary History* 1975: pp. 685-701, find some parallels in Britain, with reduction of references to obedience and mildness as virtues.

23 G. Stanley Hall, 'A Study of Anger', *American Journal of Psychology* 10, 1899: 570, 589; American Institute of Child Life, *The Problem of Temper* Philadelphia, 1914, pp. 1, 10, 11; John Anderson, *Happy Childhood: The Development and Guidance of Children and Youth* New York, 1933, p. 101; Ruth W. Washburn, *Children Have Their Reasons* New York, 1942, pp. 8, 53; William Healy, *Personality in Formation and Action* New York, 1938; Dorothy Canfield Fisher, *Mothers and Children* New York, 1914; Smiley Blanton & Margaret Blanton, *Child Guidance* New York, 1927; G. Stanley Hall, *Adolescence* New York, 1931, I, p. 221. On continuation of this motif in black child-rearing literature, see Phyllis Harrison-Ross & Barbara Wyden, *The Black Child – a parent's Guide* New York, 1983, p. 180.

24 Benjamin Spock, *The Common Sense Book of Baby and Child Care* New York, 1946, pp. 204, 252; Michael Zuckerman, 'Dr Spock, the confidence man', in Charles Rosenberg (ed.), *The Family on History* Philadelphia, 1975, pp. 179-208.

25 M. S. Smart & R. C. Smart, *Living and Learning with Children* Boston, 1949; Marion L. Faegre *et al., Child Care and Training* Minneapolis, 1928, p. 146; Emily Post, *Children Are People* New York, 1940, p. 259; George Lawton, *How To Be Happy Though Young* New York, 1949, p. 110; Esther Lloyd-James & Ruth Fedder, *Coming of Age* New York, 1941, pp. 35, 40.

26 Edwin Kirkpatrick, *Fundamentals of Child Study* New York, 1919, p. 136; Alice M. Birney (Mrs Theodore W.), *Childhood* New York, 1904, pp. 66-7, 96.

27 Marion L. Faegre & John E. Anderson, *Child Care and Training* Minneapolis, 1947; Percival M. Symonds, *The Psychology of Parent-Child Relationships* New York, 1939, p. 151.

28 Symonds, *Psychology,* p. 120; Hall, *Adolescence, passim;* American Institute of Child Life, *Problem of Temper,* p. 4 – this manual picks up the theme of growing anger in later childhood quite explicitly.

29 Jean Baker Miller, *The Construction of Anger in Women and Men* Wellesley, MA, 1983, pp. 5-7; James Averill, *Anger and Aggression: An Essay on Emotion* New York, 1982.

30 Peter Filene, *Him/Her/Self: Sex Roles in Modern America* New York, 1975.

31 Ada Hart Arlitt, *The Child from One to Twelve* New York, 1931, pp. 93-7; B. Von Haller Gilmer, *How to Help Your Child Develop Successfully* New York, 1951, pp. 82, 149-50.

32 W. Lloyd Warner, *American Life: Dream and Reality* Chicago, 1962, p. 108.

33   Caroline B. Zachry, *Personality Adjustments in School Children* New York, 1929: E. K. Wickman, *Children's Behaviour; and Teachers' Attitudes* New York, 1928, pp. 17, 127, 161; Sophie Ritholz, *Children's Behavior* Philadelphia, 1959, pp. 60-1.

34   On transitions in anger at work, a vital subject for mid- and later-20th century masculinity, see Stearns & Stearns, *Anger,* Ch. 5; William H. Whyte, Jr., *The Organization Man* New York, 1956, pp. 276ff; Arlie Hochschild, *The Managed Heart: Commercialisation of Human Feeling,* Berkeley, 1983; Loren Baritz, *The Servants of Power: A History of the Use of Social Science in American Industry* Middletown, CT, 1960.

35   Benjamin Spock, *Baby and Child Care* 4th edition, New York, 1977.

36   Dorothy Baruchi, *New Ways in Discipline: You and Your Child Today* New York, 1949, pp. 7, 45, 61; Winnifred de Kok, *Guiding Your Child Through the Formative Years* New York, 1935, pp. 78ff; Joseph D. Teich, *Your Child and His Problems* Boston, 1953, p. 142; Marion J. Radke, *The Relation of Parental Authority to Children's Behavior and Attitudes* Minneapolis, 1946, pp. 11-12, Dory Metcalf, *Bringing Up Children* New York, 1947; Sidonie Gruenberg, *The Parents' Guide to Everyday Problems of Boys and Girls* New York, 1958, p. 94; Martin Bax & Judy Bermal, *Your Child's First Five Years* New York, 1974; Irma S. Black, *Off to a Good Start* New York, 1946, p. 140; Anna W. M. Wold & Suzanne Szasz, *Helping Your Child's Emotional Growth* New York, 1954; *Parents' Magazine.*

'Passing the love of women': manly love and Victorian society

'I am distressed for thee, my brother Jonathan; very pleasant hast thou been unto me; thy love for me was wonderful, passing the love of women.'

The words of David upon hearing of the death of Jonathan (2 Samuel ch. I. v. 26) are a recurrent text in discussions of male friendship or, as the Victorians would have called it, 'manly love'. Any discussion of the subject today is fraught with difficulties. They are difficulties which Freud has a lot to answer for. Since Freud, many commentators have found it impossible to dissociate close male friendship from homosexuality. Yet it is by no means as simple as some would make out, for human relationships are crucially affected by cultural, historical and social conditions. Changes in language and modes of expression render statements of affection from previous ages highly complex and ambiguous matters. Changes in role models and value systems necessitate the careful establishment of perspective.

In many ways the twentieth century is an anomaly in its promotion of female equality, in its encouragement of male-female friendships and in its automatic post-Freudian suspicion of intense emotional friendships between men. In order to understand the concept of manly love in the nineteenth century we need to ignore twentieth century developments and examine a tradition which stretches back in Western civilisation to Ancient Greece and Rome. The lines from the Second Book of Samuel prefacing this essay seem to me to contain the essence of 'manly love' as it was understood for 2,000 years. Firstly, it constituted a form of brotherhood ('my brother Jonathan') but a brotherhood of a spiritual rather than a physical kind. Secondly, it involved notions of service and sacrifice, frequently death on behalf of the beloved. Thirdly, it is higher than and different from, rather than a substitute for, the love of women. The difference lies essentially in the fact that the love of women is sexual and therefore inferior; the love of a man for a man is spiritual, transcendent and free from base desire.

The twentieth century, obsessive about sex, has found it hard to appreciate the strength and extent of traditional Christian teaching on the subject, namely that sex interferes with the true vocation of man – the search for spiritual perfection. That is why Christian teaching exalted celibacy and virginity as the highest states of human existence and it is always within that context that we must see the true manly love which passes the love of women. It is precisely because it is spiritual that it excels. The love of women, with its inevitable sexual and reproductive element, cannot avoid inferiority within that absolute scale of values.

The nineteenth century was steeped in the past, drawing on both Ancient Greece and an idealised Middle Ages for inspiration; social, ethical and artistic.[1] But in both cases the Greek and Medieval legacies were strained through the Victorians' own moral filter. Lord Acton wrote circa 1859: 'Two great principles divide the world and contend for mastery, antiquity and the Middle Ages. These are the two civilisations that have preceded us, the two elements of which ours is composed. . . This is the great dualism that runs through our society.'[2]

It is customary to see these two traditions as being in conflict – the classical tradition in literature versus the Romantic, the classical style in architecture versus the Gothic. But there are areas in which the two traditions come together, just as they had in the Middle Ages, when elements of Platonism were incorporated into Christian philosophy and classical heroes like Hector, Alexander and Julius Caesar, garbed in the plumes and armour of the medieval knight, were celebrated along with Charlemagne, Arthur and Godfrey de Bouillon among the 'Nine Worthies of Christendom'.[3] One such area of overlap is that of romantic love between males, a concept given warrant both by classical Greek thought and by the medieval chivalric ethic, to both of which traditions the nineteenth century celebrants of manly love appealed. Complicating matters is the fact that nineteenth century homosexuals such as John Addington Symonds and Edward Carpenter drew on the same corpus of material to justify their loves.[4] Perhaps the classic case is that of Oscar Wilde, who, on trial in 1895 for homosexual offences, made his celebrated speech about the 'love that dare not speak its name':

> 'The love that dare not speak its name' in this century is such a great affection of an elder for a younger man as there was between David and Jonathan, such as Plato made the very basis of his philosophy, and such as you find in the sonnets of Michelangelo and Shakespeare. It is that deep, spiritual affection that is as pure as it is perfect. . . It is in this century misunderstood, so much misunderstood that it may be described as 'The love that dare not speak its name', and on account of it I am placed where I am now. It is beautiful, it is fine, it is the noblest form of affection. There is nothing unnatural about it, and it repeatedly exists between an elder and a younger man, when the elder has intellect, and the younger man has all the joy, hope and glamour of life before him.[5]

The speech, classically defining the Platonic ideal, earned a round of applause in the courtroom. The effect was somewhat tarnished however, by Wilde's subsequent conviction for acts of gross indecency with young men, among them male prostitutes, conduct which was the exact opposite of what he had advocated from the dock. There was concern that this might indeed discredit the ideal of manly love. As W. T. Stead wrote: 'A few more cases like Oscar Wilde's and we should find the freedom of comradeship now possible to men seriously impaired to the detriment of the race'.[6]

Plato was regularly adduced by homosexual apologists both in the nineteenth century and subsequently but while Plato undoubtedly acknowledged the centrality of the relationship between males to Greek culture and society, calling it the highest form of love, he also stressed the need to proceed from physical to spiritual communion ('The Higher Beauty') and from the particular to the general in the appreciation of beauty. In his definitive study of Greek homosexuality, Sir Kenneth Dover has concluded that homosexual relationships supplied the need for personal relations of an intensity not found in marriage or family.[7] Women were regarded as inferior intellectually, physically and emotionally and males tended to congregate in groups where pair-bonding took place. In some societies (Sparta, Crete) the men were physically segregated and in some (Thebes, Sparta) male lovers were encouraged as part of military training and discipline, an early acknowledgement of the close link of Ares and Eros, but homosexuality in Greece related closely to masculinity. The basic Greek homosexual relationship was between an older man (*erastes*) and a youth (*eromenos*). The older man admired the younger specifically for his male qualities (beauty, strength, skill, speed, endurance) and the younger man respected the older for his experience, wisdom and command. The older man was expected to train, educate and protect the younger and in due course the young man grew up and became a friend rather than lover-pupil and sought out his own *eromenos*. In sex, the older man was expected to be the active partner, the youth the passive partner. Both males were expected in due course to marry females and father children.

So Greek society was genuinely bisexual, but within certain strictly defined limits, for it disapproved of sexual relationships between men of the same age. This was deemed unnatural because one of the men adopted a passive position, thereby betraying the masculinity which required him to take the active role. The equation of women, slaves and youths in the application of legal protection from sexual assault also indicates that these are the passive partners in sexual relationships. So long as a man retained the active role and his sexual partner was a woman (naturally inferior), a slave (unfree) or a youth (not yet a fully-grown man), his masculinity was preserved. The same ethos prevailed in Rome. It was eclipsed by the rise of Christianity which embraced an entirely different sexual ethic. This was based on the primacy of celibacy, the acceptance of marriage as a necessary evil and the rejection of all forms of sex outside marriage.[8] Nevertheless society continued to devalue women, to segregate them and to preserve the social and cultural conditions of male-dominated society replete with all-male groups, not dissimilar from Greece and Rome. This was as true of the nineteenth century as it was of the ninth century.

The Christian tradition, however, willingly embraced many of the ideals of the Ancient World and one of these was of close male friendship, for Christian thought, like Platonic thought, made a clear distinction between physical and non-physical love between males. However, there was another view of male love in the Ancient World, aside from Plato's, which involved older and younger men. This was the rationale of non-sexual friendship between equals, men of similar age, rank, habits and sentiments, attracted by each other's character. It was defined and articulated by Aristotle in his *Ethics*. It could not include sex by the cultural definitions of the Greeks but could and did include love. It existed only between two men at the same time ('To have many friends in the way of perfect friendship is no more possible than to be in love with many at the same time'.) It was superior to married love, which was similar to the relations between the government and the governed, rather than the association of brotherly equals which true male friendship involved. It was a genuine spiritual bond between two good men.[9]

Aristotle's ideas were developed for the Romans by Cicero in his *De Amicitia* and in that form became one of the most influential works in the Medieval West, initiating a long and potent tradition of male friendship. Cicero saw true friendship between males as a meeting of souls attracted to each other by moral virtue, a generous simplicity of heart, good manners and conversation. It was, he believed, 'the most valuable of all human possessions'. He did not scruple to call it love but he stressed that 'true friendship can only be found among the virtuous' and he carefully defined virtue as consisting of restraint, honour, justice and beneficence. Friendship transcended rank and talent, grew over time and involved complete frankness between the friends.[10]

Cicero's ideas appealed strongly to the early Church Fathers and Jerome, Ambrose and Cassian drew on them in their own writings about friendship. Friendship was an important element in Christian thinking. St John's Gospel quoted Christ as saying: 'Greater Love hath no man than this, that a man lay down his life for his friends' (John ch. 15 v. 13): not wife nor parents nor family but friends. St Aelred of Rievaulx's *Spiritual Friendship* (c. 1130) drew directly on Cicero's *De Amicitia* and harmonised his ideas with Christian teaching. He made a distinction between the charity that was extended to all and the friendship that was reserved for a few. Spiritual friendship was based on the mutual recognition of virtue and began with 'purity of intention, the direction of reason and the restraint of moderation'. Loyalty thereafter was the 'foundation of stability and constancy in friendship' but it was unquestionably 'love' ('The fountain and source of friendship is love. There can be love without friendship but friendship without love is impossible'.)[11] Aelred cited David and Jonathan as exemplars of this kind of friendship, as well as Orestes and Pylades whom Cicero had cited.

The language that friends used to one another was extravagant and frankly erotic in the Middle Ages. St Bernard of Clairvaux wrote to Hugh of Prémentré: 'For my part, I am determined to love you, whatever you do, even if you do not return my love. I shall cling to you, even against your will; I shall cling to you even against my own will.'[12]

This love should not, however, be interpreted as necessarily homosexual. For clerics could not have written so regularly and unguardedly to each other in these terms, given the heavy penitential punishments for homosexuality at this time, if this had not been a non-sexual expression of romantic affection. The romantic male friendship was, for writers like Bernard and Aelred, part of a theology of love. Their idea was that love between friends enabled them to participate truly in the love of God. It was part of an emotional and spiritual plane transcending the flesh. As Aelred said: 'He who dwells in friendship, dwells in God and God in him.'[13]

Alongside the spiritual love of monks and clerics, there also developed in the Middle Ages a chivalric love between knights. In the Middle Ages chivalry emerged as the code of the ruling elite. There were in fact three rival schools of thought on chivalry: warrior, religious and courtly. Warrior chivalry was the oldest and the most widely practised, for it was little more than a rationalisation of the existing situation. Chivalry was fundamentally a product of war and warrior chivalry therefore exalted those qualities most prized in war: loyalty, courage, generosity, prowess in battle and skill in the martial arts. The Church, disapproving of the internecine warfare, homicide, luxury and unchastity common among members of the knightly class, proposed its own role model of knight-hood which involved chastity, austerity, humility and righteousness. To temper the savage pleasures of the warrior knights, the school of courtly chivalry was born. The object of this code was the idealised love of a noble lady. Where warrior knights fought for personal glory and religious knights for the glory of God, courtly knights fought for the glory of the lady.[14]

Around these different concepts were woven the literary elaborations. The earliest celebrations of knighthood were the *Chansons de geste,* pro-ducts of a period when Christendom was on the defensive against invad-ing hordes of infidels and they therefore exalted the qualities needed for such epic struggles: male camaraderie, courage and loyalty. C. S. Lewis wrote of this period:

> The deepest of worldly emotions in this period is the love of man for man, the mutual love of warriors who die together fighting against odds and the affection between vassal and lord. We shall never understand this last, if we think of it, in the light of our own moderated and impersonal loyalties. We must not think of officers drinking the king's health; we must think rather of a small boy's feeling for some hero in the sixth form. . . These male affections – though wholly free from the taint that hangs about 'friendship' in the ancient world – were themselves lover-like; in their intensity, their wilful exclusion of other values, and their uncertainty, they provided an exercise of the spirit not wholly unlike that which later ages have found in 'love'.[15]

The classic exemplification of this is the *Song of Roland.* Charlemagne's paladins are comprised of male pairs, the most notable of whom are Roland and Oliver. When Oliver is mortally wounded in battle he prays that God will bless France and his companion Roland above all men. He and Roland part 'with great love' and when Oliver dies, Roland weeps for him ('No man on earth felt ever such distress'). Roland declares: 'Now thou art dead I grieve to be alive' and falls swooning to the earth.[16]

The male love commemorated in the epic was overtaken in the twelfth and thirteenth century by a new poetic form – the romance; product of a time of peace, expansion and adventure. The romance eulogised courtly love, an idealised heterosexual love in which a knight performed deeds of valour for his beloved whose identity he kept secret. However, it was crucially love between an unmarried man and a woman married to some-one else and therefore perforce chaste. It stressed the qualities of gentle-ness, humility, moderation and discretion and it initiated the distinctive Western European trend of romantic love between men and women. But the earlier male love tradition continued alongside it, as seen in the twelfth century story of Amis and Amile. Amis and Amile are two knights who have sworn eternal love but their love is put to the test when Amis contracts lepresy. He is abandoned by all and his wife tries to strangle him. The Angel Gabriel tells Amis that he can be cured if Amile will slay his children and wash him in their blood. Amile does this and Amis is cured. Amile's children are then restored to life in testimony to their great love.[17]

Towards the end of the Middle Ages, synthesis was attempted and the best qualities of all three schools of thought were blended together to provide the qualities of the perfect knight. Alain Chartier's *Le Bréviaire des Nobles* listed the twelve virtues of knighthood as: nobility, loyalty, honour, righteousness, prowess, love, courtesty, diligence, cleanliness, generosity, sobriety and perseverance. This was the paragon that was recalled during the Romantic revival in the novels and poems of Sir Walter Scott where courtly love between knight and lady could exist side by side with manly love between knights. The reality of the Middle Ages, however, was that the purest ideals of manly love – between monks and between knights – persisted throughout because they were the products of the contemporary situation, an exclusively or largely male-dominated and male-centred society.

Even after the Middle Ages, manly love remained above and apart from fleshly love. The essayist Montaigne wrote feelingly about such friendship, recalling his own with Etienne de la Boétie:

Truly the name of brother is a beautiful name and full of affection and for that reason he and I made our alliance a brotherhood. . . To compare this brotherly affection with affection for women, even though it is the result of our choice – it cannot be done; nor can we put the love of women in the same category. Its ardour, I confess – is more active, more scorching and more intense. But it is an impetuous and fickle flame, undulating and variable, a fever flame, subject to fits and lulls, that holds us only by one corner. In friendship it is a general and universal warmth, moderate and even, besides, a constant and settled warmth, all gentleness and smoothness, with nothing bitter and stinging about it.[18]

He specifically distinguishes it from the love of women and from the homosexual love of youths:

To tell the truth, the ordinary capacity of women is inadequate for that communion and fellowship which is the nurse of this sacred bond; nor does their soul seem firm enough to endure the strain of so tight and durable a knot. . . And that other, licentious Greek love is justly abhorred by our morality. Since it involved, moreover, according to their practice such a necessary disparity in age and such a difference in the lovers' functions, it did not correspond closely enough with the perfect union and harmony that we require here.[19]

This continued to be society's general attitude to male friendships.

In the early nineteenth century the poet Shelley wrote:

The nature of Love and Friendship is very little understood, and the distinction betweem them ill established. This latter feeling – at least, a profound and sentimental attachment to one of the same sex, wholly divested of the smallest alloy of sensual admixture, often precedes the former. It is not right to say, merely, that it is exempt from the smallest alloy of sensuality. It rejects, with disdain, all thoughts but those of an elevated and imaginative character.[20]

Similarly Charles, Lord Metcalfe, wrote of: 'The joys. . . in the pure love which exists between man and man, which cannot, I think, be surpassed in the more alloyed attachment between the opposite sexes to which the name of love is generally exclusively applied'.[21] It is evident from just these few examples that there existed a continuous tradition of spiritual love between coeval males, something which was different from the Platonic love of an older and younger man. The latter could be interpreted also on the spiritual plane but could also lend classical justification to pederasty.

Victorian England, like Ancient Greece or the Medieval West, was a male-dominated society. For the upper middle classes, life revolved around all-male institutions: the public school, the university, the armed forces, the church, parliament, the club, the City. Marriage tended to be deferred for economic and social reasons. Women were sidelined, exploited as sex-objects or worshipped as goddesses, so male love came to seem finer, nobler and more fulfilling, just as it had in Ancient Greece and the early Middle Ages and for the same reasons. In a world in which clergymen, schoolmasters, dons and army officers were regularly bachelors, it is not surprising that many of them became enthusiastic proponents of male comradeship and male love as a central emotional factor in their existence.

One of the principal areas of overlap between the Greek and Medieval influences on Victorian society lay in the public schools. They, more than any other institutions, stand as the epitome of the Greco-Medieval value systems. They were claimed for both. Walter Pater deliberately compared the education of a Spartan youth to that in the Victorian public school:

> A young Lacedaemonian then, of the privileged class left his home, his tender nurses in those large, quiet, old suburban houses early, for a public school, a schooling all the stricter as years went on. . . And his education continued late; he could seldom think of marriage till the age of thirty. . . from the first (it) set its subjects on the thought of personal dignity, of self-command. . . The place of deference, of obedience, was large in the education of Lacedaemonian youth; and they never complained. It involved however, for the most part, as with ourselves, the government of youth by itself; an implicit subordination of the younger to the older in many degrees. Quite early in life, at school, they found that superiors and inferiors. . . there really were; and their education proceeded with systematic boldness on that fact.[22]

Pater went on to talk of the Spartan boys' 'public school slang', their meals 'in their divisions', their cold baths, the *viva voce* system which made them 'adepts in presence of mind'. However, being Pater, he could not resist noting also that: 'the beauty of these most beautiful of all people was a male beauty, far remote from feminine tenderness; had the expression of a certain *ascesis* in it; was like unsweetened wine'. This tells us as much about the Victorian tendency to interpret the past in terms of and from the perspective of the present, as well as Pater's role in promoting the aesthetic, implicitly homosexual Hellenism of youth and beauty.

Sir Henry Newbolt, on the other hand, saw in the public school the mirror of medieval chivalry. Its model was the education of the knight's squire:

> The old method of training the young squires to knighthood produced our public school system. . . The public school. . . derived the housemaster from the knights to whose castle boys were sent as pages; fagging, from the services of all kinds which they there performed; prefects, from the senior squires or 'masters of the henchmen'; athletics from the habit of out-door life; and the love of games, the 'sporting' or 'amateur' view of them, from tournaments and the chivalric rules of war. . . Its defect was that it trained boys only for one kind of career, the career of soldiering and sport. Its great merit was that it made men, and not sneaks or bookworms, and that its direct objects were character and efficiency.[23]

The public schools and chivalry provided major elements of continuity in Newbolt's verse and thought, encapsulating an important strand in Victorian culture.

When it came to male love, both the Hellenists and the Medievalists agreed on the purity and spirituality of its nature, drawing on each other's traditions to reinforce the point. John Addington Symonds explicitly compared friendship and Medieval chivalry:

> Nearly all the historians of Greece have failed to insist upon the fact that fraternity in arms played for the Greek race the same part as the idealisation of women for the knighthood of feudal Europe. Greek mythology and history are full of tales of friendship, which can only be paralleled by the story of David and Jonathan in the Bible. The legends of Herakles and Hylas, of Theseus and Peirithous, of Apollo and Hyacinth, of Orestes and Pylades, occur immediately to mind. Among the noblest patriots, tyrannicides, lawgivers and self-devoted heroes in the early times of Greece, we always find the names of friends and comrades received with peculiar honour. . . these comrades, staunch to each other in their love and elevated by friendship to the pitch of noblest enthusiasm, were among the favourite saints of Greek legend and history. In a word, the chivalry of Hellas found its motive force in friendship rather than in the love of women; and the motive force of all chivalry is a generous, soul-exalting, unselfish passion.[24]

Symonds, although himself a homosexual and homosexual apologist, chose here to list male couples representative of both homosexual *paiderastia* and of Aristotelian non-sexual fellowship and to link all to spiritual love as in chivalry. This was typical of the 'official' Victorian attitude to male couples in Greek history; their exaltation as exemplars of comradeship, virtue, partriotism and male love.

Similarly Kenelm Digby drew on the Greek tradition in *The Broadstone of Honour* (1828-9), the seminal work for the Victorian elaboration of chivalry. He pointed to heroic friendship as one of the integral elements of knighthood, giving actual historical examples, illustrations from chivalric romance ('the duty of searching after lost friends is called into constant exercise by the writers of old romance') and examples from Greek legend and history; Achilles and Patroclus, Orestes and Pylades, Euryalus and Nisus, Theseus and Pirithous, Pelopidas and Epaminondas. His definition of friendship was the same as that of Aristotle, Cicero and Aelred and he particularly stressed the appeal of chivalry to youth ('Every boy and youth is, in his mind and sentiments, a knight and essentially a son of chivalry').[25] This enormously influential work inspired writers, teachers and painters alike. It was a major influence on Baden-Powell for instance. Edward Fitzgerald popularised Digby's ideas in *Euphranor* (1851), a Platonic dialogue on the need to re-establish public schools and universities in the spirit of the Greek gymnasia, in which he equated Greek athletic heroes and medieval knights. He was against too much book-learning and in favour of swimming, drilling, riding and cricket to 'produce habitual instincts of courage, resolution, decision and good humour'.[26] He saw 'fellowship', as he called manly love, as another essential ingredient. Fitzgerald had prolonged romantic friendships, essentially extended adolescent crushes, with two younger men: William Kenworthy Browne and Joseph Fletcher. It may well be that the strength of the chivalric ethic is one of the explanations of the extended adolescence of so many Victorian males and vice versa.

The consensus clearly was then that manly love was a common element in Ancient Greece and Medieval Chivalry and its essence was spiritual. This consensus makes manly love a central strand in the definition of manliness and manliness was one of the qualities which the public schools sought to inculcate. The impact of public school education on its recipients was enormous. It shaped, taught and moulded several generations of Britain's ruling elite and its ideas filtered down the social scale via popular literature, organised sport and elementary schools.

However, manliness in the public school context went through three distinct though related manifestations. Dr Arnold's own creed and that of his circle, so influential in the early days of the reformed public school, was that so aptly described by David Newsome as 'Godliness and Good Learning'. Arnold, he says, instilled in his pupils 'a tremendous seriousness, an intense enjoyment of work and an extraordinary enthusiasm for virtue'.[27] Arnold saw education and religion as inseparably linked and both aimed at bringing the schoolboy to personal and moral maturity. He sought therefore to propel boys as rapidly as possible through boyhood and into manhood.

'The application of the doctrine of godliness and good learning to the upbringing of boys in the public school did much to create that breed of diligent, earnest, intellectual, eminent Victorians which has left its impress on almost every aspect of the age'.[28] For Arnold and company, manliness meant the pursuit and practice of the three qualities he sought to inculcate: 'first, religious and moral principle; second, gentlemanly conduct; third, intellectual ability'.[29] This was not so much an order of absolute priorities as a triple set of goals, the third being purposeless and directionless without the first two.

But in the middle of the century, a new ethos arose out of the old to challenge and supplant it – that of 'muscular Christianity', the combination of godliness and manliness. Its principal proponents were Charles Kingsley and Thomas Hughes, neither of whom was a schoolmaster but whose books were avidly read in school and whose ideas were enthusiastically taken up by sporting pedagogues. The principal themes of Kingsley's world-view were the promotion of physical strength, courage and health, the importance of family life and married love, the elements of duty and service to mankind and the scientific study of the natural world to discover the divine pattern of the moral universe.[30] Hughes took the definition 'muscular Christianity', originally applied mockingly, on board and provided a succinct definition of it in *Tom Brown at Oxford*, together with its ideological sources:

> So far as I know, the least of the muscular Christians has hold of the old chivalrous and Christian belief that a man's body is given to him to be trained and brought into subjection and then used for the protection of the weak, the advancement of all righteous causes and the subduing of the earth which God has given to the children of men.[31]

Thomas Hughes indeed claimed Christ himself for the league of muscular Christians in his book *The Manliness of Christ*. In this cause, games became increasingly important as the means of keeping fit, building strength and moulding character; intellectual pursuits in consequence lost ground.

Then, in the latter part of the century, came the final development. Games-playing and games-worship became secularised and in place of godliness and manliness there arose the cult of athleticism.[32] Manliness remained central but now it was defined by sporting ability and adherence to the creed of 'playing the game', 'team spirit', 'not letting the side down', 'being a good loser' etc. 'Fair Play' became the motto of a nation whose ideology and religious faith were subsumed into Imperialism, with its belief in the British as the elect who had a God-given duty to govern and civilise the world. In the wake of Imperialism, the public schools in particular their games fields became 'mints for the turning out of Empire-builders'.

Just as manliness, however defined, was integral to these three educational philosophies, so too was manly love. Friendship drenched in emotion was a key characteristic of the godliness and good learning brigade, where it embraced both masters and boys. David Newsome noted:

> Inseparable from this ardent craving for activity was the tendency to emotionalism and to passionate friendship. The doctrine of the stiff upper lip was no part of the public school code in the Arnoldian period. . . tears were usual, the expected consequence of reproof. . . and the word 'love' was more frequently on their lips, used with real sincerity. The association between master and pupil seems to have often been very intimate, admitting of expressions of emotion on both sides.[33]

The same was also true of the boys, where pure and earnest attachments developed quite apart from the sexual randiness that was part and parcel of boarding school life. These emotional friendships carried on into University life too. At Oxford, the Tractarians were notable for intense friendships, some of them probably sublimated homosexuality, others part of the extravagant emotionalism of the age.[34]

Kingsley was untypical of the advocates of manliness in abhorring celibacy as effeminate and eulogising married love, something which proceeded undoubtedly from his own highly-sexed nature and his passionate heterosexuality. Hughes was more typical of the apostles of manliness in enthusiastically endorsing male friendships. In *Tom Brown at Oxford* he declared: 'Blessed is the man who has the gift of making friends for it is one of God's best gifts. It involves many things but above all the power of going out of yourself and seeing and appreciating whatever is noble and living in another man'.[35] One of the continuing themes of the book is the close friendship between Tom and an older student, Jack Hardy. Hardy is an important moral influence on Tom but they quarrel when Tom starts dallying with a local barmaid. Hardy lectures him on manliness, warning 'that the crown of all real manliness, of all Christian manliness, is purity'.[36] After wrestling with his conscience, Tom gives up the barmaid and is reconciled with Hardy. Hardy admits that he loves Tom 'as David loved Jonathan' and 'Tom rushed across to his friend, dearer to him now, and threw his arm round his neck; and if the un-English truth must out, had three parts of a mind to kiss the rough face which was now working with strong emotion'.[37]

The keynote of athleticism was to reserve energy and emotion for the games field and keeping a stiff upper lip, taking defeat bravely and victory modestly became essential parts of the schoolboy's code of behaviour but love could still enter in. As J. A. Mangan has observed:

> The elements of sexual identity and legitimate sensuality are inseparable from the worship of games during the period under discussion. To be manly was a condition that exuded the physical, but, at the same time, it was an asexual physicality extended into early manhood, in which sexual knowledge and experience were taboo. . . Ironically sensuality was not only permitted, it was demanded; but it was a sensuality in which physical contact was channelled into football mauls and emotional feeling into hero worship of the athletic 'blood'.[38]

Such hero worship coupled with adolescent romanticism ensured the continuance of manly love even through the era of athleticism for, ironically, one of the consequences of the official doctrine of manliness with its stress on games, sexual purity and hero-worship was to prolong adolescence well into actual manhood.

It was Cyril Connolly who devised the theory of permanent adolescence when evaluating the importance of the public school to its alumni:

> It is a theory that the experiences undergone by boys at the great public schools, their glories and disappointments are so intense as to dominate their lives and arrest their development. From these it results that the greater part of the ruling class remains adolescent, school-minded, self-conscious, cowardly, sentimental, and in the last analysis, homosexual. . . Romanticism with its deathwish is to blame, for it lays emphasis on childhood, on a fall from grace which is not compensated for by any doctrine of future redemption; we enter the world, trailing clouds of glory, childhood and boyhood follow and we are damned. Certainly growing up seems a hurdle which most of us are unable to take.[39]

The idea that schooldays were the pinnacle of existence was certainly strongly encouraged and here popular fiction is, as so often, the mirror of the unconscious. In his novel *Gerald Eversley's Friendship*, J. E. C. Welldon, the headmaster of Harrow, has housemaster Mr Brandiston of St Anselm's tell Harry Venniker after his goal has won a key house football match: 'You will never be a greater person in life, Venniker, than you are to-day'.[40]

While one might quarrel with some of Connolly's attributions of adolescence, in particular 'cowardly' and 'homosexual', the concept of permanent adolescence is a useful and revealing one. Indeed it might even be taken further and applied to the nation at large in the Victorian era. The public school was, after all, the powerhouse of the nation, producing its ruling class, its role models, its social arbiters, stamping its imprint upon the age. Total institutions are in art notoriously microcosms of the nation and nature so frequently imitates art that the qualities so characteristic of the public school (all-male society, strict hierarchy, obsession with games, hero-worship and juvenile romanticism) can also be seen in operation in the nation particularly in the last decades of the nineteenth century.

In a very real sense the Victorian male was *puer aeternus,* the boy who never grew up. It was not just the all-male society in which he functioned, it was also his preferred activities (hunting, enpire-building, exploring, warring). It was the century which saw the invention of boys' fiction and a rich tradition of tales of adventure. Martin Green in his pioneering study of the literature of adventure pointed out that 'it (was) a striking feature of late Victorian culture that its emotional focus was on boys'.[41] Time after time the image of the boy returns. The philosopher George Santayana admiringly described the Briton as 'the sweet, just, boyish master of the world'.[42] So did Sir Henry Newbolt, who summed up the dominant ideology of the age in poetic form in *Vitae Lampada,* describing a battle in which the voice of a schoolboy rallies the ranks: 'Play up! Play up! and play the game'.[43] J. E. C. Welldon wrote with unselfconscious candour: 'no being perchance is so distinct, none so beautiful or attractive as a noble English boy'.[44] In his celebrated fantasy *Vice Versa* F. Anstey permits the pleasurable regression to boyhood when a magical Indian gemstone enables stuffy stockbroker Paul Bultitude to change places with his public schoolboy son after he utters the cri-de-coeur: 'I wish I were a boy again'. The definitive fictional embodiment of the syndrome was of course J. M. Barrie's Peter Pan, the ultimate product of an age given its name by an almost deified mother-figure, Queen Victoria.

The characteristic artistic forms of the age have all the emotion, aggression, extravagance and romanticism of the adolescent. The Gothic architecture is fantastical; a riot of towers, spires and gloriously redundant decoration. St Pancras Station is its emblem. Melodrama, the dominant theatrical form, with its vivid archetypes, bold assertion of Right and Wrong, Love and Patriotism and its lack of psychological complexity, similarly makes a direct appeal to the emotions. In art, the Pre-Raphaelites celebrated the return of chivalry with gallant knights and wilting maidens. In architecture, painting and theatre, as well as in war, ceremonial and landscape, the accent was on spectacle.

Ronald Hyam has perceptively pointed to sexual and emotional repression as one of the dynamics of Empire and expansion and it is striking how many Imperial proconsuls married late (Milner, Lugard, Baden-Powell) or not at all (Rhodes, Gordon, Kitchener). Equally striking is the devotion of many of them to boys. Explorers like Henry M. Stanley and Edward Eyre had a succession of favoured boy companions. Stanley celebrated one of his in a novel for boys, *My Kalulu: Prince, King and Slave*. Gordon was devoted to the care of boys, whom he called 'my kings'. At the heart of Victorian culture and administration were tightly knit all-male groups; Milner's 'kindergarten', Wolseley's 'ring', Kitchener's 'cubs', the Cambridge Apostles and Henley's 'regatta'.[45]

Many of the great men of Empire were essentially boy-men. Baden-Powell, with his love of practical jokes, amateur theatricals, music hall ditties and comic disguises, was perhaps the most extreme example – 'a perennial singing schoolboy, a permanent whistling adolescent, a case of arrested development *con brio*' Piers Brendon calls him.[46] Out of his instinctive identification with and understanding of boys he created the Boy Scouts. The great writers of boys' books were praised for their boyishness. Talbot Baines Reed was described as 'to the last a real boy among boys' and Gordon Stables wrote of himself: 'Thirty years ago I was myself a boy bodily. I am still a boy mentally and in heart and am likely to die a boy'.[47] 'Boy' was the highest term of approval in the vocabulary of Edward Fitzgerald: 'Plenty of the Boy in him', 'A great Boy' etc., he wrote of his friends.

This perennial boyishness had several manifestations and several consequences. There was identification with boys and the commitment of many men to the training, education and entertainment of boys, the flowering of literature and organisations for boys, almost all of them securely grounded in the concept of 'manliness'. Another consequence was the tradition of sentimental pederasty, expressed in the upsurge of Uranian poetry and writing.[48] A third was the prolonged adolescence in which for many men, married and single, passionate emotional attachments to other males were the most significant events of their lives. In so far as labels mean anything, many of these men were heterosexuals, notable proponents of manliness and would probably have greeted any suggestion of a physical realisation of their emotional attachments with horror.

Alfred, Lord Tennyson, one of the great celebrants of chivalry in his *Idylls of the King,* was so moved by the early death of his friend Arthur Hallam that he poured his grief and love into the poem *In Memoriam:*

> More than my brothers are to me. . .
> My love shall no no further range. . .
> Such friendship as had master'd time. . .
> Tis better to have loved and lost
> Than never to have loved at all.

Tennyson's biographer Robert Bernard Martin wrote of this relationship: 'Tennyson's reaction to Hallam was simple: 'He was as near perfection as mortal man can be'. . . It would be hard to exaggerate the impact Hallam made on Tennyson; their friendship was to be the most emotionally intense period he ever knew, four years probably equal in psychic importance to the other seventy-nine of his life'.[49]

Then there was the relationship between Robert Louis Stevenson and W. E. Henley, of which Henley's biographer John Connell wrote: 'It was of the utmost significance in both their lives. It was a romantic friendship, in the strict sense of the term. . . They were to part and quarrel and die unreconciled, but the power of their friendship – across and through the lives of both of them – was never finally dissipated or broken. For between them there was a strong, bitter, binding love, passing the love of women.'[50]

Finally, there was Rudyard Kipling and Wolcott Balestier. They had a brief, intense friendship, during which they collaborated on a book *The Naulakha,* but which was cut short by Balestier's death in 1891 whereupon Kipling, in the manner almost of the public schoolboy heroes of such male romances as *The Hill* and *Gerald Eversley's Friendship,* promptly married Wolcott's sister Caroline. Philip Mason called the relationship 'a romantic affection'; Lord Birkenhead called it 'love'.[51] Kipling himself in a comment to a close friend of Wolcott testified to the depth of his despair: 'He died so suddenly and so far away; we had so much to say to each other and now I have got to wait so long before I can say it'.[52]

An example from outside the world of letters is furnished by the friendship of the Christian philanthropist and evangelist F. N. Charrington, who spent much of his life working among the East End poor as Superintendent of the Tower Hamlets Mission. In his biography of Charrington, *The Great Acceptance* (1912), Guy Thorne included a chapter entitled 'David and Jonathan' in which he gave an account of Charrington's relationship with the Hon. Ion Keith-Falconer. Thorne said that it 'deserves to rank with the great friendships of the world, so uninterrupted, firm and beautiful was it'.[53] They first met when Keith-Falconer was 17 and still at Harrow, linked by their common Christian faith and commitment to working with the poor. In 1884 Keith-Falconer married and sailed to Aden to take up missionary work, dying there three years later. Charrington was and remained inconsolable ('I know that the loss is, even to-day, after so many years as fresh and keen as ever').[54]

There were so many of these relationships that space precludes further elaboration. But their importance is reflected in their regular appearance in fiction. The Leavisite Great Tradition of English literature elevated to the pantheon Jane Austen, George Eliot and Henry James, whose works were written from a female perspective and rooted in the tradition of courtly love sentimentalised. However, a rival Great Tradition of Adventure has been recovered and rehabilitated by Martin Green, centring on Defoe, Scott and Kipling, in which the central relationships are frequently between males (e.g. Crusoe and Friday, Kim and the Lama).[55] It is no coincidence that the most celebrated characters in Victorian fiction were a male couple, Sherlock Holmes and Dr Watson. Despite Watson's marriage to Mary Morstan and Holmes' reverence for *the* woman – Irene Adler, the pairing of Holmes and Watson epitomises the depth of affection, trust and loyalty that so often grew up between men in the male-dominated society of nineteenth century Britain.

The relationship is that of the bachelor clubman's world, epitomised by the habitual use of surnames, which effectively precludes a sexual intimacy which would surely have stretched to the use of Christian names. Owen Dudley Edwards has sensitively traced the development of the relationship, contrasting it pointedly with the much more emotional bond between the amateur cracksman A. J. Raffles and his chum Bunny, the erstwhile public school fagmaster and fag, created by Conan Doyle's brother-in-law E. W. Hornung.[56] While one may take issue with Dudley Edwards' description of the latter relationship as 'very obviously homosexual', it was certainly an intense romantic friendship, characteristic of public school hero-worship and prolonged adolescence.

The Holmes-Watson relationship developed with only very rare and therefore telling revelations of its emotional depth. For long periods, the relationship was not unlike a marriage. Watson observed:

> He was a man of habits, narrow and concentrated habits, and I had become one of them. As an institution, I was like the violin, the shag tobacco, the old black pipe, the index books and others perhaps less excusable. When it was a case of active work and a comrade was needed upon whose nerve he could place some reliance, my role was obvious. But apart from this I had uses. I was a whetstone for his mind. I stimulated him. He liked to think aloud in my presence.[57]

But on Watson's side the importance of the relationship was attested in the grief with which he wrote of Holmes' presumed death in *The Final Problem*, describing him as 'the best and wisest man I have ever known', the acknowledgement of his friend's great qualities of chivalry, tenacity, courage, patriotism and unfailing commitment to truth, justice and honour; qualities he shared with his creator Conan Doyle. But there came a time too when Holmes acknowledged the depth of his feeling for Watson, when Watson was shot in *The Three Garridebs:*

> My friend's wiry arms were around me and he was leading me to a chair. 'You're not hurt, Watson? For God's sake, say that you are not hurt!' It was worth a wound – it was worth many wounds – to know the depth of loyalty and love which lay behind that cold mask. The clear, hard eyes were dimmed for a moment and the firm lips were shaking. For the one and only time I caught a glimpse of a great heart as well as a great brain. All my years of humble but single-minded service culminated in that moment of revelation.
> 'It's nothing, Holmes. It's a mere scratch.'[58]

Dudley Edwards – and one cannot but agree – concluded: 'Conan Doyle has the distinction in that passage of having recorded love between male friends with more honour and more dignity than in any work in the language'.[59]

But the inculcation of manly love began at school. In their lessons, their reading, the sermons they heard, pulic schoolboys were prepared for close male friendships. Spiritual love between males, comradeship, validated by Greek and Medieval models, centred on admiration for their manliness – courage, virtue, skill, beauty, honour – was beamed at them from all sides. It channelled, directed and shaped the inherent and instinctive romanticism of the adolescent male. Alec Waugh described this state perfectly in *Public School Life:*

A boy of seventeen is passing through a highly romantic period. His emotions are searching for a focus. He is filled with wild, impossible loyalties. He longs to surrender himself to some lost cause. He hungers for adventures. On occasions he even goes so far as to express himself in verse, an indiscretion that he will never subsequently commit. . . he is, in fact, in love with love; he does not see a girl of his own age, his own class, from one end of the term to the other; it is in human nature to accept the second best.[60]

In *Coningsby,* Disraeli expressed the same view ('At school, friendship is a passion' etc.)[61]

J. R. de S. Honey has charted the rise of national concern about schoolboy friendships in the 1880s, a decade which saw the celebrated Labouchère amendment to the Criminal Law Amendment Act of 1885, which effectively brought all forms of homosexual activity whthin the scope of the law, the private publication of J. A. Symonds' *A Problem in Greek Ethics* (1883), the beginning of the scientific definition and formulation of the condition of homosexuality and the breaking of the Cleveland Street Scandal around a male brothel frequented by notable figures of the day (1889-90). The increasing concern about and attention paid to the question of homosexuality nationally flowed down to the schools.[62]

In 1884 and again in 1885 Rev J. Robertson, headmaster of Haileybury, sent a confidential circular to parents urging that they warn their boys against 'talk, example or impure solicitations' to which they might be exposed at school or elsewhere and sought to suppress the use of female nicknames among the boys and of female impersonation in school entertainments.[63] By 1900 many leading public schools officially or unofficially prohibited associations between boys from different forms or different houses but such associations went underground rather than disappearing. There was similar pressure to end too close associations between masters and boys. This was prefigured in the 1870s when Dr James Hornby, headmaster of Eton, ousted William Johnson Cory (1872) and Oscar Browning (1875), masters notorious for the crushes they had on pupils.[64]

This represents a marked change in attitude by the authorities towards the close relations which had prevailed in public schools betwen boys and between boys and masters. G. E. L. Cotton of Marlborough had preached a sermon in 1857 extolling schoolboy friendships, especially those between older and younger boys, quoting John ch. 13 v. 23 with reference to the disciple 'whom Jesus loved' and who leaned on his bosom. Cotton argued that unselfish love should inform such friendships and through them the boys would be brought nearer to God.[65] It was essentially the argument of St Aelred of Rievaulx. Similarly in *Tom Brown's Schooldays*, a friendship between Tom and the younger George Arthur is encouraged by Dr Arnold to benefit them both. Dean Farrar, author of *Eric*, wrote in a later book *St Winifred's or The World of School*: 'Of all earthly friendships few are more beautiful or in some respects more touching than a friendship between two boys.'[66] Both Hughes and Farrar, founding fathers of the school story, highlighted intense friendships but were very careful to distinguish them from more fleshly and reprehensible associations, whose existence they recognised. The friendship they were endorsing was exclusively of the manly, improving and spiritual kind.

It is against this background that we can see the importance of, and the interpretation provided by, the role models from Greek and Medieval culture. The literature of Greece in which public schoolboys of the Victorian age were steeped was rich in pairs of male friends, the tests of whose friendship was to offer or to sacrifice their lives for love of the other: Orestes and Pylades, Damon and Pythias, Nisus and Euryalus, Achilles and Patroclus, Theseus and Pirithous and Hercules and Hylas. Whether in their original Greek setting they were Platonic lovers or Aristotelian friends, for the nineteenth century they were idealised chivalric comrades.

Walter Pater rhapsodised about one such male couple: the brothers Castor and Polydeuces, one of whom was mortal and the other immortal. When Castor died in battle, Polydeuces prayed to be permitted to die with him. He was permitted but the two gallant souls became stars in the heavens:

> They were the starry patrons of all that youth was proud of, delighted in, horsemanship, games, battle; and always with that profound fraternal sentiment. Brothers, comrades, who could not live without each other, they were the most fitting patrons of a place, in which friendship, comradeship, like theirs, came to so much. Lovers of youth they remained, those enstarred types of it, arrested thus at that moment of miraculous good fortune, as a consecration of the clean, youthful friendship, 'passing even the love of women', which by system, and under the sanction of their founder's name, elaborated into a kind of art, became an elementary part of education. A part of their duty and discipline, it was also their great solace and encouragement.[67]

The elements are all there: youth as the acme of existence, athletic accomplishment, brotherhood, death. It was those idealised Greek relationships that formed the basic role models for public school boys.

F. W. Farrar begins his novel *Julian Home* (1896) with an account of the friendship of Julian and Hugh Lillyston at Horton School:

> They were continually together and never tired of each other's society; and at last when their tutor, observing and thoroughly approving of the friendship, put them in the same room, the school began in fun to call them Achilles and Patroclus, Damon and Pythias, Orestes and Pylades, David and Jonathan, Theseus and Pirithous, and as many other names of *paria amicorum* as they could remember. . . So form by form, Lillyston and Julian Home mounted up the school side by side and illustrated the noblest and holiest uses of friendship by adding to each other's happiness and advantage in every way. I am glad to dwell on such a picture knowing, O Holy Friendship, how awfully a schoolboy can sometimes *desecrate* thy name![68]

It is clear that Farrar is propagandising for spiritual friendship in the full awareness of what was darkly called 'beastliness' amongst boys. The situation that works like *Julian Home* sought to combat was the atmosphere of unrestrained sexuality such as J. A. Symonds experienced as a boy at Harrow in the 1850s:

> Every boy of good looks had a female name, and was recognised either as a public prostitute or as some bigger fellow's 'bitch'. Bitch was the word in common usage to indicate a boy who yielded his person to a lover. The talk in the dormitories and studies was incredibly obscene. Here and there one could not avoid seeing acts of onanism, mutual masturbation, the sports of naked boys in bed together. There was no refinement, no sentiment, no passion; nothing but animal lust in these occurrences. They filled me with disgust and loathing.[69]

Victorian public schools, like Victorian society in general, became just as saturated in the legends, images and ethos of chivalry as in those of Ancient Greece. The chivalric code was reformulated to provide a living and meaningful code of behaviour for the nineteenth century gentleman, who was seen as the embodiment of bravery, loyalty, courtesy, modesty, purity and honour and endowed with a sense of *noblesse oblige* towards women, children and social inferiors. The classic stories of medieval romance, among them Roland and Oliver, Amis and Amile and the Round Table, were endlessly retold.

The virtues of the new chivalry were particularly applied to games, which exalted the qualities of courage, loyalty, skill, character and manliness. J. H. Skrine, Warden of Trinity College, Glenalmond, wrote in 1898 of public school life: 'Chivalry it is again and this is the reason why the life of the school has romance'.[70] Games were yet another area where the medieval and Greek influences overlapped. For Greek athletes and athletic prowess, the *gymnasia,* the lithe bodies stripped for action, were also regularly extolled by Hellenists like Pater in his essay on Greek sculpture, 'The age of athletic prizemen'. Rev Edward Cracroft Lefroy applied Greek analogies directly to public school sport, revelling in the sight of latter-day Antinous' and Praxitelean Hermes' on the football field.[71]

Courtly love, the distant respectful adoration of a noble lady, was certainly part of the revived Victorian chivalry but it did not oust comradeship, fellowship or manly love. Even though the schools began to frown on emotional male friendships after the 1880s, they continued to be sanctioned and promoted in popular fiction. Three notable examples spring to mind of novels, which in all innocence – and therefore the stronger testimony for that – promote the ethic of manly love between boys. The chronology is interesting in that two of them postdate the Wilde trial and one the First World War, the heart of the era of the stiff upper lip. They are also interesting in that the first is the work of a famous headmaster and all three authors had been to public school themselves and were almost certainly drawing on their own memories, observations and experiences.

Gerald Eversley's Friendship (1895), subtitled 'A Study in Real Life', was the only novel by J. E. C. Welldon, headmaster of Harrow and later Bishop of Calcutta. It is by no means a great book, perhaps not even a good book, but it is a clear revelation of the philosophy and attitudes of Welldon, written with all the 'emotional fervour' which was characteristic of him.[72]

The book details the intense friendship of Gerald Eversley, bookish and bespectacled son of a poor country clergyman, and Harry Venniker, handsome, sporting and chivalric peer's son, at St Anselm's School. The school dubs them 'the inseparables'. As the friendship ripens, it deepens: 'It was in a sense, even purified, as being free from the petty frictions and bickerings which are the incidents of great and constant propinquity, which sometimes occur, it is said, even between husband and wife'.[73] On the day they leave St Anselm's, Harry declares to Gerald: 'We've learnt to love one another and St Anselm's'. Gerald meets and falls in love with Harry's sister Ethel, idealises her and through her regains the Christian faith he has lost but part of Miss Venniker's attraction is that she combines her own charm with that of her brother. Alas, she dies of diphtheria three weeks before the wedding and Harry has to save Gerald from suicide. Comforted by Harry's love, Gerald retires to the north of England, devotes himself to good works and never marries. The purity of the love of Gerald and Harry is the central theme and although it is partially transferred to Ethel, even that relationship is never consummated and is of much shorter duration anyway than the love of Harry.

It was an Old Harrovian Horace Annesley Vachell, a pupil there in the 1870s, who wrote the best-selling *The Hill: A Romance of Friendship* (1905). The story centres on the love of shy, scholarly and religious John Verney for handsome aristocratic sportsman Harry Desmond. Verney is dubbed 'Jonathan' because of his devotion to Desmond. There are rhapsodic accounts of their feelings for each other, as in the lengthy sequence where Verney is singing and Desmond's soul is drawn to his ('At that moment Desmond loved the singer – the singer who called to him out of heaven, who summoned his friend to join him, to see what he saw – the vision splendid').[74] They quarrel when Desmond falls in with bad companions but are reconciled when Verney saves Desmond from the sack.

The purity of the love of Desmond and Verney is counterpointed by an episode of 'attempted beastliness', when Verney saves young Lord Esmé Kinloch from seduction by the repulsive Beaumont-Greene. Schooldays end with Verney winning a scholarship to Christchurch and Desmond joining the Brigade of Guards. When Desmond is killed in the Boer War, the headmaster preaches a sermon on friendship: 'the heart's blood of a public school; Friendship with its delights, its perils, its peculiar graces and benedictions' and he points to Harry Desmond as a role model, whose memory 'stands in our records for all we venerate and stand for: loyalty, honour, purity, strenuousness, faithfulness in friendship'.[75] The grieving Verney is consoled by a last letter from Desmond, written on the eve of battle: 'Old Jonathan, you have been the best friend a man ever had, the only one I love as much as my own brother – *and even more*' (Vachell's italics).[76]

The conventional wisdom has it that nineteenth century chivalry and the concept of Christian manliness perished in the Great War but the success of *Tell England* (1922) is but one piece of evidence which suggests that they survived even the holocaust. *Tell England* was the first novel by Ernest Raymond, who had been educated at St Paul's School and had been an Anglican chaplain at Gallipoli. Cassells publicised it as 'a great romance of glorious youth', suggesting a direct link with *The Hill* and indeed it is redolent of almost all the strands forming the complex of ideas that I have been examining.[77]

It is rooted securely both in chivalry and the Greek classics. The very title is derived from an English version of the Spartans' epitaph at

Thermopylae. The narrator Rupert Ray is raised on tales of chivalry by his grandfather and later when Rupert is heading for Gallipoli, his commanding officer lectures him and his brother-officers on the historical significance of the campaign, reminding them that the Dardanelles Straits were the Hellespont of the Ancient World and calling the war against the Turks a new crusade.[78]

At the heart of the story is the romance between Rupert Ray and Edgar Doe, who are first boys at Kensingtowe and later subalterns at Gallipoli. It blossoms amid the usual round of raggings, canings and cricket. Rupert realises after reading Cicero's *De Amicitia* in class: 'that I loved Doe as Orestes loved Pylades'. Doe, however, falls under the influence of the unsavoury Freedham who takes drugs, gets drunk and believes that 'there must be no sensation – a law or no law – which he has not experienced'. Doe confesses to Ray: 'I believed him to be right and we – we tried everything together'. Doe breaks with Freedham, having realised the higher truth: 'Life *is* what feeling you get out of it and the highest types of feeling are mystical and intellectual'.[79] In other words, love between friends transcends sex. The friendship is broken by Doe's death at Gallipoli but Padre Monty consoles Ray, telling him that Doe died nobly and that their friendship has had the perfect end: 'your friendship is a more beautiful whole, as things are. Had there been no war, you'd have left school and gone your different roads, till each lost trace of the other. It's always the same. But, as it is, the war has held you in a deepening intimacy till – till the end. It's – it's perfect.'[80]

Ray himself is later killed in France, but goes to his death confident that he too will grasp the Holy Grail. He and Doe in the nobility of their deaths and the beauty of their friendships have accomplished the ultimate in life – a *beau geste,* which at once recalls that other post-war best-seller about duty, honour, male love and death in foreign climes, P. C. Wren's *Beau Geste* (1924), yet more evidence of the survival of these ideals.

All three novels that I have been discussing share a deeply emotional, fervently Romantic perspective, all see schooldays as a glowing idyll and schoolboy accomplishments, loves and honours as the height of existence which can only really be topped by death. In the public schools we should recognise three different levels of response to manly love: reality, ideal and reaction. One level of reality was the raw carnality of sexual relationships between boys, which was an inevitable concomitant of segregating hundreds of adolescents in an enclosed all-male environment. Scenes such as those witnessed by the young J. A. Symonds at Harrow are regularly reported throughout the history of the public schools but Havelock Ellis,

who printed accounts of such behaviour in *Sexual Inversion* (1897), concluded wisely: 'The prevalence of homosexual and erotic phenomena in
schools varies greatly at different schools and at different times in the
same school. . . As an English schoolboy I never myself saw or heard
anything of such practices'.[81] It is this aspect of public school life which
tends to preoccupy present-day commentators and much has been written
of it, as of the general question of homosexuality and sentimental
pederasty in Victorian Britain. However, it is important to reinstate in
the record the emotional and spiritual tradition of manly love, which was
in part an ideal but also for many a reality for, besides the sex at public
school, there was the frequently ennobling effect of adolescent romanticism. It was this instinct which responded most readily to the pure ideals
and spiritual role models provided by the Middle Ages and Ancient
Greece and consciously promoted in school stories.

The third level of response is the reaction of the school authorities to
manly love. Close noble friendships were encouraged until the 1880s as an
antidote to 'beastliness'. Thereafter, with perceptions sharpened and
heightened by the scientific definition of and increased legal and social
hostility to homosexuality, schools tended to become wary of such close
friendships. This concern was not, however, mirrored in popular culture,
which continued to validate them until well after the Great War.

The popular cultural manifestations of manly love were powerful propaganda for elite solidarity, especially when deviants were labelled as
social inferiors or weedy intellectuals but there was also the cross-class
promotion of manly love and comradeship, as seen in such movements as
Christian Socialism. Popular culture with its reflective and generative
process thus both reported and encouraged this manly ideology at all
levels of society. It was dominant in Victorian culture because of the existence of a strongly segregated, male-dominated society, the exaltation of
chivalry, muscular Christianity, games worship and Hellenism, the cult
of schooldays and the prolongation of adolescence which, together with
a centuries-old tradition of strong non-sexual male friendships, made for
the institutionalisation of manly love as an integral part of nineteenth
century life.

Notes

1 On the Greek heritage in Victorian Britain see Richard Jenkyns, *The Victorians and
Ancient Greece,* Oxford 1981, and Frank M.Turner, *The Greek Heritage in Victorian Britain,*
New Haven and London, 1981; on the medieval legacy, see Mark Girouard, *The Return to*

Camelot: Chivalry and the English Gentleman, New Haven and London, 1981, and Alice Chandler, *A Dream of Order: the Medieval ideal in* 19th Century English Literature, London, 1970.

2   Turner, *Greek Heritage* p. xi

3   See Raymond Klibansky, *The Continuity of the Platonic Tradition during the Middle Ages,* London, 1939, and Maurice Keen, *Medieval Chivalry,* New Haven and London, 1981.

4   J. A. Symonds, *A Problem in Greek Ethics,* London, 1883; Edward Carpenter, *Iolaus: an anthology of friendship,* London, 1902, and Edward Carpenter, *The Intermediate Sex,* 1908, in *Selected Writings* I, London, 1984, for example.

5   H. Montgomery Hyde, *The Other Love,* London, 1976, p. 1.

6   Jeffrey Weeks, *Sex, Politics and Society: The Regulation of Sexuality since* 1800, London 1981, p. 109.

7   Sir Kenneth Dover, *Greek Homosexuality,* London, 1978.

8   P. Ariès and A. Béjin ed., *Western Sexuality: Practice and Precept in Past and Present Times,* Oxford, 1985; V. Bullough, *Sexual Variance in Society and History,* New York, 1976; V. Bullough and J. A. Brundage, *Sexual Practices and the Medieval Church,* Buffalo, New York, 1982.

9   Aristotle, *Ethics,* translated by J. A. K. Thomson, Harmondsworth, 1985, p. 263.

10   Cicero, *De Amicitia,* in *Offices,* translated by T. Cockman and W. Melmoth, London, 1909, pp. 167-215

11   Aelred of Rievaulx, *Spiritual Friendship,* translated by Mary E. Laker, Kalamazoo, Michigan, 1977.

12   Colin Morris, *The Discovery of the Individual,* London, 1972, p. 102. On Christian friendship in general, see Morris pp. 98-107.

13   Aelred. *Spiritual Friendship,* quoting 1 John ch. 4 v. 16, p. 66.

14   On chivalry, see Maurice Keen, *Chivalry;* Richard Barber, *The Knight and Chivalry,* London, 1974; Sidney Painter, *French Chivalry,* Ithaca, 1957.

15   C. S. Lewis, *The Allegory of Love,* Oxford, 1936, pp. 9-10.

16   *Song of Roland,* translated by Dorothy L. Sayers, Harmondsworth, 1984, pp. 128-9.

17   The story of Amis and Amile is contained in William Morris, *Old French Romances,* London, 1896, pp. 27-58.

18   Michel de Montaigne, *Complete Essays,* translated by Donald F. Frame, Stanford, 1958, p. 137.

19   *Ibid,* p. 138.

20   Percy Bysshe Shelley, *Works,* ed. Roger Ingpen and Walter E. Peck, London, 1930, VII, p. 143.

21   Ronald Hyam, *Britain's Imperial Century,* London, 1976, p. 141.

22   Walter Pater, *Plato and Platonism,* London, 1910, pp. 220-2.

23   Henry Newbolt, *The Book of the Happy Warrior,* London 1918, pp. vii, 270.

24   J. A. Symonds, *Studies of the Greek Poets* I, London, 1873, p. 97. He develops the argument at length in 'The Dantesque and Platonic ideals of love', in *In the Key of Blue,* London, 1893, pp. 55-86.

25   Kenelm Digby, *The Broadstone of Honour,* book IV.i. *Orlandus,* London, 1876, pp. 211-77.

26   Edward Fitzgerald, *Letters and Literary Remains* VI, New York, 1966, p. 230.

27   David Newsome, *Godliness and Good Learning,* London, 1961, p. 110.

28   *Ibid.,* p. 49.

29   *Ibid.,* p. 34.

30   Norman Vance, *The Sinews of the Spirit: The Ideal of Christian Manliness in Victorian*

Literature and Religious Thought, Cambridge, 1985.

31 Thomas Hughes, *Tom Brown at Oxford*, London, 1889, p. 99.

32 J. A. Mangan, *Athleticism in the Victorian and Edwardian Public School*, Cambridge, 1981.

33 Newsome, *Godliness*, p. 83.

34 On romantic friendships at Oxford see Geoffrey Faber, *Oxford Apostles*, London, 1933, pp. 215-32; at Cambridge, David Newsome, *On the Edge of Paradise*, London, 1980, pp. 39-43, 246-7.

35 Hughes, *Tom Brown at Oxford*, p. 57.

36 *Ibid., p.* 207.

37 *Ibid., pp.* 193-4.

38 Mangan, *Athleticism*, p. 186.

39 Cyril Connolly, *Enemies of Promise*, Harmondsworth, 1979, pp. 271-2.

40 J. E. C. Welldon, *Gerald Eversley's Friendship*. London, 1895, p. 166.

41 Martin Green, *Dreams of Adventure, Deeds of Empire*, London, 1980, p. 389.

42 George Santayana,*Soliloquies in England*, London, 1922, p. 32.

43 Sir Henry Newbolt, *Poems: New and Old*, London, 1912, pp. 78-9.

44 Welldon, *Gerald Eversley's Friendship*, p. 3.

45 Hyam, *Britain's Imperial Century*, pp. 135-48.

46 Piers Brendon, *Eminent Edwardians*, London, 1979, pp. 201-2.

47 Patrick Dunae, 'British juvenile literature in an age of Enpire 1880-1914', unpublished Manchester University Ph.D. thesis, 1975, pp. 200, 300.

48 This is discussed in Timothy D'Arch Smith, *Love in Earnest*, London, 1970.

49 Robert Bernard Martin, *Tennyson – The Unquiet Heart*, London, 1983, p. 73.

50 John Connell, *W. E. Henley*, London, 1949, p. 68.

51 Philip Mason, *Kipling: The Glass, the Shadow and the Fire*, London, 1975, p. 98: Lord Birkenhead, *Rudyard Kipling*, London, 1978, p. 133.

52 Mason, *Kipling*, p. 99.

53 Guy Thorne, *The Greatest Acceptance*, London, 1912, p. 83.

54 *Ibid.*, p. 103.

55 Martin Green, *Dreams of Adventure*.

56 Owen Dudley Edwards, *The Quest for Sherlock Holmes*, Edinburgh, 1983, pp. 109-15.

57 Arthur Conan Doyle, 'The Creeping Man', *Complete Sherlock Holmes Short Stories*, London, 1963, p. 1244.

58 Conan Doyle, 'The Three Garridebs', *Complete Sherlock Holmes Short Stories*, p. 1213.

59 Owen Dudley Edwards, *Sherlock Holmes*, p. 113.

60 Alec Waugh, *Public School Life*, London, 1922, p. 137.

61 Benjamin Disraeli, *Coningsby*, Oxford, 1982, p. 38.

62 J. R. de S. Honey, *Tom Brown's Universe*, London, 1977, pp. 1781-94. On the rise in concern about homosexuality, see Weeks, *Sex, Politics and Society*, pp. 96-121.

63 Honey, *Tom Brown's Universe*, p. 181.

64 Ian Anstruther, *Oscar Browning*, London, 1983; Faith Compton Mackenzie, *William Cory*, London, 1950.

65 Honey, *Tom Brown's Universe*, p. 186.

66 *Ibid.*, p. 187.

67 Pater, *Plato and Platonism*, p. 231.

68 F. W. Farrar, *Julian Home*, London, 1896, pp. 26-7.

69 J. A. Symonds, *Memoirs*, ed. Phyllis Grosskurth, London, 1984, p. 94.

70 Girouard, *Return to Camelot*, p. 120.

Such schoolboy friendships continued into later life, as shown in Alfred Rankley's painting *Old Schoolfellows*, 1955. The catalogue entry included a quotation from Proverbs: 'A friend loveth at all times and a brother is born for adversity'. The book on the floor is Cicero's *De Amicitia*

David and Jonathan were regularly adduced as examplars of close male friendship, as here in a photograph of F. N. Charrington and the Hon. Ion Keith-Falconer, from Charrington's biography, *The Great Acceptance* by Guy Thorne

Close male friendships were celebrated in schoolboy fiction, like Talbot Baines Reed's *The Fifth Form at St Dominic's*

71   Walter Pater, 'The age of athletic prizemen', *Greek Studies,* London, 1910, pp. 269-99; J. A. Symonds, 'Edward Cracroft Lefroy', *In the Key of Blue,* London, 1893, pp. 87-110.
72   *Dictionary of National Biography,* Compact Edition, II, Oxford, 1975, p. 2957.
73   Welldon, *Gerald Eversley's Friendship,* p. 150
74   H. A. Vachell, *The Hill,* London, 1920, p. 130.
75   *Ibid.,* p. 314.
76   *Ibid.,* p. 318.
77   Ernest Raymond, *The Story of My Days,* London, 1968, p. 182.
78   Ernest Raymond, *Tell England,* London, 1973, pp. 178-9.
79   *Ibid.,* p. 118.
80   *Ibid.,* p. 298.
81   Havelock Ellis, *Studies in the Psychology of Sex,* New York, 1936, I, 4, p. 76. On sex in the public schools, see *inter alia* John Chandos, *Boys Together,* London, 1984, pp. 284-319; Jonathan Gathorne-Hardy, *The Public School Phenomenon,* Harmondsworth, 1979, pp. 158-97; Royston Lambert, *The Hothouse Society,* London, 1968, pp. 301-41.

chapter six BENJAMIN G. RADER

The recapitulation theory of play: motor behaviour, moral reflexes and manly attitudes in urban America, 1880-1920

Students of the manliness movement in the United States have neglected the importance of the recapitulation theory of play in informing and shaping the ideas and programmes of the advocates of manliness and organised sport.[1] One version or another of the recapitulation theory became part of the conventional wisdom of boy-workers in the Young Men's Christian Associations, Public School Athletic Leagues, Boy Scouts and organised city recreation programmes of the first two decades of the twentieth century. This chapter examines the origins of the theory, its implications for organised sports for boys and its uses by various adult-managed boys' organisations.

One man, Luther Halsey Gulick, Jr (1865-1918), who began his career with the Young Men's Christian Association (YMCA), played a pre-eminent role in all phases of the American adult-directed boys' sport movement. Consistent with the Darwinian temper of the time and inspired by the genetic work in psychology of his friend and mentor, G. Stanley Hall, Gulick propounded an evolutionary theory of play that exercised an immense influence on every phase of boys' work. Hall and Gulick believed that man had acquired the fundamental impulse to play during the evolution of the 'race'. Each man, as he passed from birth to adulthood, recapitulated or rehearsed in a proximate way each epoch or stage of human evolution. For example, the play of early childhood – spontaneous kicking and squirming in infancy and running and throwing when a bit older – corresponded to the play of man's primal ancestors, and tag games common to children between the ages of seven and twelve sprang from the hunting instinct, an instinct that had been acquired during the 'pre-savage' stage of evolution. Games at this stage were individualistic. Finally, the complex group games of adolescent boys – baseball, basketball, football, cricket and hockey – ultimately sprang from a combination of the earlier hunting instinct and a new instinct for co-operation. The instinct for co-operation emerged during the 'savage' epoch of evolution. The savages, Gulick explained, had hunted and fought in groups while subordinating themselves to the leadership of a chieftain.

But instincts alone did not account for the physical behaviour of the 'modern' stage. The particular 'reflexes' that had developed during the process of maturation and the racial traditions of the groups also shaped behaviour. Complex motor behaviour, Gulick explained, became reflexive through repetition. For example, the awkward, more or less conscious throwing of young children with time and practice became smooth and unconscious (or reflexive, to use Gulick's terminology), thus freeing the body for the efficient playing of adolescent ball games. Gulick speculated that the repetition of physical movements in childhood resulted in the growth of new neural centres in the spinal cord and brain.

Thus, without early experience of bountiful physical activity, adults were doubly damned. Neither their neural systems nor their motor reflexes would mature fully. Unfortunately, in the new urban age youngsters enjoyed far fewer opportunities than in earlier times to develop their neural and motor potentials. 'Everything conspires to bring the city-born upon the stage of life with an oversensitive nervous system and an undertoned physique,' wrote Gulick.[3]

But even more central to Gulick's defence of organised sport for boys was his belief that motor behaviour, if properly directed, was the primary agency of shaping moral 'reflexes'. Just as in the case of mature motor behaviour, adult morality arose initially from instincts. Young children instinctively sought to be clean, obedient and honest. When such desirable behaviour was reinforced by suggestion, example, and repetition, it became reflexive. The key, however, to nurturing moral habits was not self-examination, indoctrination, nor the learning of moral precepts. It was participation in physical activities that embodied moral principles. 'Life for others is rendered far more probable, natural and tangible,' Gulick wrote, 'when it comes as the gradual unfolding and development of that instinct that has its first great impulse of growth in the games of adolescence.'[4]

Adolescence represented the most critical stage of moral and religious growth. For at that time the instincts upon which group games rested could result in the ripening of either righteous or wicked reflexes. Too often the instincts found expression in the juvenile gang of the city, 'the most perilous force in modern civilization', rather than in group games supervised by adults. Too often adolescents recapitulated their racial history or tribal hunting and warfare by engaging in theft, depredations against property and violence rather than in the playing of team sports.

Born of missionary parents in Honolulu, Hawaii, Gulick waged a 'determined war' against the 'subjective type of religion' traditionally fostered by evangelical Protestant churches. Although he rejected the formal religious doctrines of his parents, he retained a zest for embarking on crusades. He discovered his equivalent of a spiritual 'calling' by becoming in turn the champion of muscular Christianity within the YMCA, the major proponent of a new theory of play, the founder of the Public Schools Athletic league in New York City, an organiser and the first president of the Playground Association of America, the organiser and first director of the child Hygiene Department of the Russell Sage Foundation (a philanthropic foundation), a leader of the American Boy Scout movement and the co-founder (with his wife) of the American Campfire Girls.

According to Gulick, he turned to the strenuous life partly as a way of compensating for his personal feelings of physical and psychical inadequacy. Throughout his life he suffered from severe migraine headaches, periods of dark depression and a weak physical constitution, all of which he attributed to his father. His father had been the victim of a nervous breakdown.

A quasi-mystical experience while a student at tiny Oberlin College (in Ohio) in the 1880s furnished the immediate impetus for Gulick to dedicate his life to the principle that sound morals (which include mental stability) depended on a strong, virile body. Gulick left Oberlin in 1886 without a degree to attend Dudley A. Sargent's Physical Training School in Cambridge, Massachusetts. The following year he entered New York University Medical School, where he obtained a medical degree in 1889. But Gulick never practised medicine, for in 1887 he found far more exciting work as an instructor in the Physical Department of the School of Christian Workers (renamed in 1899 the International Young Men's Christian Association Training School) located in Springfield, Massachusetts. Since the school was the main institution for preparing general secretaries and physical directors for posts with local YMCAs, it was an ideal location for Gulick to reach a national and even an international audience. Most of the pioneers in the boys' sport movement of the United States passed through the regular two-year curriculum or the summer institutes of the training school.

Impulsive, blunt, forceful and something of an autocrat, the young redhead physical director infected his students, colleagues and many followers with a zeal for the importance of organised sport for youth. As secretary of the physical work of the international committee of the YMCA, in the classroom, in the journals that he edited for the training school, in articles and books and in innumerable speeches delivered throughout the United States and in several other English-speaking nations, he unrelentingly preached the same gospel: the spiritual life of man rested on the equal development of the mind and the body. Gulick invented the famous emblem of the YMCA, the inverted triangle that symbolized the spirit supported by the mind and the body.

Unlike earlier YMCA leaders, Gulick welcomed the introduction of sport into YMCA programmes. 'We can use the drawing power of athletics a great deal more than we are doing at present,' he wrote in 1892 but he cautioned that 'we must work along our own lines and not ape the athletic organisations, whose object is the development of specialists and the breaking of records'.[5] Under his aegis competitive sport began to supplant gymnastics in many YMCA programmes. The Springfield School itself began to sponsor baseball, football, basketball and volleyball teams. They also sponsored competitions in track and field, swimming and gymnastics. The vigorous sport programme at Springfield and the experience of students there inspired YMCAs everywhere to organise their own athletics teams.

While the physical curriculum of the training school continued to centre on traditional subjects such as anatomy and motor development, Gulick added a pioneering course in the psychology of play as well as training in specific sport skills. Gulick, in his psychology of play course, asked students to experiment with new games and sports that could be played in the confined space of gymnasiums and that would be appropriate for a person's stage of maturity. The invention of both basketball and volleyball resulted from Gulick's inspiration and suggestions. In 1891 James Naismith, a young minister from Canada who was a student and part-time instructor at Springfield, put together the essentials of what became the game of basketball and in 1895 William G. Morgan, while serving as physical director of the YMCA at Holyoke, Massachusetts, invented volleyball specifically for older men who found basketball too strenuous.[6]

To Gulick and his followers team sports such as volleyball offered a superb opportunity for adults to encourage in boys the healthy growth of moral and religious reflexes. Stemming from the instinct of co-operation found in the savage stage of human evolution, team sports required the highest moral principles: teamwork, self-sacrifice, obedience, self-control and loyalty. 'These qualities appear to me,' Gulick wrote, 'to be a great pulse of beginning altruism, of self-sacrifice, of that capacity upon which Christianity is based.'[7] The churches, the YMCAs and other organisations working with boys ought to de-emphasise the teaching of feminine traits to boys and present Jesus in his 'noble heroism. . . his magnificent manliness, his denunciation of wickedness in public places, [and] his life of service to others. . .'[8] Gulick's conception of Christian manliness hardly squared with the injunction of Jesus to turn the other cheek when wronged. On one occasion he advised that a boy should have the ability and the courage to 'punch another boy's head or to stand having his own punched in a healthy and proper manner.'[9] Gulick's biological theory of play implied a far more radical departure from orthodox Protestantism than he probably recognised, for his ideas not only made the religious and moral life almost exclusively a matter of vigorous activity – almost activity for activity's sake – but also suggested a naturalistic explanation for the origins of man's religious sentiments.

In one version or another, the theory of recapitulation became part of the conventional wisdom of the boy workers in the first two decades of the twentieth century. G. Stanley Hall repeated it almost verbatim in his classic two-volume work, *Adolescence,* published in 1905. Joseph Lee, a prolific writer on play, took as his major premise the notion that play arose from an earlier stage of man's evolution, from the 'barbaric and predatory society to which the boy naturally belongs.' Henry S. Curtis, a pioneer in both the American playground and Boy Scout movements, wrote that athletics were 'the activities of our ancestors conventionalised and adapted to present conditions. They [were] reminiscent of the physical age, of the struggle for survival, of the hunt, of the chase, and of war.'[10]

William Forbush, an ardent disciple of Gulick and Hall, may have reached the largest audience of all. His *The Boy Problem,* an advice manual for boys, was reprinted eight times between 1901 and 1913. Each boy, Forbush wrote, repeated the 'history of his own race-life from savagery unto civilisation.'[11] The enthusiasm with which Forbush catalogued the instincts used by various boy organisations approached the absurd. For instance, he found that an adult-managed play school appealed effectively to the instincts of constructiveness, curiosity, emulativeness, initiative- ness, loyalty, physical activity, play and pugnacity while Sunday schools appealed only to the instinct of love. The conclusion was obvious. Organised sport was potentially far more effective than Sunday schools in developing proper moral traits among boys.

The acceptance by the boy-workers of the recapitulation theory of play had important implications for the use of play as a socialising agency. Firstly, it justified the creation of special institutions for boys that would be closely supervised by adults. Rather than relying on the unregulated, unstructured and spontaneous play of boys, the boy workers assumed that their theory revealed how adults ought to consider and adapt organised play to the instinctual tendencies of boys. For example, the preference of slum youths for punting a football up and down the street rather than playing in organised games worried G. Stanley Hall. Such unregulated activities of an expression of an instinct in his opinion failed to encourage the proper social traits. Henry Curtis became a convert to adult-directed play after realising, while observing some boys engaged in unstructured play, that no one seemed determined to win or bothered to keep careful score in the contest. While the boy workers believed that they were releasing the instinctual propensities of youths through organised athletic programmes, their theory could lend itself to a system- atic repression of juvenile impulses.[12]

Secondly, the recapitulation theory of play encouraged boy workers to relinquish the extreme forms of piety associated with the evangelical temperament. While Protestant clergymen and laymen continued to play a highly visible role in boys' work after 1900, they de-emphasised prayer meetings, sermons and demands for individual soul-searching. Several boy workers even attacked Protestant Sabbatarianism which frowned upon Sunday play. The YMCA became increasingly secular in its program- mes. YMCA leaders extended their work to include a vast number of non- members and they provided leaders and organisers for boys' sport in the churches, settlement houses and the city playgrounds. The YMCA's athletic leagues often consisted of a motley combination of secular and religious organisations. Many of the 'institutional' Protestant churches in the larger cities abandoned explicit spiritual programmes for boys in favour of organised activity which might include anything from the sponsorship of dances to baseball teams. Beginning in Brooklyn in 1904, one city after another organised Sunday school athletic leagues, usually under the guidance of YMCA Physical Directors. In 1916, through the Boys' Brigade, Roman Catholics also joined the larger adult-managed boys' sport movement.[13]

Thirdly, the play theory permitted boy workers to subordinate ethnic, religious and class differences among boys to a presumably universal experience of maturation. Thus boy leaders were optimistic that the gang tendencies of boys, regardless of their social origins, could be converted into a higher civic consciousness and a uniform set of personal values. 'The group games are, in my opinion,' wrote Joseph Lee, 'the best school of citizenship that exists.' He explained that 'to the boy playing football, the losing himself in the consciousness of the team, utterly subordinating his individual aims to the common purpose, is not a matter of self-sacrifice but of self-fulfillment, the coming into his birthright, the satisfying of his human necessity of socialization, of becoming a part of a social or political whole. What is being born in that boy is the social man.'[14] A characteristic of boys' work after the turn of the century was the concerted effort to organise athletic programmes that would include boys from slum neighbourhoods.

Finally, the recapitulation theory furnished a rationale for the sexual segregation of organised play. The boy workers agreed that children exhibited marked play preferences according to their sex. They assumed that these differences arose largely from instincts acquired over the course of human evolution. Of utmost importance to the survival of males and their offspring had been adeptness in fighting, hunting and running; activities recapitulated in the games of boys. Those females, on the other hand, who had cared best for the home were more likely to survive and produce offspring. 'So it is clear,' Gulick wrote, 'that athletics have never been either a test or a large factor in the survival of women; athletics do not test womanliness as they test manliness.'[15] Accordingly, the play activities of girls should be guided toward the acquisition of talents essential to the management of the home. Gulick and his followers formed a solid phalanx, one joined by most physical educators, against girls competing in highly organised athletic programmes. The recapitulation theory continued to be used as an argument against competitive sport for girls until past the middle of the twentieth century.

Underlying the urgency of the work of the boy workers was a deep uneasiness with both the city and the modern economy. The city was the principal home of alien peoples who held strange beliefs and often violated the behavioural codes of old-stock Americans. Traditional social restraints seemed to evaporate in the cities. Boys were vulnerable to a host of new 'perversions' – 'the mad rush for sudden wealth,' the impulse to mature too quickly, the emulation of the 'reckless fashions set by gilded youth,' membership in juvenile gangs, impure sexual thoughts and practices, the 'secret vice' (masturbation) and fornication. While the city was an unmitigated college of vice for youth, the country had furnished a wholesome, natural environment. 'The country boy roams the hills and has free access to "God's first temples",' asserted F. D. Bonyton, the superintendent of Ithaca, New York schools in 1904. 'What can we offer to the city boy in exchange for paradise lost? His only road to paradise regained is thru the gymnasium, the athletic field, and the playground'.[16] Sport, many of the boy workers came to believe, could serve as an effective surrogate for the lost rural experience.

Joseph Lee, a Boston Brahmin and a long-time leader in boys' work, believed that the modern industrial order fundamentally frustrated man's most primal instincts. 'Man is a stranger in the modern world,' he flatly declared.[17] In the barbaric stage of man's evolution the activities of hunting, fighting, striking, throwing and running had utilised man's fundamental instincts but civilisation has so altered the rules of the game that it is no longer our game as whispered to us in our inner consciousness. Some of our deepest instincts are thus left hanging in the air, calling for a fulfillment that does not exist, reaching out to do things that cannot be done and will get us into trouble if we attempt to do them.'[18] Although Lee was acutely aware of the uncreative drudgery of factory work, he saw only two practical solutions to the problem, neither of which fully satisfied man's essential nature. They were: 'fit our boys and girls to the industrial order as it exists. . . and provide an overflow.' Sport could nurture in children the delicate balance between competition and co-operation required by the world of business and industry.

Furthermore, participation by adults in sport during their leisure time could satisfy their instinctual needs, or could serve as an 'overflow' or 'safety-valve' to release harmlessly the angry frustrations of modern man. Frederic L. Paxson, in his presidential address to the American Historical Association in 1917, extended Lee's argument to formulate a major historical thesis. The rise of American sport after the Civil War, Paxson concluded, had prevented violent social unrest by the working class. Indeed, sport had saved the nation from a revolution.[19]

The modern economy also troubled Gulick. According to Gulick two great evils characterised modern life: 'the exploitation of the many by the few' and the absence of personal self-control. Both had arisen from industrialisation.[20] Yet, 'this exploitation is in itself neither good or evil,' he said.[21] Rather that recommending radical changes in the economic system, Gulick believed that most of the inequities and frustrations found in modern life could be solved by creating a new corporate conscience in which the individual would subordinate his self-interest to the good of the social whole.

The play experience of youth could enhance the nurture of both a corporate conscience and self-control. Gulick summarised the critical role of play and athletics in modern life. 'The sand pile for the small child, the playground for the middle-sized child, the athletic field for the boy and the girl in the teens, wholesome means of social relationships during adult life – these are fundamental conditions without which democracy cannot continue, because upon them rests the development of that self-control which is related to an appreciation of the needs of the rest of the group and of the corporate conscience that is rendered necessary by the complex interdependence of modern life.'[22] To Gulick, such activities encouraged the internationalisation of the norms necessary for a stable social order.

In the first two decades of the twentieth century Gulick and his followers found ample opportunities to put their recapitulation theory of play into practice. The YMCA had already begun to implement the principles of the boy workers. Shortly after becoming Director of Physical Training of the public schools of New York City, Gulick determined that 'all the boys in the city needed the physical benefits and moral lessons afforded by properly conducted games and sport.' Thus, with the assistance of prominent local citizens, he organised the Public Schools Athletic League (PSAL) in 1903. By 1910, the PSAL, hailed as 'The World's Greatest Athletic Organization,' had at least seventeen imitators in other large American cities. Moreover, in 1905, the league added a Girls' Branch but, unlike the boys' division, the Girls' Branch did not permit public inter-school competition.[23]

The playground movement furnished the boy workers with an even broader opportunity for implementing the recapitulation theory of play. Inspired by the boy workers and driven by anxieties arising from modern cities, middle and upper income taxpayers exhibited a remarkable enthusiasm for supervised recreation programmes. Between 1906 and 1917 the number of American cities with managed recreation programmes grew from forty-one to 504. The Playground Association of America, formed in 1906, published a monthly magazine, The Playground, prepared a standardised course of study for playground workers (which embodied almost verbatim the recapitulation theory) and published an extensive body of both theoretical and practical literature on playgrounds. By 1912 special courses on organised play had been offered in over sixty normal schools, colleges and cities.

The same concern, assumptions and values that shaped the YMCA and the PASL also guided the playground workers. The recapitulation theory furnished them with ready-made formulas for supervising playgrounds. For example, among the questions of the standard examination administered to all candidates for employment with the New York playgrounds was: 'What is meant by the "club or gregarious instinct"? How can it be developed and utilised with beneficial results on the playground? What athletic events are appropriate for boys aged 10-14?. . . for boys aged 14 to 16?'[24] Not only were prospective playground leaders expected to master the principles and practical implications of play theory, they also had to be able to exercise the subtle psychological techniques essential for managing youth without resorting to harsh repression. 'The men and women employed for playground service. . .' declared Edward B. de Groot, the Director of Chicago playgrounds, 'should not be regarded as mere instructors. . . but rather as *thoughtful managers,* interpreters of child and adolescent life' (my italics).[25] The playground leaders abhorred the unsupervised, unstructured play that arose from the spontaneous impulses of children. Henry S. Curtis, in the leading textbook for playground supervisors, wrote that 'scrub play,' that is, play that the children themselves initiated, 'can never give that training either of body or conduct, which organized play should give; for in order to develop the body, it must be vigorous, to train the intellect, it must be exciting, to train the social conscience, it must be socially organized. None of these results come from scrub play'.[26]

Like the YMCA, the PSAL and the playgrounds, the theory of recapitulation influenced the movement for the adult management of public high school athletics in the United States. High School educators were especially enamoured of the value of organised athletics in fostering social values. They tended to believe that activity, rather than the teaching of moral precepts, was the key to developing proper social and moral traits. Thus educators, in an influential government report prepared in 1917, concluded that the high school should give special attention to the 'participation of pupils in common activities. . . such as athletic games, social activities, and the government of the school.'[27]

Despite an enormous influence extending to the popular press and a host of organisations working with boys, by 1920 the recapitulation theory of play had reached the apex of its power. In some instances, hopes for adult-managed play had foundered. Disillusioned with the extreme forms that organised athletics had taken, the YMCA abandoned sponsor-ship of sport at the championship levels. While the PSAL did reach the younger boys who enrolled in the public schools, it could not affect the lives of the boys who presumably needed it the most – the older, ethnic youths who took full-time jobs at the age of fourteen or so. The leaders of the playground movement generally failed to extend their management of spare-time activities to the boys in the slums. Furthermore, the recapitulation theory of play was the recipient of a growing criticism. By 1920 psychologists and educators who resorted solely to instinct theory to explain childhood behaviour were clearly in the minority. Even Luther Gulick, in a publication prepared shortly before his death in 1920, played down the instinctual base of his play theory. Ironically, in the 1930s and afterwards, the vacuum created by the absence of organised sport in the schools, the YMCA and the like would be filled by national voluntary boys' work organisations such as Little League Baseball, Pop Warner Football and Biddy Basketball, over which professionally-trained boy workers exercised little influence and no control.

Notes

1 See Paul Boyer, *Urban Masses and Moral Order in America, 1820-1920*, Cambridge, MA, 1978; Lawrence A. Finfer, 'Leisure and social work in the urban community: the progressive recreation movement, 1890-1920', unpublished Ph.D., Michigan State University, 1974; Dominick J. Cavallo, *Muscles and Morals: Organized Playgrounds and Urban Reform, 1880-1920*, Philadelphia, 1981; Clarence Rainwater, *The Play Movement in the United States: The Study of Community Recreation*, Chicago, 1922. But see also Joseph F. Kett, *Rites of Passage: Adolescence in America, 1790 to the Present*, New York, 1977.

2 A full-scale biography of Gulick is much needed. See the dated and uninterpretive Ethel Josephine Dorgan, *Luther Halsey Gulick, 1865-1918*, New York, 1934.

3 Luther Gulick, 'State committees on athletics,' *Young Men's Era*, XVIII 27 October 1892, p. 1365.

4 YMCA athletic activities can be traced in the following journals: *Men, Physical Education, Triangle, Young Men's Era*, and *Athletic League Letters*, as well as the YMCA's annual yearbooks.

5 Luther Gulick, *A Philosophy of Play*, New York, 1920, p. 166.

6 Luther Gulick, 'Psychological, pedagogical, and religious aspects of group games', *Pedagogical Seminary*, VI, March 1899, p. 144. See also Gulick, 'Psychical aspects of muscular exercise,' *Popular Science Monthly*, LIII, October 1898, pp. 793-805, and 'The psychology of play', *Association Outlook*, VIII, February 1899, pp. 112-6.

7 Gulick, 'Psychological', p. 142.

8 *Athletic League Letters*, June 1901, p. 65.

9 Gulick, 'The alleged effeminization of our American boys', *American Physical Education Review*, X, September 1905, p. 217.

10 G. Stanley Hall, *Adolescence*, 2 vols, New York, 1905, I, pp. 202-23; Joseph Lee, *Play*

in Education, New York, 1915, p. 234; Henry S. Curtis, 'The proper relation of organized sports on public playgrounds and in public service,' *Playground,* III, September 1909, p. 14.

11 William Forbush, *The Boy Problem,* Boston, 1901, p. 9.

12 G. Stanley Hall, *Educational Problems,* 2 vols, New York, 1915, I, p. 109; Henry S. Curtis, 'Proper relations,' p. 14.

13 See especially, *Athletic League Letters,* January 1904, March 1906, April 1912; George D. Pratt, 'The Sunday School Athletic League,' *Work With Boys,* IV, April 1905, pp. 131-137; 'Recreation in the Church', *Literary Digest,* LIII, 29 July 1916, p. 256.

14 Lee, 'Playgrounds for schools and the importance of intelligent direction,' *American Gymnasia,* I, April 1905, p. 221. See also Lee, 'Crime or Sport?', *Work with Boys,* IV, July 1904, 152-9.

15 Gulick, *A Philosophy of Play,* p. 92.

16 F. D. Bonyton, 'Athletics and collateral activities in secondary schools,' *Proceedings and Addresses of the National Education Association,* 1904, p. 210. The anti-urban bias runs throughout all of the literature of the boy workers. A few of them explicitly asserted that adolescent sexuality was the principal problem of the city. For instance: 'I believe that sex-perversions are the most common, subtle and dangerous foes that threaten modern life.' Forbush, *The Boy Problem,* p. 147.

17 Lee, *Play in Education,* p. 436.

18 *Ibid.,* p. 434.

19 Frederic L. Paxson, 'The rise of sport', *Mississippi Valley Historical Review,* IV, September 1917, pp. 144-168.

20 Gulick, *A Philosophy of Play,* p. 256.

21 *Ibid.,* p. 265.

22 Gulick, 'Athletics for school children', *Lippincott's Monthly Magazine,* LXXXVIII, August 1911, p. 201.

23 Albert B. Reeve, 'The world's greatest athletic organization,' *Outing,* LVII, October 1910, pp. 232-5.

24 'Questions for teachers to answer,' *American Gymnasia,* II, March 1906, p. 149.

25 Edward B. de Groot, 'The management of playgrounds,' *Playground,* VIII, November 1914, p. 273.

26 Henry S. Curtis, *The Play Movement and Its Significance,* New York, 1917, p. 81.

27 *The Cardinal Principles of Secondary Education,* Bul. 1918. 35, Washington, DC, 1918, pp. 7-8. For all phases of youth organised sports see Benjamin G. Rader, *American Sports: From the Age of Folk Games to the Age of Spectators,* Englewood Cliffs, ··, 1983, Ch. 8.

Social Darwinism
and upper-class education
in late Victorian
and Edwardian England

Mrs Chris
didn't exist

From the standpoint of these equivocal times the headmasters of the late Victorian and Edwardian public schools are perhaps to be envied. They saw with clarity and spoke with conviction. Certainty subdued modesty. If they were to be believed, the products of their schools, almost to a boy, were muscular, moral and manly.

Without embarrassment or reticence a coterie of the more distinguished 'beaks' of Edwardian England made the following declaration to *The Strand*[1] in 1905. Dr Joseph Wood, headmaster of Harrow:

> Like all the rest of the world, boys have more luxury now than fifty years ago. But this does not seem to disagree with them or make them soft. Within the last year I have seen a boy stand to have a dislocated shoulder reduced, and never move a muscle or utter a sound. . . In courage and kindliness and frankness of character English public schoolboys seem as good as they ever were.

Revd Charles Tancock, headmaster of Tonbridge:

> I have no hesitation at all in saying that the public school boys of today, taken in the mass, are far more sensible, obedient, and manly than schoolboys of, say, fifty years ago. . . and although a modern boy's mind is excessively filled with talk and thoughts of his games, this has, for the most part

– in the mass, of course, taken the place not of thoughts of literature and work, but of far less desirable subjects,

Revd H. W. Moss, headmaster of Shrewsbury:

> The public schoolboy. . . is as manly, as public spirited, as devoted a lover of justice and fair-play, . . . as honourable and straightforward as those who have gone before him.

The wholly rhetorical question which stimulated this encomiastic enthusiasm was whether or not the public schoolboy had recently deteriorated!

These Edwardian pronouncements ran in a well-worn groove. Headmasters of the period never wearied of repetition. They were the keenest publicists of their product. No audience was immune. J. E. C. Welldon penned for publication panegyrics for the Oriental and homilies for the Socialist on the theme of the sterling qualities of the public schoolboy.[2]. To audiences the world over he was portrayed as a Christian gentlemen in the making, of strong arm (and leg) and chivalrous disposition – a cloned Bayard of Victorian and Edwardian Britain. Prelates designate in their antecedent role of upper-class educationist filled newspaper pieces, magazine articles and prize-day speeches with pieties, platitudes and pomposities to this effect. However improbable this image of boyhood may appear to the unromantic vision of those of the post-Golding era, the hyperbole was not necessarily hypocritical. I have argued elsewhere in defence of occasional sincerity, myopic idealism and naïve self-delusion.[3] The truth of the matter was that many pursued an ideal and turned their back on reality.

One idealist, G. G. T. Heywood, will speak for all: '. . . from a master's point of view, the ideal boy is the one who makes the most of his natural gifts of mind and body. . . a boy who can work hard and play hard. . . yet behind all this he possesses the virtues and characteristics which we all associate with a Christian gentleman. He is unselfish, modest, frank and honourable, and although he does his best to conceal it, he has a foundation of true religion.'[4] Men such as Heywood deserve some sympathy. They never recovered from the euphoric reception given in the weeklies, monthlies and quarterlies to that decent fantasy of public school life *Tom Brown's Schooldays*. Generations of subsequent headmasters naïvely or calculatedly reported fiction for fact. Thomas Hughes' image of the schoolboy had both immediate and lasting appeal. For this reason, machismo was retained yet constrained, pugnacious but pious. *In nuce*, virility was promoted but rape was proscribed.[5]

From 1857 the copper-bottomed mould for the public schoolboy was Tom Brown, and young Brown, as the *Spectator* reported admiringly in May of the same year: 'is a thoroughly English boy. Full of kindness, courage, vigour and fun – no great adept at Greek and Latin, but a first rate cricketer, climber and swimmer, fearless and skilful at football, and by no means adverse to a good stand-up fight in a good cause. . . (his) piety is of that manly order, that not even an ordinary schoolboy of the present day will find himself wearied of it'.[6] Here the substantives 'kindness' and 'piety' jostle companionably with 'courage' and 'fearlessness' in a manner in which Flashman, the fanfaron, would have found as amusingly quixotic as many do today.

The robust talisman, Tom Brown, speedily attracted the label, 'muscular Christian', the term of course used in the *Saturday Review* of February 1857 playfully and only a little maliciously, to describe Charles Kingsley's strenuous paragon who feared God and could walk a thousand miles in a thousand hours, breathed God's free air on God's rich earth and at the same time could hit a woodcock, doctor a horse and twist a poker round his finger.[7] This impressive Herculean, as the reviewer T. C. Sanders remarked, was the Faustian hunting parson transformed into 'the truest type of earthly and saintly excellence', home as usual from a good run but now, 'with a brush in one pocket and a prayer book in the other'.

As we know, Kingsley was not impressed by the expression 'muscular Christianity'.[8] Thomas Hughes, less thin-skinned and more violent, saw virtue in it and relocated and redefined it. In the first instance he transported it from 'Whitbury' to Oxford where it became personified by a schoolboy turned undergraduate – Tom Brown. This was not fortuitous. While, for Kingsley, the real joy of life was naturalistic – the lash of the rain on your cheek as you strode through the storm, the dust of the prairie swirling about you as you galloped under the sun, the raging seas off Hartland Cliffs, the thick wet mud of the flats around Finchampstead',[9] for Hughes, pleasure was gregarious:[10] cricket on the village green, the rough and tumble of a scrimmage on Bigside, stroking the Oxford boat on the Isis and perhaps, above all else, fisticuffs before cheering support 'in a good fight in a good cause'.

Although the means might differ, the end for both Kingsley and Hughes, was the same. The period 'manly Christian' (Kingsley's own preferred term) together with earlier devouts like Bertrand de Gueslin and Godfrey de Bouillon embraced mediaeval, chivalrous values: 'a man's body is given him to be trained and brought into subjection, and then used for the protection of the weak, the advancement of all righteous causes, and the subduing of the earth which God has given to the children of men'.[11] The muscularity of Kingsley and Hughes was in fact part of a more ancient 'wider theological perspective in which. . . the appalling social evils of the time were the proper sphere of man's God-given responsibility'.[12]

Few headmasters chose to see this.[13] The paradox of the socially committed athlete may have forced Kingsley to abandon Hughes' schoolboy idealism for a domestic realism which pitted sport against necessity, escape against responsibility'[14] but masters in the public schools for the most part preferred fantasy. Hughes' Christianised but fundamentally hyperborean symbol was simply interpreted; provided pugnacity took precedence over piety, it proved most acceptable. It struck a successful balance. It avoided the Hogarthian image of the pre-Clarendon Commission 'Great Schools' but it also avoided the mid-century Cuddesdon image of effeminate Puseyism. In brief, it was not too rough and not too religious. In the subsequent decades it was brought into the sharpest focus and projected by scores of headmasters acting as their own publicist.

Yet how true to life was this image and how pervasive was the influence of the ideology which underpinned it in the schools? These are most desirable questions at a time when muscular Christianity excites the growing interest of social historians and the diffusion of the concept in the wake of imperialism attracts the attention of the most distinguished students of sports history.[15]

It is interesting that the famous discussion by Fizjames Stephens of *Tom Brown's Schooldays* in the *Edinburgh Review* of January 1858 centred largely on factual rather than ficitional public school life [16] and that in the opening paragraph reality brusquely pushed aside romance.[17] Readers were informed that the book was 'a picture of the bright side of a Rugby boy's experiences'. There was a dark side; so dark that it required exceptional 'courage. . . honesty. . . (and) purity to traverse that stage of life without doing and suffering many things which can make the recollections of it painful'.[18] Much of the remainder of this historic review was given over to reflections on a style of school life that was noticeably lacking in Christian piety, kindliness and chivalry. In a significant simile the famous celebration after the great housematch — 'something between a battle and a sacrifice', was likened not to the rejoicing of robust saints in God's Heaven but to a carousal of rapacious einhergers in Odin's Valhalla. In fact, references in the review to Christian morality were noticeably parisimonious and frequently critical, while reference to the merits of a seemingly secular school of hard knocks which generated sensible realism and dissipated foolish romanticism were continuous and unambiguous. Here is a typical example:

> A public school affords a boy. . . an excellent opportunity of learning his own place in life. He will find that talents and accomplishments do not govern the world. . . He will learn to estimate the power, whatever he may think of the merits, of a hard coarse temperament and he will discover the immunities which a light heart and a thick skin confer on their possessors. He will learn how to go through life without undertaking what he is not fit for, without repining at what cannot be helped.[19]

At best this is Stoicism not Christianity. What was considered in much of this celebrated article was not the 'muscular Christianity' embraced by Thomas Hugues and disavowed by Charles Kingsley, but a hard, secular morality much more akin to the tenets of the Social Darwinism preached by Herbert Spencer or favoured by William Graham Sumner.[20] *This is the heart of the matter*. Consideration of public school life in Victorian and Edwardian England, reveals that the public image seldom mirrored the private morality. Too frequently, there was an ideology for public consumption and an ideology for personal practice; in a phrase muscular Christianity for the consumer, Social Darwinism for the constrained.

Darwinism has spawned a multitude of contradictory social theories. It is the ancestor of 'Laissey-fairism and socialism, racism and anti-racism, segregation and desegregation, militarism and anti-militarism, Marxism and evolutionary socialism, social engineering and eugenics'.[21] It has attracted the attention of the most curious conceptual bedfellows: Horton Stewart Chamberlain and T. H. Huxley, Lothrop Stoddard and Teilhard de Chardin. Consequently, for some the concept is too tolerant of contradiction, for others too diffuse, for many too replete with repulsive values. Yet for all this, as Gertrude Himmelfarb had remarked, its very complexity demonstrates its significance. As an analytical tool it cannot be lightly dismissed; 'intelligent men,' Himmelfarb warns us, 'do not argue passionately about matters of little consequence'.[22] To put this another way, one indication of the value of an idea is revealed in the extent to which it has been attacked, defended, borrowed, distorted, extended and restricted.

Michael Ruse has argued recently that, however varied its interpretation over time, there are attached to the term Social Darwinism certain common components. Certainly it 'tends to mean all things to all people, but if one has to abstract what people take to be the crucial elements. . . two things in particular would tend to stand out: on the one hand, some sort of evolutionary progress as man and his culture push teleologically towards some better state, and, on the other hand, a bloody struggle for existence – 'nature red in tooth and claw' – as the weakest in society (or the weakest societies) go to the wall'.[23]

Others have perceived the essential truth at the heart of this observation. Robert Bannister has drawn attention to a common denominator amid many definitions, namely the theoretical predisposition 'to describe and explain phenomena in terms of competition and conflict'.[24] It should not go unnoticed either that Richard Hofstadter has linked Darwinism and related biological concepts concerning the struggle for existence and the survival of the fittest not merely with the technical vocabulary of philosophers but with enacted social ideologies.[25]

In the unambiguous terms of Ruse, Bannister and Hofstadter, Social Darwinism is at least as valuable a conceptual instrument for probing the hermetic world of the English public school as the concept of muscular Christianity. The fact is that a religious ideal has become confused with a secular reality. David Newsome has suggested 'that up to the end of the First World War the public schools very conspicuously moved with the times. Their ideal of Christian manliness corresponded closely to the prevailing sentiments and opinions of the middle classes, especially the upper middle class, who were the chief patrons of these schools. Since 1919 this unanimity in ideals has not been pronounced. It proved easier to convert Arnoldianism into muscular Christianity than to correct the deficiencies of a code which inevitably led to athleticism, the glorification of aggressive patriotism and a distorted sense of values'.[26] This is an over-estimation both of the intensity of religious sentiment of the upper middle classes of the period as a whole[27] and of the corresponding unanimity of idealism between these classes and the schools. Furthermore, conversion from Arnoldianism to muscular Christianity was far less complete than is implied above. One member of the audience commenting on a parable recounted by David Newsome in an address to the Headmasters' Conference of 1972 in which Newsome described the community of a school, destroyed in an appalling catastrophe and successfully rebuilt but without a chapel, as 'lifeless', has remarked in response:

Dr Newsome was a distinguished historian of Victorian society and for his audience his parable had a distinctly Victorian, even archaic ring. Had the chapel ever been the heart of the school or had that been the initial intention but ultimate delusion of the great Victorian headmaster? The headmasters of the sixties and seventies often used the Christian foundation argument as a means of discrediting Labour plans to take over their schools. Religious freedom is a powerful rallying cry in a country that does not take its religion too seriously. But the headmasters were honest enough to admit that they could not altogether share Dr Newsome's vision. There was no doubt that chapel services had influenced generations of public schoolboys but not perhaps in the way that headmasters such as Newsome imagined. Chapel was part of the routine, like lessons, games and field days; and as part of the routine it became an element in the grown man's nostalgia for boyhood. It was not so much Christian truth that he took away from all those compulsory services but a longing for atmosphere, for the faces of young friends, for the familiar hymns, above all for a sense of belonging.'[28]

There is much truth in this comment and we shall return to the issue.

In the interim the point should be made that the situation in the schools of the period was in fact complex. A constellation of ideologies existed: secular ideologies found favour partly because they reflected attitudes in the wider society where secularism at the lowest level meant simply that attention was not focused on the religious issues which so preoccupied the churchmen.[29] The concerns of a few should not be regarded as the predilections of the many. Clerical schoolmasters were not necessarily admired or emulated by the parvenus of late Victorian England or their sons who populated the schools in large numbers. The schools moved with the times by embracing athleticism, adopting aggressive patriotism and reflecting a post-Darwinian agnosticism.[30] It is simply misleading to imply, as Newsome has done, that abundant playing-fields, 'cock' house matches, a Rifle Corps and a flourishing Old Boys' Association among other things, were the exclusive appurtenances of an ideology which he favours with the title 'public school muscular Christianity'.[31] They were more. They were the instruments of a form of Social Darwinism which 'embodied a vision of life, and if the phrase will be admitted, expressed a kind of secular piety that commands our attention. . . a kind of naturalistic Calvinism in which man's relation to nature (and man) is as hard and demanding as man's relation to God under the Calvinistic system'.[32] They were also the tools of athleticism: a profound belief in the value of physical exercise, especially the team games, for developing instrumental and expressive skills which did not necessarily require a religious dimension.[33]

These various ideologies *co-existed* in the public schools. They over-lapped, even fused on occasion, but certain of their elements were discrete even contradictory. To fail to recognise this is to neglect a real complexity in favour of an unreal simplicity. There is a need to develop a fuller set of concepts to do justice to actuality, to employ a more extensive vocabulary to recapture the past, to expand our categories in order to comprehend the full range of values of masters and boys in the public schools of the late nineteenth and early twentieth centuries. In taking such steps in the case of Social Darwinism and the schools, we shall certainly be seeking both a *post facto* legitimacy for a well-used idea and brighter illumination of a well-lit edifice. However, as Himmelfarb argues in *Victorian Minds*, the act of retrospective legitimisation may well be as important to the well-being of an idea as it is to a child[34] and, I argue here, the act of increased illumination may well add significant detail to an already well-scanned image. Much of public school life before the Great War had more in common with the harsh Nietzschean imperatives of *The Will to Power* than with the sanguine Darwinian prophecies of the concluding pages of *Origin of Species* and what some claim to be a religious condition was sometimes no more than a secular instinct. What frequently characterised the public schools of this period was an implicit, if not explicit, crude Darwinism encapsulated in simplistic aphorisms: life is conflict, strength comes through struggle and success is the prerogative of the strong. In consequence, conditions in the schools were, to adapt the classic Hobbe-sian expression, nasty, brutish and for some not short enough. The public school world was often a godless world of cold, hunger, competition and endurance. There was frequently little kindness and less piety. John Honey descibes a historical contrast particularly well in this comment:

> Everything I know of the evolution of the English boarding school tradi-tion convinces me that they operated from a very, very different starting-point from so many schools today, certainly state schools where all the talk is of the happiness of the pupils and the flowering of the pupils' abilities. All the machinery of nineteenth-century boarding school life was designed for something quite different. It was designed for a toughening, extending process where your character was forged like steel in the fire. . . Nothing 'soft', nothing 'permissive', nothing egalitarian; nothing remotely 'child-centred'.[35]

A mere glimpse of the effectiveness of this toughening process is pro-vided by C. R. Nevinson in his autobiography *Paint and Prejudice*. He was at Uppingham at the time of the Boer War. This Midland public school, living off the reputation of Edward Thring, its first headmaster who had died in 1887, was considered liberal and in Nevinson's own words:

> I had no wish to go to any such school at all, but nevertheless Uppingham did seem to be the best. Since then I have often wondered what the worst was like. No qualms of mine gave me an inkling of the horrors I was to undergo. . . the brutality and bestiality in the dormitories made life a hell on earth. An apathy settled on me. I withered. I learned nothing: I did nothing. I was kicked, hounded, caned, flogged, hairbrushed, morning, noon and night. The more I suffered, the less I cared. The longer I stayed, the harder I grew.[36]

He suffered most at the hands of the athletic 'bloods' – the heroes of the system.

It is important to be clear that before 1850 hardship in the schools was largely the product of adult indifference; after this date it was mostly the product of adult calculation. Fittingly the following rationale for public school privation came hard on the heels of the publication of *Origin of Species*:

> To the boy or to the community alike, the constant reliance upon another for aid in difficulties, guidance in perplexities, shelter from temptations, fatally weakens the fibre of the character. Boys, like nations, can only attain to the genuine stout self-reliance which is true manliness by battling for themselves against their difficulties, and forming their own characters by the light of their own blunders and their own troubles. It is the great benefit of our public schools that they help them – a benefit that would be wholly lost if their system were not based on a salutary neglect. The object of the public school is to introduce a boy early to the world, that he may be trained in due time for the struggle that lies before him.[37]

In time such Darwinian arguments became commonplace. This is understandable. They represented a contemporary Samuel Smiles upper-middle-class view of the world: 'So far as the public was concerned. . . the idea of evolution by natural selection of the fittest was a view that particularly appealed to industrialist and the upper class who saw in the doctrine a universal law of nature that would serve to justify their own. . . practices.'[38] More than this, schools and society were all of a whole. The schools were simply microcosms[39] of the social macrocosm:

Fortunate indeed the man who retained good health, knew not pain, lost no children, was never unemployed, and never had less than enough to maintain family life at the level he felt appropriate. Such painless security of life is not nowadays uncommon. It was then extremely so; and the mid-Victorians' common philosophy of independence, sensibly accepting the fact that life was on the whole a painful and arduous affair, justified its rigours as a proving-ground for character. Experience of adversities and temptations sifted out the tough characters from the feeble.[40]

Circumstances defined the nature of man in society, dictated human needs and resulted in the appropriate institutional arrangements in the schools.[41]

Evolution, as Bronowski once observed, was a Victorian intellectual crisis which no one could escape[42] but while Darwinism and its offshoots were widely discussed and debated among the upper middle classes of late Victorian England, there was little direct reference to them and a shortage of open advocates for them in the public school community. The notable exception was Hely Hutchinson Almond who adopted a Spencerian functionalism in his organisation of Loretto.[43] Reticence in the schools should not surprise us. Darwinism was widely considered the property of the ungodly: 'it seemed to strike from more than one direction at the very heart of traditional theology. For nearly a century the argument for design, as popularised by the English theologian William Paley, had been standard proof of the existence of God. Now it seemed to many that Darwinism, by blasting this theological foundation stone, must inevitably lead to atheism. The new theory also exploded traditional conceptions of sin and, with them, the moral sanctions of the past. At the very least it clearly impaired the authority of Scripture by discrediting the Genesis version of creation.'[44] For ambitious Victorian clerics the English public school was an Establishment staging post in the occupational journey from priest to prelate and, for their own good reasons, the conventional appear to have been tongue-tied and the progressive, circumspect. At the same time the latter were not without influence. In the second half of Victoria's reign a painful scepticism spread among the English intelligentsia:

Neither a disintegrating Evangelicalism nor a failing Oxford movement could relieve powerful minds of doubts resulting from the findings of natural scientists and German theologians. Many intellectuals went into the wilderness in search of something in which they might believe. J. A. Froude, the historian, once a disciple of Newman, took refuge in Carlylism:

Arthur Hugh Clough, the poet, broke away from Oxford and resigned his fellowship: F. W. Newman wrote the Phases of Faith and gave up his early Evangelicalism: Matthew Arnold broke with orthodoxy and wrote poems of divine despair: Frederick Robertson struggled for his faith and John Sterling's faith disappeared.[45]

Positivism increasingly characterised Oxford and Cambridge[46] and issues, we learn, were more and more regarded 'without reference to fundamental Christian beliefs'.[47] These universities provided the masters for the public schools. Edward Bowen, for one, learnt his Agnosticism from Leslie Stephen at Trinity College, Cambridge and took it to Harrow school.

Despite the urging of Leslie Stephen, T. H. Huxley and Frederic Harrison, within the schools the dominant rhetoric was that of the fashionable and acceptable muscular Christianity but the reality was more often atheistic. It was frequently Stoicism making bland use of Christian phraseology[48] with the same purpose and deceit as the fifteenth century *chevalier*! In reality, as in idealism, the relationship between Mediaeval Chivalry and Victorian muscular Christianity was close. The words of Marina Warner written with reference to the one, apply equally to both:

> The fifteenth century used emblems to express its values with a refinement that escapes us today: the sense of allegory and of the import of a device ran very deep; a motto or a family crest was not a hollow conceit, chosen for its sonority or charm. It embodied the owner's image of himself and his ultimate quest. By creating a personal poetic language, a knight could maintain the fiction that the internecine struggles of his house were gallant undertakings approved by God. Maréchal Boucicuat invested his characteristically ambitious and cruel enterprises on the field of battle with piety and courtliness by calling the chivalric order he founded the order of the Ecu Vert à la Dame Blanche.[49]

The *Dublin Review* of July 1860 clearly discerned a contrast between emblem and action. It had hard and perceptive words to say on the subject of the English public schoolboy and his beliefs. The reality, in its view, was 'an attempt to keep up the mask of a religion'. The aim of creating a boy in the likeness of his God was reduced to 'a mere question of tissues and tendons – to bring out muscle, pluck, self-reliance, independence – the animal man'.[50]

It passed scathing comment on the Clarendon Commission's emphasis on a narrow manliness, which contained not a breath about 'proficiency in the love of God', and on the Commission's view that home rather than school was the source of religious instruction. It came to the conclusion, not unreasonably as we shall see, that 'religion in the public schools of England was a poor, blighted sickly weed. . . strangled by the luxurious growth of animal vigour which overpowers it'.[51] Consequently, the issue was clear: 'The Character of Christ, and of an Englisman formed by the Public School system are very opposite. Will you sacrifice the Englishman to Christ, or Christ to the Englishman? On which will you model? The clay cannot be made to resemble both!'[52] The reason was equally clear. The whole process of public school education was to ensure survival in a materialistic world:

> No boy can elbow his way up from the lower remove of the fourth, to the upper division of the sixth, through the common system of 'trials' and 're-moves', wihout being broken in to many things, and hardened simply by a process of friction to endure, to suffer, to be patient, to bide his time, without having learnt, (as beings in a lower order of creation learn), to take care of himself, to hold his own, to fight his way, to trust to his own best, his own determination, and coolness, and pluck, without, in a word, being prepared for 'the great world of business and society'.[53]

The *Dublin Review*, of course, had its own sectarian hobby-horse to ride. It was left to those with no bishoprics to covet and no beatitudes to defend, to note with qualified approval the 'Darwinian' resemblance between life in a public school and in society. The agnostic Leslie Stephen found the cosmic process of the struggle for existence quite defensible:

> I hold, then, that the 'struggle for existence' belongs to an underlying order of facts to which moral epithets cannot be properly applied. It denotes a condition of which the moralist has to take account and to which morality has to be adapted, but which, just because it is a 'cosmic process' cannot be altered, however much we may alter the conduct which it dictates. Under all conceivable circumstances, the race has to adapt itself to the environment, and that necessarily implies a conflict as well as an alliance. The pre-servation of the fittest, which is surely a good thing, is merely another aspect of the dying of the unfit, which is hardly a bad thing.[54]

and viewed with considerable complacency the harsh facts of public school existence:

> And English public school. . . is a miniature world; and certainly, the world is in many respects a big public school. The training it gives is of the rough

and ready order, with plenty of hard blows and little allowance for senti-ment. The men who succeed in later life generally owe that good fortune to the same qualities which raise a boy to be the leader among his fellows.[55]

The attitude to religion in the schools which the *Dublin Review* found so uncongenial can be fruitfully explored at a later date in the both honest and well-intentioned autobiographical novels of two public schoolboys who wrote of their schooldays in the flush of youthful indignation before the mellow, selective and guarded nostalgia of old age held them fast in its grip. In Alec Waugh's famous *Loom of Youth* (described by Thomas Seccombe in his preface to the 1947 edition as possessing a rare quality for a book on the public schools, namely 'objective reality') religion looms small in the lives of the boys. The hero Gordon Caruthers, a resident incidentally of an 'entirely pagan house', was wholly typical of many of his peers – an uncomplicated hedonist:

pagan

> He was not an atheist; he acceptd Christianity in much the same way as he accepted the Conservative Party. All the best people believed in it, so it was bound to be all right; but at the same time it had not the slightest influence over his actions. If he had any religion at this time it was House football; but for the most part, he lived merely to enjoy himself, and his pleasures were, on the whole, quite innocuous.[56]

Religion was not a spiritual commitment but a social habit. After all, as no less an authority than Halèvy has remarked, English piety was no more than a superficial phenomenon, the property of a select few.[57] It is interesting to note also in Waugh's book that the most famous 'Games Master' of *fiction*, The Bull, while splendidly muscular, was not noticeably Christian. For Caruthers, he was a figure in the Roman not the Christian tradition.[58] And, in passing, perhaps we should note again that probably the most famous Victorian schoolmaster-athlete in *fact*,[59] Edward Bowen of Harrow, was not a Christian but an unbeliever. Waugh returned to the question of public school religion in a later book, *Public School Life*, observing that 'religion plays, and will play, a small part in a boy's life at school. A boy has been told to believe certain things by his parents, and he has accepted these beliefs unquestioningly and without enthusiasm. They have not been tested by experience. They are not real to him. . . I do not think you can expect the average small boy to be deeply influenced by religion. His religion, if he has one, is an unswerving devotion to his house and school'.[60]

Halevy

Of equal value in determining the substance of schoolboy religion in the Victorian and Edwardian public school is Arnold Lunn's autobiographical novel *The Harrovians*. At several points in the book, Lunn highlights actual Harrovian values, ironically juxtaposing them with institutional orthodoxy but nowhere more pointedly than in this passage:

> The Chapel is the scene of the offical religion. . . . far removed from the rough and tumble of school life which cares nothing for the ethics of non-resistance and humility and for whom Christ is an ideal which they cannot be expected to appreciate. Here under the elms is the real temple of the School, and the hope of a place in the XI gives that incentive to a cleanly life which the pulpit so rarely provides.[61]

The public schoolboy's hero, Lunn remarks elsewhere in the book, is not Judaic but Gothic and the schoolboy himself 'simple pagan and just as the pagan may use traditional machinery of sacrifice to his gods, so the boy may say his prayers and bellow his hymns without damage to his sincerity. He remains throughout a pagan. . . . Christianity does not sit easily on his shoulders'.[62]

When in a whimsical passage Lunn's autobiographical hero, Peter O'Neil, troubled momentarily by obvious contradictions between Christian and Chaw (Old Harrovian), tried to imagine Christ in a public school:

> He felt that he would hardly be a success; he could see His House-master lecturing Him on His indiscreet behaviour. 'New boys are expected to keep in the background, and not lecture their elders on their supposed lapses from virtue. Your views, my dear boy, are Quixotic. They might go down in a Quaker School, but they won't help you in the rough and tumble of Harrow life'.[63]

Muscular Christianity itself got short shrift on the Hill. Lunn's merciless description of the foolish Bishop's sermon in which he attempted to curry favour by means of athletic metaphors and portraits of sporting parsons, ends as follows:

> 'I wish you could have know that curate. You would have thought him a jolly good Christian. . . . You simply couldn't get a ball past him. Yes, Tom Bayley, Christian and cricketer, you won't find many like him.' The School began to hate Bayley rather worse than the Bishop. Boys dislike muscular Christians, and do not respect a man for being more proud of his cricket, which is not his job, than his profession as a parson, which is.[64]

Blessed are the meek in Christian cosmology but at Harrow the meek only turned the other cheek, observed Lunn, in case they got hit in the same place twice!

A final word on public school religion. Just as Jean de Meung in the *Roman de la Rose* savages 'the entire mediaeval world's pretence at chivalry'[65] so Howard Whitehouse in *The English Public School: A Symposium* exposed in the schools 'a life of false issues given to worship of the athletic god' in which religion is simply 'good form'.[66] Both demythologised conventional myths revealing that the reality denied the rhetoric. It must never be thought of course that the Victorian and Edwardian public schools were without convinced 'muscular Christians' any more than it can be argued that the Middle Ages were barren of the chivalrous. Kitson Clark's reminder that there were men in even the worst public schools trying 'often in a very muddled sort of way. . . to turn Barbarian virtues into Christian good'[67] is both salutary and pertinent. To consider their influence exclusive or even predominant however, would be inexcusably naïve.

The ambivalence towards the intellect among some later nineteenth and early twentieth century public school headmasters certainly caused confusion in the school.[68] Perhaps the same was true with regard to their Christianity. Stalwart and less stalwart Christians adopted a Darwinian posture when it suited them. Kingsley himself was a strong supporter of Darwin's scientific theories and did all he could to publicise them.[69] Less admiringly of course, Kingsley loathed Papists to the point of annihilation. Most curiously, that meek Christian headmaster, writer and priest, who by no stretch of the imagination could be called muscular, Frederick Farrar, proved to be a most cold-blood Darwinian racist who could contemplate with satisfaction the disappearance of the whole 'degenerate' negro race from the face of the earth.[70]

The scarcely Christian adherence to the view that Might is Right, typical of apparently confused and simple-minded muscular Christians, earned a rebuke in *Tait's Edinburgh Review* as early as 1857.[71] In a sardonic article on muscular Christianity dressed up as the Philosophy of Force, a *soi-disant* muscular Christian correspondent to *The Times* was called to task for writing in the following terms about the death of a Westminster schoolboy after rowing:

> I regret to observe the invasion of what may be called the flannel-waistcoat and comforter element, and I grieve that with regard to sports, which really are half public school education, a course is pursued which resolves itself

into a fear lest the boys should take cold. . . . a Westminster boy ought to take the water like a duck, and. . . it does not much matter whether a weak boy or two is removed, before the cares of life fall upon him, . . . I sympathise with the whole blithe, healthy company of boys, who are bereaved of their boating because some one's pet lamb has turned sick and been cut off. I think it is a pity that we have now-a-days no Eton and Westminster boat-race, simply because in some race a boy over-heated himself, caught cold, and died. There is a wear and tear of public school life just as there is a wear and tear of public life. Here and there a wheel stops, a spring snaps, as this great engine of life whirls on; now and then a champion even in the fore-front of the battle of life totters and falls, and many in the rear rank totter and fall behind him; but these losses are soon repaired and the machine, taken as a whole, is as strong as ever.[72]

A tart reminder was issued to all readers that the 'very essence of Christianity is to care for everybody, especially to make the most of the weak and the sickly'.[73]

The Hobbesian conditions of the ante-bellum public school have already received passing mention. These brief but colourful passages from the autobiographies of Marlburians add evidence to assertion. Each represents many more from Marlborough and elsewhere.[74] Marlborough College was a substantial and successful nineteenth century proprietary school with something of a reputation for scholarship in those philistine times. It represented the better class of school. This made little difference to conditions there.

Edward Lockwood (1843-1851) entered the school at its opening in 1843. His abiding memories were of hunger, religiosity and brutality. The 'wolf of hunger', always prowling, stalked him with special tenacity during Lent:

> A much dreaded time at school. . . there was enough tyranny and humbug mixed up with it to last one for a lifetime. . . On Wednesdays and Fridays my only food was stale bread washed down by water from the pump, and we used to search for pignuts to satisfy our craving. Salt fish occasionally was put upon the table, but an edict had gone forth that it was not fit for human food, so no one ever touched it. . . Then we had to attend long services in chapel, and listen to dreary sermons which no one but the pulpit orator himself could possible enjoy.[75]

His beatings were fully licensed and spectacular:

The knoutings which I received from my master's reverend arm, turned my back all the colours of the rainbow; and when I screamed from the fearful torture they produced, the headmaster would send a prefect down to say, that if I made such a horrid noise, he also would have a go-in at me, when my master had done his worst. Occasionally two masters would be caning at the same time with the rhythms of blacksmiths hammering on an anvil. . . When on my arrival home, I was undressed and put to bed by my tender-hearted nurse, she viewed my back with the utmost horror and indignation. But she was told that as the punishment had been administered by reverend men called to the ministry, I must have deserved every blow I got.[76]

Some twenty years later Roland Prothero (1864-1871) found his options lay between the physical necessities of food and warmth, cold and hunger. Kept from the two fires in the Upper School (a large study-room for over one hundred pupils) by bigger and stronger boys for most of the day, his only chance of warmth in the freezing Wiltshire winters was during meal-times. Breakfast somewhat reduced his dilemma; it was a 'square wad of bread, a small pat of butter, and tea or coffee' – quite unappetising. Unhappily it was not wholly unwelcome: '. . . before breakfast, every morning, we had already attended chapel and done an hour's school. and had tasted no food since the previous evening at 6.30, when a similar wad of bread and a pat of butter had been provided for tea'.[77]

Beverly Nichols (1912-1916) found things little changed in the period immediately before the Great War: 'There was no nonsense about Marlborough; it was a school where they made full use of the cane and where, throughout winter's rages, the windows of the dormitories were always kept wide open so that one sometimes woke up to find that one was sleeping under a coverlet of snow. That is my sharpest and most immediate reaction in recalling those desolate years. Cold. We were always cold.'[78] 'After the cold,' he added, 'the accent was on cruelty.' New boys, it transpired, were given six weeks to learn to perform on steel gymnastic rings hanging from the dormitory ceiling: 'We were expected to have developed our small biceps to a degree that would enable us to leap up, grip the rings, and twist about in a series of complicated gymnastic exercises. If we failed we were bent over the bed and given ten strokes in pyjamas, in the presence of the rest of the dormitory. If we cried out in pain, the strokes came harder.'[79] As far as Christian training was concerned, Nichol's experience is instructive. The boys were left to formulate their own ethics and to construct their own code of conduct 'under the guidance of a gang of gauleiters disguised as senior prefects'.[80] Dennis

Vidler (1928-1933) remembered a Marlborough in the nineteen thirties which even then was 'still a pretty harsh, arid place'. He recalled that a contemporary, Sir Peter Medawar, once described it in a *Sunday Times* interview as 'fit only to train commandants of Concentration Camps' and reflected, 'I don't know about Commandants of Concentration Camps but you learnt how to live in one and survive.'[82]

This was not the whole of life at Marlborough nor were boys perpetually unhappy but,[82] as in the other public schools, life was frequently a physical and psychological struggle for survival against hunger, cold and callousness in one form or another. It resembled the annealing process of an iron foundry: intense 'heat' in the initial stages, gradually lessening in intensity. As such it was part and parcel of a calculated toughening technique arising out of a contemporary view of childhood, education, society and destiny. As A. J. Hartley has stated, at one level *Tom Brown's Schooldays* is a social blueprint 'depicting a polity as a model for national society. . . as boys act and live, so will act and live the men they become!'[83] Newbolt made the same point, more enduringly, in his 'Clifton Chapel', a poem overflowing with Darwinian mandates:

> My son; the oath is yours: the end
> Is His Who built the world of strife
> Who gave his childhood pain for friend,
> And death for surest hope of life.
> To-day and here the fight's begun,
> Of the great fellowship you're free;
> Henceforth the School and you are one,
> And what you are, the race shall be.[84]

In conclusion, within the late Victorian and Edwardian public schools the ideological shibboleths of Thomas Hughes may have been widely disseminated, Kingsleian muscular Christians may have won headmasterships since fashion demanded a clerical collar and a 'varsity blue', some schoolboys may have prayed zealously in the chapel and made half-centuries at the wicket in preparation for the slums of Southwark but life in the schools frequently owed little to the Christian values and can be better understood by reference to a simplistically decoded Darwinian interpretation of existence which harmonised with wider social values of the time.

Public school life of the period reflected the imperatives of Spencer and Sumner as often as the exhortations of Kingsley and Hughes. Attitudes were often secular not spiritual, beliefs were often materialistic not idealistic, custom was often callous not Christian. It is questionable whether ideals

changed simply from godliness and good learning to godliness and manliness; a prevalent secular precept was strength through struggle. To
understand the schools as they were, not as some wished them to be seen,
to deal in reality not romance, it is necessary to add to our analytical
tools, to extend our conceptual horizons, to consider a wider set of
ideological possibilities. Such flexibility will help recapture more accurately the complexity of the past in these hugely influential, much discussed but still not fully penetrated establishments.

Notes

1   See 'Has the public schoolboy deteriorated?', *The Strand Magazine*, 29, 170, 1905, p.
189. I am indebted to Dr David Newsome for this reference. See D. Newsome, 'Public
schools and Christian ideals', *Theology*, 64, December, 1961, p. 486.

2   See J. E. C. Welldon, 'The public school spirit in public life', *Contemporary Review*,
132, 313, October 1927, p. 620 and 'The training of an English gentleman in the public
schools', *Nineteenth Century and After*, CCCLV, 355, September, 1906, pp. 396-413. Welldon
was a prolific publicist for the public schools. He celebrated their virtues in sermons,
autogiographies, fiction and numerous newspaper and journal articles.

3   See J. A. Mangan, *Athleticism in the Victorian and Edwardian Public School: the
Emergence and Consolidation of an Educational Ideology*, Cambridge, Cambridge University
Press, 1981, *passim* but especially Chapter 1.

4   G. G. T. Heywood, 'Ideals of schoolboy life' in E. H. Pitcairn, *Unwritten Laws and
Ideals of Active Careers*, London, Smith, Elder, 1899, p. 242.

5   Despite this, rape in its homosexual form was not unknown in the late Victorian
public school, see C. E. Tyndale-Biscoe, *Tyndale Biscoe of Kashmir. An Autobiography*,
London, Seeley, Service & Co., p. 24; for a brutal, symbolic act of rape at Marlborough
see T. C. Worsley, *Flannelled Fool*, London, Ross, 1967, p. 46.

6   *Spectator*, 2 May 1857, p. 477.

7   *Saturday Review*, 21 February 1857, p. 176.

8   See Charles Kingsley, *The Roman and the Teuton: a Series of Lectures Delivered before
the University of Cambridge*, London, Macmillan, 1875, p. 100; *Charles Kingsley. His Letters
and Memories of his Life*, edited by his wife (F. E. K.) London, 1901, pp. 26-7. For an
interesting comment on Kingsley's reaction to the term, see Henry R. Harrington, 'Charles
Kingsley's fallen athlete', *Victorian Studies*, 21, 1, Autumn 1973, pp. 73-4. Clearly the expression is still viewed with some distaste in certain religious quarters. It fails to get a mention
in either the *New International Dictionary of the Christian Church*, 1974, or the *Oxford
Dictionary of the Christian Church*, 1974.

9   D. Newsome, *Godliness and Good Learning*, London, Murray, 1961, p. 211.

10   Bruce Haley, 'Sports and the Victorians, *Western Humanities Review*, 22, Spring
1968, p. 119.

11   Newsome, *Godliness and Good Learning*, p. 214.

12   Norman Vance, 'The ideal of manliness' in B. Simon & I. Bradley (eds.) *The Victorian Public School*, Gill & MacMillan, Dublin, 1975, pp. 121-2.

13   The Christian Socialism of F. D. Maurice as might be expected found few supporters
in the highly conservative public schools, while late nineteenth century public school

missions in the slums of Britain's cities, the product of 'a curious alliance between High Church sacramentalism and muscular Christianity' (Newsome, *Theology*, p. 490), although laudable, were of marginal interest to most boys.

14 Harrington, *Victorian Studies*, p. 76.

15 For a seminal and particularly stimulating paper on this topic, see G. Redmond '"Muscular Christianity" in Colonial Canada, 1830-1912', *Annual Conference of the American Historical Association*, Los Angeles, December 1981.

16 *Edinburgh Review*, CVII, 217, January 1858, pp. 172-93.

17 *Edinburgh Review*, p. 172.

18 *Edinburgh Review*, p. 172.

19 *Edinburgh Review*, p. 180.

20 See D. Martindale, *The Nature and Types of Sociological Theory*, London, Routledge and Kegan Paul, 1970, pp. 162-8; Gertrude Himmelfarb, *Victorian Minds*, London, Weidenfeld and Nicolson, 1968, pp. 313-32; Richard Hofsfadter, *Social Darwinism in American Thought*, Boston, Beacon Press, 1955 (revised edition).

21 Himmelfarb, *Victorian Minds*, p. 327.

22 Himmelfarb, *Victorian Minds*, p. 332.

23 Michael Ruse, 'Social Darwinism: the two sources', *Albion*, 12, 1, Spring 1980, p. 32.

24 Robert C. Bannister. *Social Darwinism: Science and Myth in Anglo-American Social Thought*, Philadelphia, Temple University Press, 2980, p. 4.

25 Bannister, *Social Darwinism: Science and Myth*, p. 5.

26 Newsome, *Theology*, p. 489.

27 For a description of the materialistic parents of the public schoolboys of the period, see Mangan, *Athleticism*, pp. 127-34.

28 John Rae, *The Public School Revolution*, London, Faber and Faber. 1981, p. 100.

29 Helen Merrell Lynd, *England in the Eighteen Eighties*, Oxford, Oxford University Press, 1945, p. 340.

30 For a contemporary assessment of the influence of Agnosticism and its prospects, in educated English society, see Frederic Harrison, 'The future of Agnosticism', *Fortnightly Review*, CCLXV, January 1889, pp. 145-56.

31 Newsome, *Godliness and Good Learning*, p. 223.

32 Hofstadter, *Social Darwinism in American Thought*, p. 10.

33 Mangan, *Athleticism*, pp. 6-9.

34 Himmelfarb, *Victorian Minds*, p. 315.

35 John Honey, 'The English public school: its dismal past and doubtful future', *Proceedings of the Conference of Boarding Schools Association at University College*, Oxford, January 1979, p. 25.

36 C. R. Nevinson, *Paint and Prejudice*, London, 1937, p. 7. It is interesting to compare the following description of Nevinson's experiences at Uppingham circa 1905 with the statements of Wood, Tancock and Moss in the opening part of this paper:

As a result of my sojourn in this establishment for the training of sportsmen I possessed at the age of fifteen a more extensive knowledge of 'sexual manifestations' than many a 'gentleman of the centre'. It is possible that the masters did not know what was going on. . . It is now the fashion to exclude 'the hearties' from accusations of sexual interest or sadism, or masochism; but in my day it was they, the athletes, and above all the cricketers, who were allowed these traditional privileges. Boys were bullied, coerced and tortured for their diversion, and many a lad was started on strange things through no fault nor inclination of his own.

Games and the practice of games were the order of the day. . . Fortunately, . . . I was a good runner, and I seldom was whipped by the hunting crops of the 'hearties', who would ride beside us lashing out at any fellow with stitch or cramp. I was also able to follow the hounds on foot in that great hunting county and thereby escape many a flogging.

I think it was the kicking which finally settled matters. In this popular pastime known as the 'flying kick' the cricket eleven wore their white shoes and any junior was captured and bent over for their sport. They took running kicks at our posteriors, their white shoes marking the score and a certain place counting as a bull. A period of this marksmanship left me inflamed and constipated, and eventually I developed acute appendicitis, an illness much dreaded in those days, as the operation was thought to be extremely dangerous.

Thank God, I became so ill that I was moved to London. . . . I was in wretched state, septic in mind and body (pp. 7-8).

37   *Saturday Review*, 8 December 1860, p. 727, quoted in Mangan, *Athleticism*, p. 135.

38   Robert E. D. Clark, *Darwin: Before and After*, London, Paternoster Press, 1966, p. 72.

39   See G. M. Trevelyan, *English Social History*, London, Longmans, Green & Co., 1944, pp. 563-9.

40   G. Best, *Mid-Victorian Britain* 1851-1875, London, Weidenfeld and Nicolson, 1971, p. 258.

41   For a fuller discussion of this point, see R. J. Halliday, 'Social Darwinism: a definition', *Victorian Studies*, XIV, 4 June 1971, pp. 389-405.

42   J. Bronowski, 'Unbelief and science', in *Ideas and Beliefs of the Victorians,* London, Sylvan Press, 1949, p. 165.

43   Mangan, *Athleticism* pp. 48-58. For a fuller outline of Almond's Spencerian beliefs see R. J. Mackenzie, *Almond of Loretto*, London, Collins, 1905.

44   Hofstadter, *Social Darwinism in American Thought*, p. 25.

45   William E. Winn, 'Tom Brown's School Days and the development of "Muscular Christianity"', *Church History*, 21, 1960, pp. 64-5.

46   For an illuminating consideration of English Positivism and its political and social influence, see Royden Harrison, *Before the Socialists: Studies in Labour and Politics*, London, Routledge and Kegan Paul, 1965, pp. 251-342.

47   Newsome, *Godliness and Good Learning*, p. 229. For a personal reaction to the atmosphere of religious scepticism at the universities, see Walter Leaf, *Some Chapters of Autobiography*, London, Murray 1932, pp. 106-8. Leaf was at Cambridge from 1870-4.

48   G. Kitson Clark, *The English Inheritance*, London, SCM Press, 1950, p. 142.

49   Marina Warner, *Joan of Arc. The Image of Female Heroism*, London, Weidenfeld and Nicolson, 1981, p. 166.

50   'Public school education, *Dublin Review*, 5, 57, July 1865, p. 36.

51   *Dublin Review*, p. 42.

52   *Dublin Review*, p. 570.

53   *Dublin Review*, p. 31.

54   Leslie Stephen, 'Ethics and the struggle for existence', *Contemporary Review*, 64, July 1893, p. 169.

55   Leslie Stephen, 'Thoughts of an outsider: public schools', *Cornhill Magazine*, 27, 159, March 1873, p. 283. In this article Stephen provides an admiring but unsurprisingly, wholly *secular* view of public school manliness:

Standing in the Eton playing-fields, one would perhaps rather not talk about the battle of Waterloo, and ask too curiously whether the training woud be equally adapted to produce the heroes of some future Gravelotte or Sedan. But one cannot resist the spirit of the place. There is a certain fine stoicism, a sturdy, tough-fibred sense of manly duty, which seems to pervade the atmosphere; and, with all its sacred absurdities, one feels that lads brought up under such influences have a chance of carrying on the old traditon with fair credit to themselves and their country. After all, the old maxim holds true that one virtue lies at the base of all others; call it force, energy, vitality, or manliness, or whatever you please, it has perhaps a better chance at a public school than at most places. (p. 290).

For an interesting discussion of the Victorian worship of force, see Walter E. Houghton, *The Victorian Frame of Mind* 1830-1870, New Haven, Yale University Press, 1957, pp. 196-217.

56 Alec Waugh, *The Loom of Youth*, London, Grant-Richard, 1917, (1947 edition) pp. 96-7. In this novel Waugh wrote of *The Harrovians* in these terms:

This book, as no other book has done, photographs the life of a Public School boy stripped of all sentiment, crude and raw. . . It may have may artistic blunders; it may be shapeless and disconnected, but it is true to life in every detail;' (p. 153).

57 Waugh, *The Loom of Youth*, p. 325.

58 Elie Halèvy, *Imperialism and the Rise of Labour*, (*A History of the English People in the Nineteenth Century*) V. London, Benn, (2nd ed. 1951), p. 168.

59 J. A. Mangan, 'Philathlete extraordinary: a portrait of the Victorian schoolmaster Edward Bowen', *Journal of Sports History*, 9, Winter, 1982, pp. 23-40.

60 Alec Waugh, *Public School Life*, London, Collins, 1922, p. 246.

61 Arnold Lunn, *The Harrovians*, London, Methuen, 1913, pp. 109-10.

62 Lunn, *Harrovians*, pp. 141-2.

63 Lunn, *Harrovians*, p. 140.

64 Lunn, *Harrovians*, p. 104.

65 Warner, *Joan of Arc*, p. 219.

66 J. Howard Whitehouse (ed.), *The English Public School: A Symposium*, London, Grant-Richards, 1919. G. E. L. Cotton is an excellent example of a headmaster who used games as an instrument of social control, see Mangan, *Athleticism*, pp. 24-7.

67 Kitson Clark, *English Inheritance*, p. 143. Some idea of the mishmash of theological jingoism served up on occasion is provided by C. R. Nevinson. At Uppingham he recalled:

I attended endless divine services; listened to strange sermons delivered by doctors of divinity in which Englishmen were confused with God, Nelson with Jesus Christ, Lady Hamilton with the Virgin Mary. The German Fascists. . . are fed on no greater confusion of patriotism and religion. (*Paint and Prejudice*, pp. 8-9)

68 Mangan, *Athleticism*, pp. 109-10.

69 See Darwinism, *Encyclopaedia Britannica*, 1970, XIII, p. 366.

70 See Frederick Farrar 'Aptitudes of race, transactions of the ethnological society' (V), 1867 quoted in M. D. Biddis, *Images of Race*, Leicester, 1979, pp. 150-1.

71 'Muscular Christianity', *Tait's Edinburgh Review*, 25 January 1858, pp. 100-2.

72 *Tait's Edinburgh Review*, p. 101.

73 *Tait's Edinburgh Reveiw*, p. 102.

74 Details of the harshness of life within the nineteenth century public school system as a whole are succinctly and graphically described by John Honey in his *Tom Brown's Universe*, London, Millington, 1977. See especially pp. 209-22.

75 Edward Lockwood, *The Early Days of Marlborough College*, Simpkin, Marshall, Hamilton and Kent, London, 1893, pp. 91-2.

76 Lockwood, *Marlborough College*, pp. 25-6. The violence of the beatings in the early years is also recorded vividly in F. A. Brown, *Family Notes*, Genoa, Instituto Sordomuti,

Forging characters of steel in the English public school

'A school run'

The 'Blood' in his glory

1917, p. 96. Brown was at Marlborough from 1849 to 1855.

77 Rowland Prothero (Lord Ernie), *From Whippingham to Westminster*, London, Murray, 1938, p. 32.

78 Beverly Nichols, *The Unforgiving Minute*, Allen, London, 1978, p. 20.

79 Nichols, *Unforgiving Minute*, p. 21.

80 Nichols, *Unforgiving Minute*, p. 21.

81 Letter to the author from Mr Dennis Vidler dated 26 September 1981. Evolution tends to be a slow process in the public school system. Consider this comment:

In the early sixties it was still the norm that a boy had to attend chapel every day and twice on Sunday; play the major sport whether he liked it or not; join the Combined Cadet Force; and wear a school uniform, every item of which was prescribed in the school rules. He was probably compelled to attend the school play and the school concert. His movements were strictly controlled by bounds and bells. Fagging and corporal punishment were common practice; in many schools the prefects had the power to beat other boys. A hierarchy of prefects or monitors kept the machinery of compulsion running and in return enjoyed privileges that allowed them to escape the more disagreeable aspects of the machine themselves. For all pupils, whatever their position in the hierarchy, the secret of success – and survival – was to conform.

The 'early sixties' were the 1960s. The comment is by John Rae. See *The Public School Revolution*, p. 96.

82 Beverley Nichols described a common condition among public schoolboys which I leave others to explain. He wrote in *The Unforgiving Minute*: 'In spite of the cold, the cruelty, the barbarism. . . I must have been in love with the place when the time came to leave.' (p. 28). This eventual love for Marlborough is made very clear in *Prelude*, the novel about Marlborough he wrote shortly after leaving the school. For a Christian and more gentle assessment of Marlborough a little earlier see W. Keble Martin, *Over the Hills*, London, Joseph, 1968, pp. 22-24.

83 A. J. Hartley, 'Christian socialism and Victorian moralty: the inner meaning of *Tom Brown's Schooldays*', *Dalhousie Review*, XLIX, 1969, p. 266.

84 Sir Henry Newbolt, 'Clifton Chapel' quoted in T. C. Worsley, *Barbarians and Philistines*, London, Hale, 1940, p. 89.

chapter eight ROBERT J. HIGGS

Yale and the heroic ideal, *Götterdämmerung* and palingenesis, 1865-1914

On 19 October, 1869, President Charles W. Eliot of Harvard articulated the ideal of Harvard in his age in a famous inaugural address that has been called 'a turning point in higher education', '. . . there is an aristocracy to which the sons of Harvard have belonged, and let us hope will ever aspire to belong – the aristocracy which excells in manly sports, carries off the honors and prizes of the learned professions, and bears itself with distinction in all fields of intellectual labor and combat; the aristocracy which in peace stands for the public honor and renown, and in war rides first into the murderous thickets.'[1]

The sons of Yale also belonged to this heroic aristocracy. In fact, Yale had perhaps an even better claim on the old-fashioned virtues than did Harvard. When in 1859, just ten years before Eliot's inauguration and only two years before Fort Sumpter, a Harvard professor asked a Yale graduate what college spirit was, he was told: 'It is a combination of various elements – inspiration or faith with enthusiasm, sacrifice, or self-denial, fidelity and loyalty, cooperation and patriotism.' The response of the Harvard professor: 'We have not got that here.'[2]

Harvard did have those qualities, to a significant degree, as Eliot makes clear, but they had long been enshrined at Yale. One of the great heroes of the American revolution and 'the Hero' of Yale, Nathan Hale, possessed them in great abundance. 'No graduate', says Anson Phelps Stokes in *Memorials of Eminent Yale Men* (1915) 'so symbolizes to the undergraduate of today [1914] the highest manifestation of the Yale spirit as this able student and manly youth who gladly gave up his life for his country's service.'[3]

Hale's diary, says Stokes, written while on duty in the Boston area in the early months of 1776, was full of 'references to his fine spirit and to his devotion. Westling, 'chequers', and football were among his diversions, but his main work was improving the efficiency of his men.'[4] 'Manly'was a favourite word of Eliot in 1869, of Stokes in 1914 and apparently of Hale's contemporaries as seen, for example, in the following elegy by a companion of his undergraduate days:

> Erect and tall, his well-proportioned frame,
> Vig'rous and active, as electric flame;
> His manly limbs had symmetry and grace,
> And innate goodness marked his beauteous face;
> His fancy lively, and his genius great,
> His solid judgment shone in grave debate;
> For erudition far beyond his years;
> At Yale distinguish'd above all his peers, . .
> Removed from envy, malice, pride and strife,
> He walked through goodness as he walked through life;
> A kinder brother nature never knew,
> A child more duteous or a friend more true.[5]

In his own description of Hale, Stokes links the words 'spirit' and 'football' and the linkage in 1914 is probably deliberate. By this time 'spirit' has become the distinguishing feature of Yale, especially in contrast to Harvard and especialy in sports. 'From 1872 through 1909 in all games of soccer, rugby and American football, the fantastic Yale teams ran up a record of 324 victories, 17 losses, and 18 ties. Yale's success against Harvard was so great that Cambridge men began to think of Yalies as nothing but muckers while Yale men had serious doubts about the manliness of the Harvards.'[6] It was in fact the Yale dominance in sports that led to such clichés as Yale 'spirit' and Harvard 'reserve' and Yale 'brawn' and Harvard 'brains'. Both universities, of course, valued both brain and brawn in accordance with the heroic myth of the age but Yale men, for whatever combination of reasons, seems to have emerged as the victor in the image of success. Note for example, the following description of Andy Lockheart in 'The Captured Shadow' by F. Scott Fitzgerald: 'Winner of the Western Golf Championship at eighteen, captain of the freshman baseball team, handsome, successful at everything he tried, a living symbol of the splendid, glamorous world of Yale.'[7]

If Yale by 1892 had become, in the view of George Santayana, what Harvard once was and 'a great deal more',[8] then it should not surprise us that Theodore Roosevelt (Harvard, 1880) was more at home at Yale by the end of the century than he would have been at Harvard, where people like William James gave lectures with such titles as 'Is Life Worth Living?' 'When in 1902 the Public Orator presented Theodore Roosevelt for an honorary degree [at Yale] he explained that the president "is a Harvard man by nature, but in his democratic spirit, his breadth of national feeling, and his earnest pursuit of what is true and right, he possesses those qualities which represent the distinctive ideals of Yale".' This was received not with gales of laughter, but with prolonged applause.[9]

At the turn of the century Yale seemed to be at the height of its glory but all was not well within the ivied walls of America's most famous colleges or in America itself. Santayana, while heaping praise upon both Yale and Harvard, asked if both weren't 'partly going in the wrong direction' and the country itself in the view of many was headed very much in the wrong direction. The dominant tone of the times, especially among artists and intellectuals, was that of *Götterdämmerung*, the twilight of the gods. To paraphrase Matthew Arnold, one world was dead and another was powerless to be born. The malaise has been called *fin-de-siècle* despair and its high priest was Henry Adams (Harvard, 1859). In a letter to Charles Milnes Gaskell in 1894, he wrote:

> . . . My generation has been cleaned out. My brother and their contemporaries are old men. I am myself more at odds with the time. I detest it, and everything that belongs to it, and live only in the wish to see the end of it, with all its infernal Jewry. I want to put every money-lender to death, and to sink Lombard Street and Wall Street under the ocean. Then, perhaps, men of our kind might have some chance of being honorably killed in battle and eaten by our enemies. I want to go to India,and be a Brahmin, and worship a monkey.[10]

In his diatribe Adams was expressing a widespread attitude among Harvard Alumni – Lodge, Roosevelt, Wister – who wanted to revive the warrior ideal as an alternative to that of the businessman.[11] It was an attitude of caste, class and exclusion. The anti-semitism, which Adams regretted expressing even in private, was merely one of several characteristics of *Götterdämmerung*. Among the others was a sophisticated primitivism that exalted the natural man and manliness and indicted polite society, a stereotyping of woman into one role, namely wife and mother, the belief that men of talent or genius were doomed in a society devoted to the dollar, and the certainty that the old west was dead or dying and that the east was also on the way to ruin.

Judging from the serious writings of the time, it was not a period of hope. Juvenile literature, however, presents a different picture. The contrast of pessimism and optimism is quite evident in a brief look at four Yale men, two real, Clarence King and Frederic Remington, and two fictional, Frank Merriwell and Dink Stover. All were athletes and manly men of action but they present to us two entirely different attitudes towards life in America around the turn of the century and two different sets of values as well.

Clarence King, in Adams' view, was the most remarkable man of his age, which the testimony of their contemporaries tends to confirm. Founder of the U.S. Geologic Survey, he was not only a scientist but a prolific writer of science (mainly Geology, for example, his 'epochal' *Systematic Geology* (1878) and other topics as well; his *Mountaineering in the Sierra Nevada* (1872) was regarded as a minor literary classic. He was also a lover of art, a patron and collector, at home in the great galleries of Europe as in the Sierra. He was, however, more (judging from accounts) than the sum of his achievements. Says Adams,

> . . . the charm of King was that he saw what others did and a great deal more. His wit and humor; his bubbling energy which swept everyone into the current of his interest: his personal charm of youth and manners; his faculty of giving and taking, profusely, lavishly whether in thought or money as though he were nature herself, marked him almost alone among Americans. He had in him something of the Greek – a touch of Alcibiades or Alexander. One Clarence King only existed in the world.[12]

Indeed King (Yale, 1862) epitomised the excellence that Eliot defined in the opening sentences of his address since he was 'almost equally' at home, in the words of Anson Phelps Stokes, 'in the world of art, letters, and science'. At Yale, according to Stokes, King 'was a good student, had a taste of field work in his vacations, derived an enthusiasm for science from his instructors, and was prominent in the social and athletic life of the college community, being stroke oar of one of the crews, and captain of the baseball team'.[13]

King lived up to his promise sufficiently to be invited to give the commencement address at Sheffield School (Yale Scientific School) in 1877 and to gain seven laudatory pages in Stokes' *Memorials of Eminent Yale Men* but he himself became increasingly disappointed in his own efforts to succeed in the fashion of the Renaissance man. Utilising his vast knowledge of geology and mining, King wanted to turn a fortune but not for the mere purpose of making money. Says his biographer Clarence Wilkins: 'He dreamed of gaining millions from his Mexican mines; he dreamed, too, of turning millions to the uses of contemporary artists, and of making himself a new Lorenzo'.[14]

What Henry Adams deplored in others, the preoccupation with wealth, he quickly excused in King, whom he idolised, and from King's example drew the familiar conclusion 'that the theory of scientific education failed where most theory failed – for want of money'.[15] In King, Adams had further proof that while the ideal, as defined by Eliot, posited an integration, the drive for wealth and the love of learning (as seen, for example, in Eliot's mix at Harvard of poor ambitious boys and rich boys of 'manly delicacy') the two instincts were virtually irreconcilable; and if King couldn't reconcile them, Adams and his friends seemed to say, then there is no need for anyone else to try. Though King maintained his sense of humour to the last, he slipped more and more, says Wilkins, into 'enervating spells of depression in a hostile milieu in which William James's 'Bright Bitch Goddess' reigned supreme, a goddess that attracted and repelled King at once'.[16] Just as King was of two minds about money, so he was too about society, celebrating the natural man and woman, Indian and Negro, being secretly married to a black woman yet remaining extremely proud of his 'blue blood' and his aristocratic status.

If the surveys of Clarence King provided a comprehensive view of the geologic history of mountain regions of the West, Frederic Remington provided, through his painting, sculpture and fiction, a comprehensive view of the natural man of the West that King also admired. His achievement in art, like King's in science, staggers the imagination, considering the fact that Remington died in 1909 when he was only forty-eight. (Remington did not receive his degree from Yale until 1900 but his studies in the Art School, as Stokes points out, were carried out from 1878 to 1880.) While King's pioneering work has been overshadowed and dated by the advances of science, Remington's art becomes more valuable with the passage of time. Few people would disagree with Owen Wister who called him 'a national treasure' or with Roosevelt who said:

I regard Frederic Remington as one of the Americans who has done real work for his country, and we all owe him a debt of gratitude. It is no small thing that such an artist and man of letters should arise to make permanent record of certain of the most interesting features of our national life. . . . [Remington] is, of course, one of the most typical American artists we ever had, and he has portrayed a most characteristic and yet vanishing type of American life. The soldier, the cowboy, and rancher, the Indian, the horses and the cattle of the plains, will live in his bronzes for all time.[17]

Roosevelt had a special admiration for the manliness of Remington's art as he did for that in Wister's fiction. Indeed Roosevelt admired manliness wherever he found it. He was in fact its most vocal advocate, devoting an essay to the very topic entitled 'The manly virtues and practical ideals'. Here he claimed that any man 'desirous of doing good political work' stands in need for 'the rougher, manlier virtues and above all the virtue of personal courage, physical as well as moral'.[18] Henry Cabot Lodge believed that ' the time given to athletic contests and the injuries incurred on the playing field are part of the price which the English-speaking race has paid for being world-conquerors',[19] and it was a view which Roosevelt soundly endorsed in relating his own practical experience in 'raising the regiment' among athletes at Harvard, Yale and Princeton for his venture in Cuba. When the Rough Riders gathered for the last time in September 1898, at Montauk Beach on Long Island, 'they presented Roosevelt with a bronze copy of Remington's 'Bronco Buster' which, Roosevelt told his men, 'represented "the foundation of their regiment"'.[20]

The manliness which Remington portrayed in his art was partly a 'cowboy philosophy which seemed almost reserved for Anglo-Saxons.[21] Like Clarence King, he denounced the 'torrential vulgarity flooding America' and, like Henry Adams, he was ready to do violence to the culprits:

> Jews, Injuns, Chinamen, Italians, Huns – the rubbish of the Earth I hate – I've got some Winchesters and when the massacring begins, I can get my share of 'em, and what's more, I will. . . Our race is full of sentiment. We invite the rinsins, the scourins, and the Devil's lavings to come to us and be *men* (Remington's emphasis) something they haven't been most of them, these hundreds of years. I don't care a damn how a man gets to Heaven – how he takes care of his soul – whether he has one or not. It's all nothing to me. But I do care how he votes and lives and fights.[22]

For Remington, manliness meant actual physical strength and ability and almost a love of fighting, certainly a love of sports. He especially loved football and was glad to see Roosevelt defending it during the trial of the game in 1905. He even loved the destructive side of football and hoped it would never be changed to suit critics such as Charles W. Eliot.

According to Peter H. Harrick, Remington was 'a natural athlete, displaying strength and skill which enabled him to excel in all sports, including boxing and horsemanship. As a rusher he knocked heads in the line, and although his brawn should have been sufficient, he employed psychological tactics as a means of bringing his team to victory. On the occasion of the 1879 Prince-Yale game, Remington reputedly dipped his jersey in blood at a local slaughterhouse to make it look more business-like'.[23] Stokes in *Memorials* mentions his 'fine physique' and membership on the football team. He also cites one authority who called Remington 'the authoritative chronicler of the whole western land. . . . and of all men and beasts dwelling therein. . . .'[24]

Remington chronicled the West in *Crooked Trails*, the *Sundown* stories and *John Ermine of the Yellowstone*, published only a few months after *The Virginian* and by the same company. Just as Adams was a close friend of Yale man King, so Remington was a friend of Harvard Wister for fifteen years and illustrator of his work, including an edition of *The Virginian*. Indeed, the friendship of the two men and similarity of *The Virginian* and *John Ermine* raised several questions about influence but there were differences between the novels, if not 'a thousand' as one reviewer said, at least some that were significant. Both John Ermine, the hero of *Yellowstone*, and *The Virginian* were 'historical' characters but they 'operated under different laws'. Though both were manly, natural men, the Virginian was a southerner while John Ermine 'was born white. . . . but had a crow heart'.[25]

The final lament of John Ermine, 'I am all alone', applies to Frederic Remington as well in his last years. Predictably, he had been drawn to the Cuban war at the beginning because of an unending desire for physical action but 'he became inreasingly convinced that the impulse which won the West was not identical with that which guided the Cuban campaign. Roosevelt was wrong in stating that the Bronco Buster formed the 'foundation' of the Rough Riders. For Remington, the 'Buster' came to represent his youth and the youth of his country. The war had shown him that both were over'.[26] 'Cowboys,' he would cry. 'There are no cowboys anymore!'[27]

All was not completely lost, however. While *Götterdämmerung* was in vogue in the late nineteenth and early twentieth centuries, so was another romantic term, its opposite 'palingenesis', which means 'a new or second birth, the state of being born again; regeneration'. *The Dictionary of Philosophy and Psychology* (Vol.11) defines it, in addition to 'regeneration', as 'the doctrine that the soul passes through a succession of rebirths, and is closely akin to 'metempsychosis', transference of souls'. In the case of the heroic ideal of Yale, palingenesis occurred in the popular literature at the same time that *Götterdämmerung* weighed most heavily on the brightest minds. Gilbert Patten's Frank Merriwell, for example, made his appearance in 1896 at approximately the same time that the frontier of Remington and Wister was becoming legend and myth.

Palingenesis also means 'breeding true', the refinement of ancestral type, and this is essentially what Patten intended to do with his Merriwell stories.

> Believing the old-fashioned dime novel was on its way out, I decided to set a new style with my stories and make them different and more in step with the times. As the first issues were to be stories of American school life, I saw in them the opportunity to feature all kinds of athletic sports, with baseball, about which I was best informed, predominating.
>
> Such stories would give me the opportunity to preach – by example – the doctrine of a clean mind in a clean and healthy body.[28]

What Patten wished to revive was not the stock theatrics of the plains which had served as the testing ground for manliness of the graduates of Harvard and Yale but the simpler and older form of entertainment centred on 'athletic sports'. With Frank, Patten started where the old order finished. He started with a dying West and went East, back to roots, to tradition, to Yale, the school of Nathan Hale. There in the person of Merriwell he produced an innocent hero that was truer to Hale's and Eliot's dream in many ways than were the distinguished graduates who left their marks upon the nation's arts, letters and political destiny. Indeed Frank had all the sterling attributes that Yale held dear:

> Frank Merriwell. . . stood for truth, faith, justice, the triumph of right, mother, home, friendship, loyalty, patriotism, the love of *alma mater*, duty, sacrifice, retribution and strength of soul as well as body. Frank was manly; he had 'sand'. He was tolerant. . . He was honest. When some prankish classmates stole a turkey from a farmer's coop, Frank risked capture to stay behind to nail a five-dollar bill to the roost. 'Have all the sport you like over it', he told his laughing friends, 'but I feel easy in my mind'.[29]

He was, of course, a great athlete, as was his brother Dick. 'Frank won every big game in Fardale's history and Yale's, and so did Dick after him. Each was at Yale nine years, and each graduated with honors. Both were fullbacks, both were pitchers, both stroked the crew – Frank threw a "doubleshoot" ball that curved twice before it reached the plate, while Dick possessed a "jumpball" that rose a full foot as it approached the batter. In track meets the Merriwells ran the dashes, the half mile, the mile, did the pole vault, the broad jump, the high jump, and threw the hammer. In vacation periods they hunted big game, punched cows, explored the jungle, mined gold, and so on.'[30]

Where the dream of dollars wrecked the lives of others such as Clarence King, Frank rose easily above such temptation.

Says Russell B. Nye:

> . . . implicit in the Merriwell books is a concept of success markedly differ-
> ent from that stated in Alger. The Alger hero's rise is measurable in
> accountable material terms; we know where our hero starts, where he will
> end, and we can measure his progress in the size of his wallet. The Mer-
> riwell books recognise success as something quite different, in terms of the
> personal satisfaction of excellence, of the assumption of authority through
> virtue, of establishing leadership by example, of excelling under the rule of
> 'doing the right thing' and 'playing the game'.[31]

Frank also seems an improvement over some of his real-life contemporaries in other ways. Sports were a form of democracy at work and
success called for compliment. 'Frank once outraged a crowd by shaking
hands with a Negro jockey who had ridden a good race' and in 1939 in a
radio script for the Council Against Intolerance 'Frank defended a Jewish
baseball player at Fardale'.[32] Say the editors of *Frank Merriwell's 'Father'*,
'by being friendly with characters who happened to be Negro or Jewish
or members of other minority groups, Frank helped to erase prejudice
and intolerance from growing minds without preaching'.

Only in the area of academic excellence does Frank seem to lag behind
the real graduates of Yale. One simply cannot imagine him matching the
achievement of either King or Remington possibly because, though
bright, he was not really that interested in either sciences or arts.

His strengths lay not in the intellectual virtues but in the heroic ones
which accounted for his wide appeal. One whom Frank influenced was
Eddie Eagan, 'outstanding Yale athletic star and college boxing champion', Rhodes Scholar and later United States attorney in New York. Said
Egan, 'I lived way out in Colorado where Yale was something you did
when you shouted good and loud – that's all it meant to us – and college
was a place where sissies went. It wasn't until I began sneaking in your
novels on Frank Merriwell that I got the big yearn to be like him, and
that's how I came to go to Yale – something I'll never regret'.[33] Here is

an example of the eternal cycle, the expectant youth, as opposed to ageing and despairing intellectuals, going East to play and to learn and, later, to enter into public service.

Another Yale man of fiction, Dink Stover, highlighted the ideal not so much by attempt at imitation but by scepticism, by noting the discrepancy between the ideal and the actual. Owen Johnson's novel, *Stover at Yale,* first appeared in *McClure's Magazine* in 1911, three years before Frank disappeared from the pages of *Tip Top Weekly* after a run of seventeen years. Like Frank, Stover is a star athlete and a leader on campus but, unlike Frank, he is credible.

In his review of a modern edition of *Stover*, Michel J. Halberstam calls the book 'bitter, almost subversive', which 'starts us thinking about our own condition'. It is a book, says Halberstam, 'where American higher education is split open like a Delicious apple and then allowed to turn brown and rot under the reader's eye'.[34] That such will happen with every reader is unlikely but that the values and assumptions of Yale and America are called into question cannot be denied, as, for example, when one of the characters, Brockhurst, gives the following opinion of football, as timely today as in 1911:

> I say our colleges today are business colleges – Yale more so, perhaps, because it is more sensitively American. Let's take up any side of our life here. Begin with athletics. What has become of the natural, spontaneous joy of contest? Instead you have one of the most perfectly organized business systems for achieving a required result – success. Football is driving, slavish work; there isn't one man in twenty who gets any real pleasure out of it. Professional baseball is not more rigorously disciplined and driven than our "amateur" teams. Add the crew and the track. Play, the fun of the thing itself, doesn't exist; and why? Because we have made a business out of it all, and the college is scoured for material just as drummers are sent out to bring in business.[35]

Johnson merely uses Brockhurst to illustrate certain points – giving him, says Halberstam, 'the best lines in the novel' – but does not use him to express doctrine. Certainly Johnson did not want a war every ten years as Brockhurst would, nor even a return to the warrior ideal. What he did want he makes clear at the end of the novel, giving the lines to Brockhurst, appropriately, since he had been the most critical of Yale.

> I'm not satisfied with Yale as a magnificent factory on democratic business lines; I dream of something else, something visionary, a great institution

not of boys, clean, loyal, and honest, but of men of brains, of courage, of leadership, a great center of thought, to stir the country and bring it back to the understanding of what man creates with his imagination, and dares with his will. It's visionary – it will come.[36]

Brockhurst, though he ends the novel on an optimistic note, is for the most part an extremist who, by virtue of his independence and intelligence, directs a withering attack at Yale and America. Stover, by contrast, is a moderate who, impressed by Brockhurst, must work out for himself the conflicts he finds at Yale between quality and equality. Like Frank Merriwell, he is thoroughly decent and a distinct improvement in terms of democratic idealism over his real-life contemporaries. Likeable and open-minded, he is drawn, as Halberstam points out, to the outsiders, 'to Regan, a gruff older freshman, working his way through Yale in order to go into reform politics back West. He comes to respect Gimbel, a classmate who is politicking to overthrow the sophomore societies (Johnson hints that Gimbel may be Jewish – despite being an Andover athlete he has no chance of making a society – but never used the word.) He makes a condescending visit to a couple of grinds from a small New England town and finds a respect for Yale and for learning unknown among his own carefree friends'.[37]

When the book appeared, says Brooks Mather Kelly, faculty, students and alumni were aware of what was happening and the situation was 'already changing' for the better. How rapidly it was changing toward equality of opportunity may remain a matter of opinion forever but that positive change occurred over the long run seems undeniable, at least in the eyes of Kingman Brewster, Jr, former president of Yale who wrote the introduction for the modern edition. Johnson, he thinks, 'perhaps. . . would like the new Yale better than his own'.[38]

On the metaphysical level, 'Götterdämmerung' and 'paligenesis' at the turn of the century suggest the thought of the two nineteenth-century German philosophers, Nietzsche and Schopenhauer, respectively.[39] While elements of both of their contrasting theories of recurrence may be seen in the evolution of heroism at the turn of the century, Frank Merriwell and Dink Stover themselves partake neither of Nietzsche's will to power on the one hand, which is evident to some degree in King's obsession with wealth and Remington's ethnic prejudice, nor of Schopenhauer's pessimism resulting from a belief in the gradual abolishment of the will by the 'pale cast of thought'. Though their emergence on the American scene seems to illustrate certain 'Laws' of recurrence described by both

Nietzsche and Schopenhauer, philosophically they are closer to the optimistic and self-reliant romanticism of Ralph Waldo Emerson and Henry David Thoreau.

What they represent is a hearty affirmation of the democratic principles. In many ways they educate their alma mater instead of the other way around. We may need excellence in America, they seem to say, but we need just as much equality of opportunity.

If the belief in equal opportunity is measured by the presence of minorities in roles of leadership, then Yale definitely lagged behind its older rival in providing equality of opportunity, at least as seen in the manly sport of football. Harvard had a Black captain in football in 1893, but it was not until 1949 that a Black , Levi Jackson, was captain at Yale and also Yale's first Black player. In 'To the Game: Happy Birthday' Thomas G. Bergin, Sterling professor of Romance languages and literature emeritus at Yale, writing on the occasion of the one-hundredth birthday of the Harvard-Yale football game, says that 'the past four decades have witnessed an impressive enrichment in the ethnic origins of combatants. Slavs, Scandinavians, Hungarians, Lithuanians, Greeks, and Hispanics have joined the ever-more prominent Ausonian segment (Yale's Pagliaro and Diana, Harvard's Gatto and Champi) and the already comfortably installed Irish to reinforce the original Yankee stock'.[40] At the same time there has been no relaxation, in Bergin's view, of academic standards:

> The roll call of players over the years includes poets, men of letters, governors, senators, diplomats, college presidents, and more distinguished doctors, lawyers, and captains of industry then you can shake a goal post at. And doubt not, gentle reader, that the delegations of '83 though the elite is not so restricted as of yore, will achieve their share of renown in the years to come.[41]

Here is an optimism that would have warmed the heart of Charles W. Eliot, in spite of his scepticism of the values of football, and Nathan Hale in site of the primary emphasis he put upon home and church. Both would be able to recognize the heroic ideal at the hundredth anniversary of 'The Game', but both would have been puzzled as to why soldiers and sailors had not also been included in the list of endeavours or occupations in which Harvard and Yale men had distinguished themselves.

The old heroic ideal, then, has been democratised, demilitarised, and 'demasculinised', for want of a better term, though emphasis upon competitive sport and academic achievement remains high. Both women and ethnic minorities may now strive for the ideal with reasonable assurance of being evaluated on their own merits, as is the case now in competition for the Rhodes Scholarship. The drive, though, for financial success and power, which troubled Owen Johnson so much, is still held in high esteem and still calls forth critics, as for example Kurt Vonnegut in *Jail Bird*, in which Harvard graduates show up in all sorts of strange and questionable positions; one, a Chinese Communist in charge of a military prison in North Korea.

We may take comfort in the fact that elements of the heroic ideal are still evident at Harvard and Yale, and more democratic elements at that it might be added, but the gentle scepticism of George Santayana of a century ago does not go away. Are we still going 'partly in the wrong direction?' Even the resurrected ideal seems closely tied to the corporate world and is as far removed from the world of nature as was the older, more aristocratic ideal with its emphasis upon military valour. The transcendental ideal of Henry David Thoreau (Harvard, 1837) seems to have made no more impact upon American educators than it did in the latter half of the nineteenth century. Are not knowledge of nature and knowledge of self the only alternatives of war on the one hand and a bland business ideal on the other? Owen Johnson, for one, seemed to think so.

Eliot was, of course, an admirer of Ralph Waldo Emerson (Harvard, 1821) but on some matters there was a gulf between Emerson and Thoreau, whom Eliot strangely never mentions. Emerson may well have been the founder of 'the cult of athletics', as Eliot argues,[42] but Emerson's enthusiasm for sport was not shared by Thoreau who saw beneath 'the games and amusements of mankind' an 'unconscious despair'.

Both Thoreau and Walt Whitman, whom Thoreau admired, emphasised the union of body and soul throughout their works but it was a synthesis that placed great emphasis upon the instructive power of nature. Thoreau loved to spend afternoons doing nothing but sitting in his doorway and Whitman wanted to 'loafe and invite' his soul. Yet both celebrated the active life, Thoreau going on long walks every day and Whitman chanting the beauties of the open road.

Both Thoreau and Whitman exalted the individual, Whitman making a special point of including women and placing them on a level equal to men. Indeed, while Roosevelt and others promoted manliness, Whitman, largely rejected by his society, also sang the praises of woman even in sports or especially in sports. In 'To a Woman Waits for Me', he says, 'The drops I distil upon you shall grow fierce and athletic girls, new artists, musicians, and singers'. Where the transcendental idealism of Thoreau and Whitman really clashes with heroic idealism, old and new, is not so much along sexual lines as on material wealth and worldly honour. Bergin is obviously proud of 'the captains of industry' who have played for Yale and Harvard, but the highest rank that Thoreau ever attained was 'captain of a huckleberry party', a position that apparently did not impress Eliot or many other Harvards or Yalies. For the most part, he, like Whitman, was simply a party of one.

In the heroic ideal, duty and service are often indistinguishable from the desire for power and glory; in the transcendental ideal little or no emphasis is placed on service but much on the simple joy of living attainable for every individual who wants to grow in self-understanding. One ideal celebrates becoming, the other being. The advice of Thoreau is 'simplify, simplify'; that of Roosevelt 'achieve, achieve' in academics, sports, business or war. Thoreau and Roosevelt both were Harvard men and conservationists, yet the latter, who became an adopted hero of Yale, was never able to appreciate or perhaps even understand the dying words of the former: 'Moose. . . Indians'.[43]

Notes

1 *A Turning Point in Higher Education: The Inaugural Address of Charles William Eliot as President of Harvard College. Oct. 19. 1869*, with an introduction by Nathan M. Pusey, (Cambridge, Mass., Harvard University Press, 1969, p. 17. For a discussion of Eliot's influence upon American culture, see Hugh Hawkins, *Between Harvard and America: The Educational Leadership of Charles W. Eliot*, New York, Oxford University Press, 1971.

2 Brooks Mather Kelley, *Yale: A History*, New Haven and London, Yale University Press, 1974, p. 305.

3 *Memorials of Eminent Yale Men*, New Haven, Conn., Yale University Press, 1915, p. 317.

4 Stokes, pp. 324-5

5 Stokes, p. 319.

6 Kelley, p. 302.

7 *The Stories of F. Scott Fitzgerald*, New York, Scribners, 1951, p. 351.

8 'A Glimpse of Yale', *George Santayana's America: Essays on Literature and Culture*, ed. James Ballowe, Urbana, Ill., University of Illinois Press, 1967, p. 54. See also in this collection 'The Spirit and Ideals of Harvard University'.

9 Kelley, p. 314. See also Roosevelt, 'Yale Men in the Rough Riders', *Works*, 17, pp. 170-3.

10 *Letters of Henry Adams*, 1892-1918, 2, ed. Worthington Chauncey Ford, 1938; reprint ed., Boston, Houghton Mifflin Co., 1969, pp. 34-5.

11 See Larzer Ziff, *The American 1890's*; *Life and Times of a Lost Generation*, New York, The Viking Press, 1966, p. 220.

12 *The Education of Henry Adams*, ed. Ernest Samuels, Boston, Houghton Mifflin, 1973, p. 311.

13 Stokes, p. 76.

14 *Clarence King: A Biography*, New York, The Macmillan Company, 1958, p. 297

15 *Education*, p. 346.

16 Wilkins, pp. 308-9.

17 Quoted in G. Edward White, *The Eastern Establishment and the Western Experience: The West of Frederic Remington, Theodore Roosevelt, and Owen Wister*, New Haven, Yale University Press, 1968, p. 197-8.

18 *The Works of Theodore Roosevelt*, National Edition, 13, New York, Charles Scribner's Sons, 1926, p. 32.

19 Quoted in Hawkins, p. 114.

20 *Rough Riders, Works*, vol. XI, pp. 157.

21 Ben Merchant Vorpahl, *My Dear Wister: The Frederic Remington-Owen Wister Letters*, (Palo Alto, Cal., American West Publishing Co., 1972, p. xviii. For an excellent discussion of the search for the natural aristocrat in early American fiction and culture, see William R. Taylor, Chapter 11, 'From Natural Aristocrat to Country Squire', *Cavalier and Yankee: The Old South and American National Character*, New York, Anchor Books, 1963.

22 White, p. 109.

23 *Frederic Remington: Paintings, Drawings, and Sculpture in the Amon Carter Museum and the Sid W. Richardson Foundation Collections*, New York, Harry N. Abrams, 1973, p. 19. Also see p. 101. A book depicting the 'manliness' theme in Remington's art is *The Illustrations of Frederic Remington* with an introduction by Owen Wister and edited by Marta Jackson, New York, Crown, 1970.

24 Stokes, p. 127.

25 Quoted in Vorpahl, p. 312.

26 Vorpahl, p. 237.

27 White, p. 121.

28 *Frank Merriwell's 'Father': An Autobiography* by Gilbert Patten (Burt L. Standish), eds. Harriet Hinsdale and Tony London, Norman, Oklahoma, University of Oklahoma Press, 1964, p. 178.

29 Robert Boyle, 'The unreal ideal: Frank Merriwell', *Sport-Mirror of American Life*, Boston, Little Brown Co., 1963, p. 242. See particularly in Boyle the Section 'At Yale'. See Also Patten, ch. 23, 'The Yale Spirit', *Frank Merriwell at Yale*, Philadelphia, David McKay, 1903.

30 Russel B. Nye, 'The Juvenile Approach to American Culture, *1870*-1930', *New Voices in American Studies*, eds. Ray B. Browne, Donald M. Winkleman and Allen Hayman, Lafayette, Indiana, Purdue Research Foundation, 1966, p. 75. As Robert Boyle points out, Frank was a 'halfback' as a freshman and the length of time that Frank matriculated at Yale seems unsettled. Nye says nine, while Heywood Hale Broun said eight, to which claim Patten objected in good humour. 'Tain't so, Heywood, 'tain't so. Either there was malice in your assertion or your memory played you a bum trick. He got only the usual four years, much as I would like to have stretched it. Of course in a later yarn he did go back to Yale as a Coach. . . I allowed Frank to do a lot of things a college man couldn't do. . . but I didn't keep him in Yale eight or ten years, honest I didn't'. *Frank Merriwell's "Father"*, p. 306.

31 Nye, p. 76.

32 Nye, pp. 77, 84.

33 *Frank Merriwell's "Father"*, p. 307. Boyle confirms the story and says that 'any number of students have gone to Yale because of him [Frank], ranging from the athletic to the intellectual. . ., among them Jordan Oliver, the Yale coach from 1952-62, who said he

would make Frank his quarterback, (Boyle, pp. 245-6). Frank, quite obviously, could play anwhere in the backfield – and the line too, no doubt.

34   Michael J. Halberstam, 'Stover at the Barricades', *American Scholar* 38, Summer 1969, p. 470.

35   *Stover at Yale*, 1912; reprint ed. New York, The Macmillan Company, 1968, p. 195.

36   Johnson, p. 308.

37   Halberstam, pp. 472-3.

38   Kingman Brewster, Jr, Introduction to *Stover at Yale*, p. vii.

39   See, for example, 'Twilight of the Idols', *The Portable Nietzsche*, Walter Kaufmann, trans. & ed., New York, Viking Press, 1964, pp. 540-1 and *The World as Will and Idea*, 3 vols., trans. R. B. Haldane and J. Kemp, London, Routledge, & Kegan Paul, 1883, 3, pp. 300-1. For discussion of the differences between Nietzsche and Schopenhauer in regard to recurrence, see Joan Stambaugh, *Nietzsche's Thought of Eternal Return*, Baltimore, The John Hopkins Universiy Press, 1972, pp. 77-9 and 97-9.

40   Thomas G. Bergin, 'To the Game: Happy Birthday', *Harvard Magazine*, November-December 1983, p. 33. See also Bergin's book, *The Game: The Harvard-Yale Football Rivalry*, 1875-1983, New Haven and London, Yale University Press, 1984, p. 73, and 'The Upper Class: Harvard-Yale Weekend' in Boyle, Ch. 6.

41   Bergin, pp. 29-30.

42   Charles W. Eliot, *Four American Leaders*, Folcraft, Pa., Folcraft Library Editins, 1907, p. 95.

43   Joseph Wood Krutch, Introduction, *Walden and Other Writings*, New York, Bantam, 1965, p. 19. That Theodore Roosevelt seemed almost oblivious to the works of Thoreau is also a point made by Henry A. Beers in *Four Americans: Roosevelt, Hawthorne, Emerson, Whitman*, New Haven, Yale University Press, 1919. Beers says that he doesn't even mention Thoreau, but a member of the Roosevelt Memorial Committee brought one reference to his attention in *The Wilderness Hunter*, p. 261: 'As a woodland writer Thoreau comes second only to Burroughs'. Beers says that Francis Parkman had contempt for philosophers like Emerson and Thoreau and that Roosevelt had a similar inclination. Beers, pp. 13-14. There is no mention of Thoreau's name in the index of the national edition of Roosevelt's works in 1919 – nor of Emerson's or Eliot's. Roosevelt was too far to the right of all of them to take much notice of what they were saying, to say nothing of the differences between them. Roosevelt, after all, did not dwell on philosophical distinctions but manly action.

The imperial pioneer and hunter and the British masculine stereotype in late Victorian and Edwardian times

'Every boy ought to learn how to shoot and to obey orders, else he is no more good when war breaks out than an old woman.'[1]

This injunction appeared in the opening camp fire yarn of the first edition of R. S. S. Baden-Powell's *Scouting for Boys* of 1908. It perfectly encapsulates concepts of manliness which were conveyed through youth organisations, popular images, juvenile literature and many other texts in the late Victorian and Edwardian periods. Discipline for the young was to take precise forms: obeying orders from elders and superiors, training in firearms, acceptance of violence as part of the natural order, preparation for war and a strict separation of sexual roles.

Baden-Powell's ideas on the training of boys emerged out of Lord Edward Cecil's Boy Scout troop formed in Mafeking during the siege of 1899-1900 and almost all his notions came from the imperial frontier. In distinguishing between war and peace scouts, his examples of the latter were drawn entirely from that frontier. He defined them as 'men who in peace time carry out work which requires the same type of abilities' as in war:

These are the frontiersmen of all parts of our Empire. The 'trappers' of North America, hunters of Central Africa, the British pioneers, explorers,

THE IMPERIAL PIONEER AND HUNTER 177

and missionaries over Asia and all the wild parts of the world, the bushmen and drovers of Australia, the constabulary of North-West Canada and of South Africa – all are peace scouts, real *men* in every sense of the word, and thoroughly up on scout craft, i.e. they understand living out in the jungles, and they can find their way anywhere, are able to read meaning from the smallest signs and foot-tracks; they know how to look after their health when far away from any doctors, are strong and plucky, and ready to face any danger, and always keen to help each other. They are accustomed to take their lives in their hands, and to fling them down without hesitation if they can help their country by doing so.[2]

They give up their personal comforts and desires, he went on, because it is their duty to their King and the history of the Empire has been made by such men. Pioneering attributes appear on many other pages of *Scouting for Boys*. The men who come from the furthest frontiers of the Empire, wrote Baden-Powell, are 'the most generous and chivalrous of their race'. Their moral worth was acquired through their 'contact with Nature'. They cultivated 'truth, independence, and self-reliance'. Boxing, wrestling, and Japanese martial arts were recommended to Scouts in pursuit of these virtues, as was, above all, the importance of marksmanship: 'the Colonial boys consider marksmanship the most important thing to practise, because it is for their country. They put cricket and football second, because these are for their own amusement.'[3]

Scouting for Boys became one of the twentieth century's best-sellers and several generations of boys were initiated into frontier lore through secret signs, animal names and calls, woodcraft, stalking and spooring. The current edition (1981) contains the paragraph on frontiersmen quoted above almost in its entirety, with just a few geographical adjustments to fit modern scouting, and with all mention of Empire excised. The passage is now accompanied by a drawing of 'frontiersmen' that modern boys would immediately associate with the 'Wild West'. This indeed perfectly represents the transformation wrought in the image of the frontier by popular culture, primarily the cinema, in the twentieth century.

Baden-Powell's manual for boys did not of course manufacture the frontier stereotype, nor was it the first to hold it up as a prime model for boys at home. Rather did it mark the climax of a process in which images of frontier manliness were fed back into the metropolis and became an established feature of a variety of popular cultural forms. Britain's imperial frontier was not a continental one, like the American, but a highly dispersed phenomenon in different continents and highly varied environments. Baden-Powell's own experience had been primarily in India and southern Africa, but he was at pains to include examples from North America, Australasia and other parts of the Empire. Yet a composite image was established in which different conditions nonetheless contributed to a set of characteristics Baden-Powell wished to inculcate. In examining masculine stereotypes in the late Victorian and Edwardian periods, their transmission through popular culture and youth organisations and their effects on such phenomena as the dramatic recruitment for the First World War, we shall be formulating something approaching a cultural frontier thesis for British attitudes to masculinity.

There was indeed a close interaction between British and American concepts of the frontier and no one created the bridge between them more effectively than Theodore Roosevelt. Rancher, soldier, big-game hunter and President, Roosevelt seemed to typify the frontier spirit and he was an untiring propagandist for it. Baden-Powell referred to his example and his works with approval. For Roosevelt, the pioneer and cowboy 'possesses, in fact, few of the emasculated, milk-and-water moralities of the pseudo-philanthropist; but he does possess, to a very high degree, the stern, manly qualities that are invaluable to a nation'.[4] Above all, the pioneer is a hunter and the hunter is 'the archetype of freedom'.[5] He is self-sufficient not just in food, but, if needs be, in clothing and deer-skins for his bunk. Roosevelt was an Anglophile whose admiration for the British Empire is apparent in a number of his works. His closest contacts were with British big-game hunters, for whose works he supplied an apparently endless stream of introductions, and he liked to compare himself as a naturalist with them.[6] For Baden-Powell hunting also constituted the essence of the pioneering spirit, the source of all the attributes that prepared the peace scout for war. This is apparent in his list of frontiersmen above; it was also depicted as a source of fun and adventure:

> All the fun of hunting lies in the adventurous life in the jungle, the chance in many cases of the animal hunting *you* instead of you hunting the animal, the interest of tracking him up, stalking him and watching all that he does and learning his habits. The actual shooting the animal that follows is only a very small part of the fun.[7]

He recommended as further reading the works of the big-game hunter, Colonel Stigand, and *Deer-Stalking* in the Badminton Library.

Treitschke saw imperialism as the mark of 'virile nations'.[8] The nationals of these nations expressed their virility through their capacity to dominate their environment and they did that largely by a combination of hunting, killing and classification. It was in hunting that the most perfect expression of global dominance could be discovered in the late nineteenth century. Hunting required all the most virile attributes of the imperial male; courage, endurance, individualism, sportsmanship (combining the moral etiquette of the sportsman with both horsemanship and marksmanship), resourcefulness, a mastery of environmental signs and a knowledge of natural history. It was indeed that scientific dimension, the acquisition of zoological, botanical, meteorological and ballistic knowledge, and the ordering and classifying of natural phenomena which went with it, which helped to give hunting its supreme acceptability among late Victorians.

It was, moreover, capacity in the Hunt which marked out the virile from the 'effeminate' imperialist. The Germans were confident and effective hunters. So were the Americans, particularly as expressed in the stereotype Roosevelt created in his many works on hunting and pioneering. The Portuguese, on the other hand, were not great hunters and for contemporaries it showed in their empire. Spanish imperial decline was accelerated, according to one hunter, when the Spanish aristocracy gave up hunting and bullfighting and became 'frenchified and effeminate'.[9] With some individual exceptions, neither the French nor the Belgians were among the first ranks of hunters either. They were too epicurean, waxing fat on food and wine and preferring the sexual expression of native harems to the sexual sublimation of the hunt.[10]

The connections between hunting and sex and between imperialism and sexual separation are indeed close. The Hunt has always been a masculine affair, though there has never been any taboo, in Europe at least, on high-born women being present as spectators as well as, occasionally, participants. Fox-hunting had been virtually an all-male preserve until the middle of the nineteenth century.[11] From the 1860s and 70s more and more women followed the hounds, but, at the same time, other forms of hunting became more exclusively male. The immense popularity of stag-hunting in Scotland, which saw some two million acres of Highlands turned over to deer forests by 1884, placed renewed emphasis on masculinty,[12] as did big-game hunting and the pioneering life in general. Many hunters stressed the fact that the imperial hunt was no place for a women, though some women did participate and some turned it into a powerful expression of female emancipation of sorts. By Edwardian times more women were hunting and by the 1920s Sir Iain Colquhoun of Luss was putting down the declining popularity of stag-hunting to the revolt of women.[13] They could participate in fox-hunting and in grouse and pheasant shooting since, even if they themselves did not shoot, they could converse with the men at the butts between drives. In India, only the most senior of women had participated in the tiger shoot from the relatively safe perch of an elephant's back.

In any case, the presence of some women only served to emphasise the sexual symbolism of the Hunt. Generally the object of the Hunt was the male of the species. The Hunt became a vital part of the collecting mania of the period, the collection of horns and skins representing in their very inutility western man's dominance of the world. Horns perfectly symbolised the war of males for sexual conquest. They indicated to a Darwinian age the sexual selection of the fittest. The fascination with horn size and the achievement of record dimensions, stimulated by the publication of the taxidermist Rowland Ward's books of records, had deeply sexual connotations, implicitly recognised at the time, which Sir Richard Burton took to logical human lengths in his anatomical studies. When two women went big-game hunting in the Horn of North-East Africa in 1907 and published their adventures in a spirited and amusing volume *Two Dianas in Somaliland*, their bringing down of males of the species and their search for notable trophies had a particular piquancy.[14] Diana was, after all, the goddess not only of the hunt but also of chastity.

Hunting can readily be interpreted as sexual sublimation. Hunting works are full of descriptions of the physical agonies of the Hunt, of 'the exaltation no civilised world can supply', the tensions induced by the great risk and the ecstasy of release when the hunter prevails and stands over his kill.[15] Hunting created a link with man's primeval past, a contact with 'matters primitive and elemental'.[16] Moreover, collecting is invariably an emotional substitute and the collection of animal trophies came to be inseparably bound up with the separate male worlds of the Victorian and Edwardian periods.

Sexual separation is often a characteristic of dominant societies. The military, administrative and travelling imperatives of imperialism dictated it and, no less than in Sparta or among the Zulu, the training and socialisation of the young became increasingly directed towards this end. Public schools, youth organisations, juvenile literature, the club and the army mess were all expressions of it, as were strictly segregated working-men's clubs and school staff-rooms. In the extending and building of country houses and public buildings in this period, the provision of the male sanctum became an architectural necessity.[17] The billiard room, the game itself redolent of sexual symbolism, became the male preserve, asserting its masculinity through the dark browns and green baize of its decoration and, above all, the animal skins on the floor and the horns around its walls. The officers' messes of barracks at home and in the empire were similarly adorned and the fashion reached public buildings, hotels, pubs, middle-class homes, schools and even ships at sea.[18] Horns were everywhere, if often relegated to the indignity of acting merely as hatstands. The vast sale of antlers, skins and curious items like elephant feet (used as umbrella stands or stools) and trays made of oryx skin illustrated the manner in which non-hunters wished to bask in the reflected glory of the Hunt. The contrast in interior decoration between the billiard room or the smoking room – dark, sombre and assertively adorned – and the ladies' boudoir – softer, pastel-shaded and chintz bedecked – represents sexual separation through domestic aesthetics.

Hunting was closely bound up with the symbolism of imperialism. Many a literary nimrod summoned up St George as his exemplar.[19] The iconography of St George, ubiquitous in the period, with all its military, equestrian, moral and sexually protective, chivalric overtones, was repeatedly linked to the Hunt. The slaying of the dragon represented the ultimate in justified killing which, when transferred to big-game hunting, represented the victory of civilised man over the darker, primeval and untamed forces still at work in the world. The other was the lion, the king of beasts that the British tried so successfully to annex as a national and imperial symbol. The lion was everywhere; rampant, couchant, passant, in a whole variety of moods – the epitome of the virile Empire itself. The lion lies at the centre of hunting books too. F. C. Selous, one of the greatest of the late-nineteenth-century hunters and the model for Rider Haggard's Allan Quatermain, extolled the excitement of lion hunting above all others.[20] The lion, he wrote, had been a souce of fascination and awe to him since he had been a child. He revelled in his thirty-one lion kills and in the collection of skins he had made. His sentiments were echoed in a host of other hunting books. It was as though the virile imperialist and the lion – or in India the tiger – were locked in deadly contest for control of the natural world. One hunter, exercising the god-like power of the imperial nimrod, allowed a beautiful lesser kudu to go free.[21] Later its carcase was found, killed by a lion. Control, thus flouted, had to be reasserted. The lion was hunted down and killed. If St George with his dragon and the lion were the most notable imperial icons of the age, heraldry too carried a host of animal and hunting symbols and families like the Grosvenors tried to establish their links with great hunters of the past.

Such symbols and icons were the stock-in-trade of publishing and there were few areas of that rapidly expanding trade that were more overloaded with works than hunting and sport. A survey of the bibliography of hunting uncovers a vast literature in which almost all publishers participated.[22] There were complete libraries of sport, in which hunting always figured prominently, like the Badminton and Lonsdale libraries. Some publishers, like Seeley Service, issued large numbers of sporting accounts and anthologies of hunting stories were compiled for younger readers. The proliferation of such works was noted by contemporaries. One hunter suggested that 'Few subjects have elicited more literature than has Indian sport'.[23] Another wrote: 'I am aware that of the making of sporting books there is no end.'[24] In each case, 'sport' in fact meant hunting and, indeed, nothing is more indicative of the importance of hunting in the period than the manner in which 'sport', in certain contexts, became synonymous with it. The percolation downwards of this kind of material into juvenile literature will be examined below.

The great wealth of hunting publications was supplemented by the iconography of the Hunt. It was of course Sir Edwin Landseer who did most to establish hunting images as among the prime popular visual experiences of the age.[25] His stags at bay, being killed, or as carcases in the process of being transformed into venison, together with his stream of animal paintings, almost all associated with hunting, enjoyed an immense vogue as prints. In them he successfully conveyed the sensuality of killing, as well as converting gore into an everyday, sacramental experience. He also helped – with their entire approval – to associate the Royal Family with hunting images. A veritable army of engravers turned out sub-Landseer depictions of hunting scenes for juvenile literature and journals. Well-authenticated events, like the attack of the lion upon David Livingstone, were illustrated repeatedly to demonstrate the heroism of the missionary-explorer. In the craze for natural history it was never enough simply to provide neutral representations of wild animals; they were usually shown in conjunction with humans so the moral of human dominance and danger through discovery and understanding could be drawn. Tins, packagings, plates, textiles and furniture also became repositories of hunting images.

The etiquette of hunting was equally extensive and elaborate and it marked the shift from an 'economic' hunting, hunting as a subsidy for imperial advance, to the Hunt as an elite code. Of course there remained in many places a great gulf between theory and reality but the often indiscriminate hunting of pioneer and settler was generally kept from the cultural record. The rules were laid out repeatedly in the vast hunting literature and adherence to them was the mark of the imperial gentleman, distinguishing the sportsman from the butcher.[26] The 'sporting' code was a crucial identifier not only of the ruling race but of class, training and breeding within that race. As 'conservation' policies developed, the tendency of game laws was to restrict access to game precisely to the 'sportsman' class. This tendency to upward exclusiveness in participation in the Hunt had occurred in most societies with developed elites in both Europe and the wider world. Now it occurred on a global scale, with the upper echelon of a white imperial elite gradually attempting to restrict access to game to itself. As in Britain in the eighteenth and nineteenth centuries, 'preservation' and 'conservation' were used as the justificatory ideologies for this process. Hunting was transformed from a pioneering survival system into an elite ritual.[27]

The most 'sporting' way to hunt game was to stalk it; to use, paradoxically enough, all the techniques of the 'primitive' hunter to 'spoor' game, understand its habits, and attempt by stealth to approach to a range at which a shot had a good chance of producing an instantaneous kill. It was at this point, in the realm of advanced technology, that the 'sporting' hunter diverged from the native hunters whom he invariably used as his auxiliaries. When the object was ivory, their intentions were the same – economic gain – but by the end of the century the object was more likely to be the acquisition of trophies and specimens. Increasingly, the African hunter found the objectives of the European inexplicable. Large quantities of meat were left on the hoof while immense labour was put into the singling out and securing of a particular trophy. The achievement of the latter introduced the next range of rules.

Generally the sporting hunter was interested only in males. In some species the females carried horns and consequently made themselves vulnerable. One hunter remarked that it served them right for taking on male characteristics. In the case of the big cats, the skins of either sex were equally desirable. To kill a female with cubs was, however, distinctly unsporting. In pig-sticking in India, sows were always left alone, It was only the boar, marked by his great tushes, which was fair game. In shooting, the hunter had to approach close enough to identify sex, age and quality of trophy of the animal. He had to shoot to kill and not to wound. He had to understand the anatomy of his quarry sufficiently well to know where to place a heart or a brain shot. If he inflicted a wound which was not mortal he was under an obligation to follow the animal to deliver the *coup de grâce*, however far it took him and however much discomfort he had to endure in the process. The mark of the ungentlemanly hunter was to fire indiscriminately into herds, as Americans tended to do (at least so it was thought), to hand over firearms to Africans and expect them to do the hunting or to charge African trackers with the task of following wounded animals. Although Theodore Roosevelt was often held up for emulation as a model pioneering and hunting figure who also became an imperial politician, the true gentlemanly sportsmen, like Sir Frederick Jackson, disapproved of his somewhat indiscriminate methods.[28] Later, technology created new hazards for the sporting code. Denis Lyell expressed horror at the practice of chasing animals in motor vehicles, using mechanical devices to run animals to a stop before killing them.[29] In the First World War young aviators had even attempted to shoot and bomb animals from the air. Shooting from river steamers and trains had been quite common in the 1890s before animals fled from transportation routes but incurred the wrath of the true hunter.

Other hunting techniques received the stamp of disapproval too. White hunters were sometimes, but not always, respectful of African bushcraft but they deprecated African hunting methods which they saw as haphazard and cruel. That helped to justify restrictive game laws as well as keep modern firearms out of African hands. In India, some of the Indian princes kept cheetahs and leopards and used them to hunt black buck. In 1921 the Prince of Wales was taken to view such a hunt in Baroda but one account of his journeys described the technique as a distinctly unsporting and un-British way of doing things and the experience was not repeated.[30]

Hunting from a machan, a tree platform, using a live animal or carcase as bait was also not considered sporting. Luring the animal (in this case always the big cats) to the hunter was not considered to be giving the animal a 'sporting' chance. Indeed, it was the supposed effort to even the odds, giving the quarry the chance to pit its skill against that of the hunter, which was the essence of sportsmanship. All hunters relished the dangers of hunting and retold in macabre and admiring detail tales of serious injury and deaths among their fellow hunters.[31] (They tended to be phlegmatic about the deaths of African trackers, which occurred frequently.) Hunting with bait from a platform was acceptable only in the case of securing a man-eater that might have been terrorising a local community. Big-game hunters in Africa (at least those who published) were particularly scathing about these methods, although there seems to have been fewer scruples about them in India. In the ultimate in elite hunting, the Indian tiger shoot, the very essence of the hunt was driving the tiger into the range of the distinguished nimrods on elephant-back.

The true hunter, according to many of the African authorities, hunted alone (apart from local trackers, bearers etc.). It was a much more satisfying experience and it avoided bickering over kills. If a party went on a hunting expedition, then it was recommended that they should separate, sometimes for weeks on end, for the actual business of hunting. Where the imperial hunters did hunt together (which was more common in India), then there were elaborate rules as to who took the first shot and who secured the kill. 'First blood' was the vital honour and ought to receive the prize even if another hunter actually did the killing. This was particularly true in team hunting such as pig-sticking. There were also territorial rules. As parties of hunters began to spread out into many parts of Africa and India, inevitably they encountered rival groups. In the appropriate season of the year a small army of hunters would head up into the northern fastnesses of Kashmir in search of ibex, bear and markhor. The sporting hunter never impinged on a rival's territory. If it was clear that a hunter had begun to shoot in a particular valley or region, then it was the new arrival's duty to move on to find another hunting ground for himself. For this reason, one military hunter heading for some weeks' leave in Kashmir indulged in forced marches in order to overhaul other hunting parties en route.[32]

The true sportsman was unselfish in other respects too. An Indian hunter who claimed to have shot a hundred tigers was considered a 'selfish old swine' by a rival.[33] Sir John Hewitt was held up for emulation. Although he was described as being keen on the preservation of game, it was said that 250 tigers had been shot in his presence, only forty to his own rifle.[34] He liked to see to it that subalterns being trained in the Hunt had their proper opportunity. Sir Bindon Blood, G.O.C. Northern Command in India had been present at the killing of 150 tigers, fifty-two to his own rifle, a somewhat less meritorious proportion it would seem and commensurate, perhaps, with his name.

The genuine sportsman also took the leading role in preparing and caring for his trophies. Whether horns, head or skins, great care had to be taken with the removal, preservation and transportation so that perfect specimens could be returned for wall mounting, floor covering or handing over to the taxidermist for stuffing. While it was permissible for the sportsman to leave the heaviest labour to his many helpers, the essential work should be his responsibility, a test of patience and skill. At home, taxidermy remained a high street service, with taxidermists active in most towns. The elite went to Rowland Ward of Piccadilly or Edward Gerrard and Sons of Camden Town, each having their devotees. Others, like Colonel Harrison of Cumbria who eventually handed over all his collection to Kendal Museum, took their trophies to a local taxidermist like H. Murray and Sons of Carnforth, who often spoilt the exotic effect by using local grasses and mosses in casing the smaller animals.[35]

This elaborate code was vital to the hunting ethos and it was used to illustrate the moral training aspects of the Hunt. Baden-Powell frequently alluded to the code in *Scouting for Boys*: 'No scout should ever kill an animal unless there is some real reason for doing so, and in that case he should kill it quickly and effectively, so as to give it as little pain as possible.'[36] It is interesting that the main exception he gave was: 'when you and your natives are hungry, then you must of course kill your game'. The code was a central part of the juvenile literature of the Hunt at one end of the class spectrum, vital in the identification of the imperial elite at the other.

Hunting, as well as representing the prime activity and survival technique of the pioneering figure, had two vital functions for an imperial 'race'. It was a distinguishing characteristic and a vital training for the imperial elite and, as in so many societies throughout the ages, distinctiveness was sanctioned by legal restrictions. The second role of hunting, one much stressed in the late nineteenth and early twentieth centuries, was as a training ground for war. These two functions of the Hunt will be examined in turn.

Hunting in India , and later in Africa, perfectly represented the class and racial relationships of the imperial social structure. While there were gradations of status among local porters, trackers, beaters, bearers and hunters, the different forms of hunting also marked gradations of status among the elite. Pig-sticking was primarily a military sport which helped, according to Baden-Powell, to bring soldiers and peasants together into a common pursuit, offering opportunities for earnings to local peoples.[37] Most district administrators hunted, partly to assert their status, partly to protect the communities of their human charges, partly to supply themselves with trophies and sometimes to augment their salaries. The upper elite partook of tiger hunting or duck and wildfowl shooting on the lakes and marshes of the Indian princely states. Planters and box wallahs of the towns attempted to break in on the charmed circle but were invariably rejected as indifferent shots and inadequate hunting parvenus. In Africa, white settler access to hunting was progressively restricted by game laws and hunting again became the perquisite of the administrative and military elite joined by the end of the century by visiting members of the aristo-military caste from home. The white Dominions, on the other hand, generally had a more democratic approach to hunting opportunities. This was, for example, one of the stated attractions of New Zealand as a territory for settlement. There, ordinary people had access to hunting and equestrianism such as would be beyond their legal and economic reach at home. Though there were game laws, hunting was 'almost unrestricted and unpoliced'.[38]

In such a hierarchical scheme of things it was essential that the most notable hunting feats were performed by those at the apex of the social order. The Prince of Wales, the future Edward VII, devoted much time to hunting on his visit to India and Ceylon in 1875. George V on his 1911 tour of India for the Coronation Durbar was sufficiently adept with the rifle to be proclaimed a great shikari (a 'Bayard in the Realm of Sport') in the dedication of one hunting book.[39] Another Prince of Wales, the future Edward VIII, hunted frequently on his visit to India in 1921-2. The distaste of his party for hunting by means of surrogate cheetahs has already been described but all other forms of hunting were acceptable. Sixty 'loyal duck' (as the Maharajah put it in an after-dinner speech) fell to his gun at Bikaner.[40] His first tiger was shot in Nepal to earn him the plaudits of the notable tiger hunters, while Baden-Powell dedicated a later edition of his book on pig-sticking to him. The Prince of Wales had 'in the pig-sticking field proved himself in the fuller sense of the word a Prince among Sportsmen'.[41] The Prince had killed boars in Jodhpur and Patiala, while he had participated in, and won, the finals of the Kadir Cup pig-sticking competition at Meerut. He had shown his 'pluck' in 'ding-dong horsemanship'.[42] One account of the Prince's tours took care to justify pig-sticking ('a wild, exhilarating sport' in which 'the pig has a better chance than in any other form of big-game chase' and those who take part run 'considerable risk') and went on to quote a speech in which the Prince had lectured Indian students on the importance of games.[43] On his arrival in Nepal the Prince was greeted by the ultimate in welcoming banners: 'Hearty Welcome to Britain's Sporting Prince'. All of these exploits were lovingly retold in the many popular works for adults and children which described his world tours.

In the absence of royalty, governors and viceroys had to display similar prowess in the Hunt. Many of the most famous African governors, Sir Frederick Lugard, Sir Alfred Sharpe, Sir Robert Coryndon, Sir Frederick Jackson and Sir Geoffrey Archer, had begun their careers as hunters and built their political power, in effect, on their hunting expertise. Some of the Indian viceroys, like the Marquis of Ripon, were among the most distinguished hunters of their day. There are many fascinating records of the social relations and markers of prestige in the Hunt but one example will suffice. At Hopetoun House in the Lothians, the great Adam Palace of the Marquises of Linlithgow, there are detailed records of the hunting bags of the third Marquis when he was viceroy in the 1930s. He made frequent visits to the princely states to shoot and printed records of each day's activity indicate the social etiquette powerfully at work. The viceroy, with rare exceptions, always secured the largest bag, followed by the Maharajah and then by the vicereine (if shooting) and the Maharajah's heir apparent. On one occasion, in the state of Bikaner, the heir apparent got so far above himself as to shoot more duck than the viceroy, a social solecism no doubt attended by a combination of family recrimination and wry comment on the part of the British.[44] In all of these exploits it is clear that hunting was a vital mediator in the feudal relationship of crown, viceroy and princes or, in Africa, governors, black kings, chiefs and askaris. The connections with the social relations of the mediaeval Hunt are apparent. It was not the least of the atavisms of imperialism.

Just as Baden-Powell exphasised the connections between war and peace scouting, so was the role of hunting as a preparation for war frequently stressed. A number of military hunters, Baden-Powell included, wrote books on these connections.[45] They regarded hunting as an essential training in the understanding of terrain, analysing the reactions of foe, courage, endurance, horsemanship and marksmanship. Pig-sticking brought out a combination of competitiveness with *esprit de corps*. Many colonial campaigns became a mixture of hunting and warfare. Troops had to be supplied with meat and officers required relaxation. In guerrilla campaigns, like that against the Shona and Ndebele of 1896-7, Africans swiftly became the human substitute for the usual animal prey. Baden-Powell constantly stressed that the scouting and stalking techniques of the Hunt could immediately be transferred to human quarry in times of war. Hunting was also, though this was never explicitly stated, a preparation for the violence and brutalities of war.[46] By brutalising themselves in the blood of the chase, the military prepared themselves for an easy adjustment to human warfare, particularly in an age so strongly conditioned by social Darwinian ideas on race. Moreover, colonial campaigns were frequently described in the language of sport. The irony is of course that war in the twentieth-century was to be very different from the colonial campaigns of late Victorian and Edwardian times and all the training of the Hunt was to count for nothing in trench warfare. Nevertheless, the code remained in place and, on the outbreak of the First World War, it was frequently averred that 'war was the highest form of all sport'.[47] Again, it is easy to give the last word to Baden-Powell. For him, pig-sticking was essential training for subalterns because it was the 'brutal and most primitive of all hunts' in which death was 'the whole aim of the run'. It combined the 'mêlée of the polo-field' with a 'savage quarry to be warily hunted and boldly fought'. It was a sport in which 'blind to all else but the strong and angered foe before you, with your good spear in your hand, you rush for blood with all the ecstasy of a fight to the death'.[48]

Alarming though that sounds, Baden-Powell was always anxious to temper bloodlusts wih humour. He quoted with approval one old shikari's motto: 'Dum Spiro Spearo' and part of the hunting code seems to have been a love of japes, jokes and ruses. Baden Powell loved them and other hunters like Lyell and de Crespigny found them an essential part of sportsmanship. It is an interesting fact that one of the greatest artistic figures of the age, Sir Edward Elgar, was also an enthusiastic perpetrator of japes. It was all part of the 'boyish masters' effect, a concern to avoid a too serious approach to imperial rule. Many administrators were thoroughly irritated when interrupted by work when out hunting. The Indian official, Sir Henry Ramsay, known as the 'King of Kumaon', was enraged at having to deal with urgent business on a tiger hunt.[49] Sir Frederick Jackson was notoriously bored by his administration in East Africa, merely writing on each unopened file 'I concur'.[50] It is not surprising that he fell out with the scholar, linguist and administrator, Sir Charles Eliot, who disapproved of hunting. It was a tradition of easygoing administration, carefully avoiding the stigma of the 'swot', continued by the celebrated Colonial Office recruiter Ralph Furse in the inter-war years. It was an essential part of the public-school code of athleticism which was pressed upon the other, imitative, educational sectors.

It has indeed frequently been noticed that the late Victorian and Edwardian periods were a time when the framers of educational policies, popular literary tastes and youth organisations were intent on a 'downward filtration' effect. There was a conscious effort to sweep up the lower class into a fascination with the pursuits and moral codes of the elite. The fact that these could be placed in a context of romance and adventure greatly helped the process. Schools were caught up in the natural history craze, making collections of birds eggs, insects and even stuffed animals. The iconography of the Hunt appeared upon their walls. The universities promoted these interests too. A Master of Brasenose College, Oxford in the late nineteenth century was noted for insisting that his students hunted. 'Ride, Sir, ride,' he told the future Earl Haig, 'we like to see our gentlemen here in top boots'.[51]

There was a long tradition of highlighting hunting as a wellspring of the pioneering and adventure tradition in juvenile literature. From America, the works of Fenimore Cooper, like *The Deerslayer* or *The Pioneers* perfectly reflected it. They date from the 1820s and 30s and were invariably set in the eighteenth century but by the end of the nineteenth century they embarked on a new period of immense popularity. There were cheap editions of Fenimore Cooper from a variety of publishers and they became a favourite staple of the prize and present market. Cooper's description of young Deerslayer, dressed in his deerskins, was the image all hunters liked to convey: he stood six feet tall in his moccasins, his frame 'comparatively light and slender; showing muscles, however, that promised unusual agility, if not unusual strength'.[52] His facial expression was that of 'guileless truth, sustained by an earnestness of purpose, and a sincerity of feeling, that rendered it remarkable'. The code was there too. When Deerslayer's companion offered him some venison, the manly young hunter responded 'Nay, nay, Hurry, there's little manhood in killing a doe, and that, too, out of season'. An illustrated Collins edition which enjoyed large sales early this century had colour pictures not only of Red Indian foes but also of stags attempting to escape the hunters' bullets. At the end of Cooper's *The Pioneers*, the old hunter stands on the verge of the wood, the symbolic edge of civilisation, before disappearing for ever. 'He had gone far towards the setting sun – the foremost in that band of Pioneers who are opening the way for the march of the nation across the continent'.[53]

Youth and age, guileless, noble, self-reliant, killing to survive and to spread civilisation, illustrating at every turn the mastery that was wrought of technical advance, environmental knowledge and moral worth: these were the images conveyed by a host of works written for children in the later nineteenth century. W. H. G. Kingston, who was himself a propagandist for emigration and settlement in the Empire, pioneered this taste for the British market.[54] His works included *Peter the Whaler, Hendricks the Hunter, In the Wilds of Africa* and *In the Wilds of Florida*. R. M. Ballantyne, who had spent his early career as a fur trapper and factor in the Hudson's Bay Company, incorporated hunting into almost all his works. Many of his titles were explicit, as in *The Gorilla Hunters, The Walrus Hunters, The Buffalo Runners* and *Hunting the Lion*.[55] Captain Mayne Reid, another of the classic boys' writers from the third quarter of the nineteenth century, was equally obsessed with hunting; *The Boy Hunters, The Young Voyageurs, The Young Yägers, Bruin or the Grand Bear Hunt, The Giraffe Hunters* and *The Wild Horse Hunters* are but a selection from his hunting titles. Contemporary obsessions with all forms of natural history were reflected in his *The Plant Hunters*. In the later period, H. Rider Haggard's books, a popular staple for British boys until at least the 1950s, are full of hunting. His principal characters were based on famous hunters of the day: Allan Quatermain on F. C. Selous and Captain Goode on Sir Frederick Jackson.[56] Haggard's brother was a vice-consul in East Africa and Jackson, a family friend and Norfolk neighbour who went to Africa as a hunter, was employed by the Imperial British East Africa Company and later became Governor of Uganda, fed Haggard with hunting stories for inclusion in his novels.

These are but the most obvious examples of the immense juvenile hunting literature of the period, a tradition carried on today by some of the boys' books of Willard Price. Perhaps even more importantly, hunting – in both factual and fictional accounts – became a prime subject for the boys' journals which struck a winning formula after the founding of the *Boy's Own Paper* in 1879. Patrick Dunae, who has closely studied the periodical juvenilia, has noted the obsession with hunting within their pages.[57] The Ballantyne tradition, which never spared any gory detail, was continued there. The moral and 'sporting' code of hunting was repeatedly laid out for junior edification. Detailed descriptions of taxidermy were offered at just the time that the natural history craze was reaching schools and local museums everywhere. Such hunting material offered a bloody substitute for the penny dreadfuls which one hunter described as 'manlier stuff' than the melodrama of the twentieth century cinema.[58]

Youthful fascination with animals and hunting is a significant element in many memoirs of the day. Baden-Powell had been gripped by the natural history craze as a boy. It was an important component in Charles Kingsley's muscular Christianity. Gordon Stables, one of the most popular of boys' writers, collected natural history specimens, while G. A. Henty, the most celebrated of them all, had a considerable natural history collection.[59] The study in which he dictated his works to an amanuensis was filled with spears, guns, skins and other animal trophies – constant reminders of adventure. For Henty, hunting lay at the centre of the imperial experience and he had a horror of lads who shrank from shedding blood.[60] Natives, he wrote, were uninterested in learning or intelligence: it was pluck and fighting power that impressed them.[61] Moreover, sportsmen could speedily diminish the numbers of wild beasts that were the scourge of cultivators. The attributes of the hunter, therefore, were crucial both in establishing mastery and in creating patterns of patronage.

Many hunters and just as many stay-at-homes remarked on the influences of the classic hunting works, again both factual and fictional, on their lives. Public school boys were celebrated for their hunting and poaching activities, in which they were often encouraged by their masters. In these ways the public schools offered an 'antidote to effeminacy'.[62] Denis Lyell suggested more than once that every boy's prime excitements in adolescence consisted of bagging his first blackbird with a catapult or taking potshots at local cats, imagining they were lions or tigers.[63] In South Africa, Lyell noted with approval that Boer children fought each other for the right to kill fowls.[64]

According to E. S. Grogan it was 'the norm of adventurous life which was the general ambition of Victorian youth.[65] The use of books of heroes as material for moral emulation was designed to the same end. Boys should be given 'manly' rather than 'refined' books, which should help to create 'manly boys, uttering manly thoughts, and performing manly actions'.[66] Such actions consisted of pioneering and hunting activities which constituted the training for war which was 'the antipodes. . . of an effeminate sentimentalism'.[67] Popular anthologies of hunting stories carried these ideas to a wider audience. The coloured frontispieces of *Pictorial Sport and Adventure* consist of a tigress on one page and Landseer's African Lion on the other.[68] It is filled with details of hunting exploits and the copy in the author's possession was given as a Sunday School prize in Shipley in 1900. *The Romance of Modern Pathfinders*, published in the early Thirties, was filled with accounts of hunting from Africa to Kamchatka, Baffin Land to the Amazon.[69]

By that time, however, a whole generation of hunters was lamenting the fact that the opportunities which had hardened them and had provided much romance and adventure in violence were at an end. Game stocks were seriously depleted, licences cost a great deal of money and the railways and the internal combustion engine had brought tourists to the remotest corners of the wilder continents. Subalterns in India were giving up pig-sticking for (in Baden-Powell's words) 'poodle-faking at the hill-stations'.[70] Claude Champion de Crespigny, who had devoted decades to hunting, boxing, bull-fighting and other violent pastimes, saw the craze for dancing, night clubs and 'the pernicious cocktail habit' as the greatest sappers of the moral fibre of the young in the 1920s.[71] Denis Lyell dreaded a time when youth would fail to respond to the 'call of the wild'.[72] Always eager to apply Darwinian ideas derived from the wild to human society, he saw the incipient welfare state as the prime threat to the British as a virile and imperial nation. Civilisation 'with its false policy of nurturing the diseased and unfit' was upsetting 'the balance of nature'.[73] Certain African species were at risk, Marcus Daly had written, because they allowed defeated males to continue to run with the herd.[74] The weakest characteristics, he believed, alway predominated. Similarly, allowing the weak to survive at home and removing the opportunities for gaining virility and strength through pioneering and hunting would ultimately extinguish the British race. But these are the final echoes of the Edwardian passion for eugenics, about to be thoroughly discredited in Nazi Germany.

Although Baden-Powell was still extolling the joys of a bloody kill at pig-sticking, the scouts were making adjustments. Just as they attempted to make an accommodation with the new internationalism of the inter-war years, tempering the imperial and militarist attitudes of the pre-1914 era, so did they tone down the hunting imagery.[75] Baden-Powell had always argued that it was as meritorious to hunt with the camera as with the gun (influenced no doubt by his brother, a distinguished naturalist) and this strand in his thinking was now stressed by the official publications of the Scouts.[76] Baden-Powell and his associates hoped that moral training could be effected by using all the techniques of the Hunt while removing the emphasis on the ultimate kill. In doing so they made the gulf between the sexes more bridgeable. By toning down the image of the male as the killer destroying primarily the males of other species, they began to eliminate the strict sexual roles that Baden-Powell had originally envisaged. In any case, women had either broken in on the Hunt or were making strenuous efforts to restrict their husbands' activities in that direction. Moreover, as emigration opportunities contracted and frontiers in North America, Southern Africa and Australasia closed, the sturdy individualist pioneer began to lose his relevance as an exemplar.

In the British tradition the confusion between hunting as the pioneering archetype of freedom and the role of the Hunt as an elite ritual with an elaborate code was never fully resolved. There can be no doubt that between the 1870s and the 1920s there was a shift from the former to the latter and popular culture found it difficult to accommodate that shift. The increased elitism of the British imperial hunt helped to destroy its effectiveness in the 'romance and adventure' tradition, while the gore and violence it symbolised became hard to stomach in the post-Great War years. The fashionable images of Empire of both official propaganda and some aspects of popular culture in the inter-war years were of the 'economic' and 'peace' Empire, the Empire of 'builders' rather than 'makers' as the BBC liked to put it.[77]

The British imperial frontier, in at least some of its complexity, was depicted in the cinema, with beneficent white rule portrayed repeatedly in films like *Sanders of the River* and *Rhodes of Africa*.[78] Hunting as a symbol of white mastery inevitably makes its appearance. There is a pig-sticking sequence in *Lives of a Bengal Lancer* (1935), a tiger hunt in *The Charge of the Light Brigade* (1936) and an elephant hunt in *King Solomon's Mines* (1950). There are also hunting scenes in *The Maneater of Kumaon* and *Harry Black and the Tiger*, while a whole clutch of films was inspired by J. H. Patterson's *The Maneaters of Tsavo* – *Men Against the Sun*, *Bwana Devil* and *Killers of Kilimanjaro*. But it was the coherence and relative simplicity of the American frontier that was to become the prime cinematic expression of the hunting and pioneerng tradition. Yet it was a mythic image of the American West that came to predominate, a land of make-believe in which most of the wildness was human, bearing little relation to Baden-Powell's colonial boys or Theodore Roosevelt's hunting pioneer.

Notes

1   R. S. S. Baden-Powell, *Scouting for Boys*, London, 1908, p. 3.

2   Baden Powell, *Scouting*, p. 5.

3   Baden-Powell, *Scouting*, p. 248

4   Theodore Rossevelt, *Ranch Life and the Hunting Trail*, Gloucester, 1985 (reprint of 1896 edition), p. 56.

5   Roosevelt, *Ranch Life*, p. 83.

6   Among others, Roosevelt wrote introductions to F. C. Selous, *African Nature Notes and Reminiscences*, London, 1908, and C. H. Stigand, *Hunting the Elephant in Africa and other Recollections of Thirteen Years Wanderings*, London, 1913.

7   Baden-Powell, *Scouting*, p. 90.

8   Quoted in R. Coupland, *The Exploitation of East Africa, 1856-90*, London, 1939, p. 396.

9   Sir Claude Champion de Crespigny, *Forty Years of a Sportsman's Life*, London, 1925, pp. 182-3.

10   Marcus Daly, *Big-Game Hunting and Adventure, 1897-1936*, London, 1937, p. 84, C. H. Stigand and Denis D. Lyell, *Central African Game and its Spoor*, London, 1906, p. 3, and W. Hogarth Todd, *Work, Sport, and Play*, London, 1928, p. 53.

11   David C. Itzkowitz, *Peculiar Privilege, a Social History of English Foxhunting, 1753-1885*, Hassocks, 1977, pp. 48, 55-6.

12   Willie Orr, *Deer Forests, Landlords, and Crofters, the Western Highlands in Victorian and Edwardian Times*, Edinburgh, 1982.

13   John Ross (ed.), *The Book of the Red Deer*, London, 1925, pp. 109-10.

14   Agnes Herbert, *Two Dianas in Somaliland*, London, 1908.

15   Denis D. Lyell, *Memoirs of an African Hunter*, London, 1923, pp. 129-30; Stigand and Lyell, *Central African Game,* p. iv.

16   Theodore Roosevelt, *The African Elephant and its Hunters*, London 1924, p. 97.

17   Clive Aslet, *The Last Country Houses*, New Haven and London, 1982.

18   For example, the Cunard-White Star S.S. *Berengaria*, perhaps also trying to establish a link with the Middle Ages associated with her name, was decorated with antlers in her smoking room.

19   R. S. S. Baden-Powell, *Pig Sticking or Hog Hunting*, London, 1924, p. 21. See also J. S. Bratton, 'Of England, home, and duty, the image of England in Victorian and Edwardian juvenile fiction' in John M. MacKenzie (ed.), *Imperialism and Popular Culture*, Manchester, 1986, pp. 90-1.

20   Selous, *Afrian Nature Notes*.

21   Herbert, *Two Dianas*, pp. 202-9.

22   This literature will be surveyed in John M. MacKenzie, *Imperialism and the Hunting Ethos*, Manchester, forthcoming.

23   A.I.R. Glasfurd, *Rifle and Romance in the Indian Jungle*, London, 1921, p.v (first published 1905 and reprinted several times).

24   Herbert, *Two Dianas*, p. 9.

25   Harry Hopkins, *The Long Affray, the Poachers' Wars in Britain, 1760-1914*, London, 1985, pp. 216-7. Campbell Lennie, *Landseer*, London, 1976. One follower of Landseer was Archibald Thorburn, on whom see *The Field*, 23, November 1985, pp. 64-7.

26   Denis D. Lyell, *The Hunting and Spoor of Central African Game*, London, 1929, pp. 1-2.

27   John M. MacKenzie, 'Chivalry, Social Darwinism, and ritualised killing: the hunting ethos in Central Africa to 1914' in D. Anderson and R. Grove, *Conservation in Africa*, Cambridge, forthcoming. For the increasing elaboration of social rituals as a marker of class, see Leonore Davidoff, *The Best Circles*, London, 1973.

28   Sir Frederick Jackson, *Early Days in East Africa*, London, 1969 (first published 1930), p. 381.

29   Lyell, *Hunting and Spoor*, p. 2. Lyell, *Memories, p.* 261.

30   Charles Turley, *With the Prince Round the Empire*, London, 1926, p. 71; J. W. Best, *Indian Shikar Notes,* Lahore 1931 (first edition 1920), p. 16.

31   Daly, *Big-Game Hunting*, pp. 161-2.

32   Anon, 'Ibex shooting', *King's Royal Rifle Corps Chronicle*, 1913, p. 35. Stigand and Lyell, *Central African Game*, p. 5, used Kashmir as an example of a place where etiquette on the matter of sporting room was highly developed.

33   Nigel Woodyatt, *My Sporting Memories*, London, 1923, p. 12.

34   Woodyatt, *Sporting Memories*, pp. 18-19.

35   I am grateful to Phillip Dalziel for information about Colonel Harrison.

36   Baden-Powell, *Scouting*, p. 90.

37   Baden-Powell, *Pig Sticking*, pp. 38 and 46.

38   Rollo Arnold, *The Farthest Promised Land*, Wellington, 1981, p. 246.

39   This is the dedication of Woodyatt, *Sporting Memories*.

40   Turley, *With the Prince*, p. 76.

41   Baden-Powell, *Pig Sticking*,. dedication.

42   Baden-Powell, *Pig Sticking*, pp. 47-9.

43   Turley, *With the Prince*, pp. 74 and 78.

44   These albums and accounts of bags can be seen in the library of Hopetoun House, the Lothians.

'A bit of bravado'   (*Right*) 'Perils of the chase'

'His first stag'

45   R. S. S. Baden-Powell, *Sport in War*, London 1900. E.A.H. Alderson, *Pink and Scarlet or Hunting as a School for Soldiering*, London, 1900. See also R. S. S. Baden-Powell, *The Matabele Campaign*, London, 1897.

46   For the scale of colonial violence, see Phyllis M. Martin, 'The violence of empire' in David Birmingham and Phyllis M. Martin, *History of Central Africa*, volume II, pp. 1-26.

47   W. J. Reader, *Call to Arms*, Manchester, forthcoming.

48   Baden-Powell, *Pig Sticking*, p. 27.

49   Woodyatt, *Sporting Memories*, p. 16.

50   Jackson, *Early Days*, introduction by H. B. Thomas, p. ix.

51   Ian S. Wood, 'Haig: the last judgment', *The Scotsman*, 2 November 1985.

52   J. Fenimore Cooper, *The Deerslayer*, London, n.d., pp. 8-9.

53   J. Fenimore Cooper, *The Pioneers*, London, n.d., p. 386.

54   J.S. Bratton, *The Impact of Victorian Children's Fiction*, London, 1981, pp. 115-33.

55   Eric Quayle, *R.M. Ballantyne: A Bibliography of First Editions*, London 1968.

56   Jackson, *Early Days*, pp. vi, 1, 124.

57   Patrick A. Dunae, 'British juvenile literature in an age of Empire, 1880-1914', unpublished Ph.D thesis, University of Manchester, 1975, pp. 157, 179, 182, 245, 327, 375-6.

58   Lyell, *Memories*, p. 14.

59   Dunae, 'British juvenile literature', p. 182.

60   Dunae, 'British juvenile literature', p. 179.

61   When Charlie Marryat was fitted out for India by his uncle, Joshua Tufton, he was given 'a brace of pistols, a rifle, and a double barrel shot gun'. G. A. Henty, *With Clive in India*, London, n.d., p. 27.

62   Dunae, 'British juvenile literature', p. 475. The remark was made by Edmund Warre, Headmaster of Eton, in 1898.

63   Stigand and Lyell, *Central African Game*, pp. 1 and 4.

64   Lyell, *Memories*, p. 44.

65   Preface by Grogan to H.F. Varian, *Some African Milestones*, Oxford, 1953, vii.

66   Dunae, 'British juvenile literature', p. 39.

67   The remark was made by Dr Hutchison on the stories and books of Talbot Baines Reed. Dunae, 'British juvenile literature', p. 294.

68   *Pictorial Sport and Adventure, Being a Record of Deeds of Daring and Marvellous Escapes by Field and Flood*, London, Frederick Warne, n.d. (1890s?).

69   Norman J. Davidson, *The Romance of Modern Pathfinders* London, Seeley Service, n.d.

70   Baden-Powell, *Pig Sticking*, p. 34.

71   de Crespigny, *Forty Years*, pp. 295-6 and *passim*.

72   Lyell, *Hunting and Spoor*, p. 16.

73   Lyell, *Memories*, p. 19.

74   Daly, *Big-Game Hunting*, pp. 279-80.

75   Allen Warren, 'Citizens of the Empire, Baden-Powell, Scouts, Guides, and an imperial ideal', in MacKenzie (ed.), *Imperialism*, pp. 232-6.

76   The Boy Scouts Association, *The Story of Baden-Powell*, London, n. d., p. 9. Baden-Powell *Scouting*, pp. 90-1

77   MacKenzie, *Imperialism*, p. 183.

78   These films are examined in Jeffrey Richards, *Visions of Yesterday*, London, 1973.

Popular manliness:
Baden-Powell, scouting,
and the development
of manly character[1]

Introduction

It is now almost a commonplace among historians that during the second
half of the nineteenth century the notion of manliness became widely
accepted in English public schools and lay behind many of the impulses
stimulating voluntary work among boys and young men. Prompted at
first by the Christian concerns of Charles Kingsley and Thomas Hughes,
the ideal of manly conduct quickly became more extensive and comprehensive, comprising in Norman Vance's phrase 'a fascinating medley
of Victorian ideals and responses'. But despite its many forms, certain
common elements of feeling and attitude can be isolated which informed
almost all its varied social manifestations. There is firstly the close connection between manliness and good health, both physical and moral, a link
at times seen in the obsessive debates over the value of team games or in
the spread of gymnastic training as well as in the growing interest in
personal health education, rational diet, along with self-denial in respect
of cigarettes and alcohol. There was a widely held belief that a healthy
physique was more important than a veneer of social culture. Linked to
these concerns was the value of a simple and spartan life away from the
debilitating materialism of the city and in response to the natural challenges of the rural and colonial frontier. In such an environment the
emphasis was likely to be on energetic action rather than unhealthy reflec-

200 MANLINESS AND MORALITY

tion and in much of the writing on manliness there is a persistent strain of anti-intellectualism, a suspicion of fine discrimination or expressed emotion. This vigour and sense of purpose was itself often linked to the values of self-improvement, the ghost of Samuel Smiles hovering behind much of the writing on popular manliness, and was similarly associated with the straightforward qualities of directness, honesty, decency, duty and honour. What such treatments rarely contain is any social or political critique in answer to the question of why the ladder of self-propelled advancement is steeped the way it is. Finally the ideal of manliness was frequently tied to a reworked Christian code of knightly conduct, itself placed within a newly articulated national tradition. As a medley of aspirations, manliness was only partially destroyed by the traumatising experience of the First World War and many of its elements can be found in later attempts to create a similarly comprehensive ideology in the Fitness enthusiasm of the inter-war years.[2] This essay is concerned with one of the major attempts to give manliness a popular dimension amongst boys and young men – the Boy Scouts, whose founder Robert Baden-Powell expressed many of the ideals which were summed up in the phrase 'true manliness'. In particular, it will concentrate on the Rover Scouts, the section specifically devoted to young men over the age of eighteen and which reached its peak in terms of membership in the early 1930s. The first section will concentrate on the writings of Baden-Powell and in particular on *Scouting for Boys* and his later *Rovering to Success* and will examine how the founder of the Scouts saw the manly ideal. The second part will describe how the national headquarters of the Scout movement responded to the demand for a section for young men and what hopes they had for it. The concluding third of the essay analyses what it was like to be a Rover Scout and how far it lived up to its aim of being 'a Brotherhood of Open Air and Service' and, finally, how those hopes fared in the very different social conditions of Britain after 1945.[3]

Baden-Powell and the development of manly character

As a career soldier Baden-Powell had had little experience of civilian conditions in Britain before his return from South Africa in 1902 following his 'heroic' defence of Mafeking in the early stages of the Boer War. His writings were largely confined to sporting journalism and military handbooks and were directed at a largely non-military audience. Not until his tour as Inspector General of Cavalry from 1903 until 1907 did Baden-Powell become aware of the 'boy problem' and it was only slowly that he saw that his own individual enthusiasm for military reconnaissance and scouting could be translated into a training scheme for boys. Encouraged by Pearsons, the publising house, Baden-Powell agreed to redraft his earlier manual, *Aids to Scouting*, for boys' use and to run an experimental camp on Brownsea Island in Dorset in July 1907 on scouting lines. The resulting *Scouting for Boys* was published in early 1908 and proved to be the catalyst for the emergence of a separate organisation in that year, dedicted to the character training of boys. *Scouting for Boys* therefore provides an essential insight into how Baden-Powell saw the ideal of manliness.[4]

From its opening pages there is a direct association between manliness and the life and training of the military scout, trapper and colonial frontiersman. These are the 'real men', who do their duty to the King and their countrymen and who form part of a heroic national tradition stretching back to the knights of King Arthur and Richard 1 and including Raleigh, Drake and Captain Cook. For boys the exemplar is Kipling's character Kim, the model young scout training himself in personal health and for public service. But the scout is no superman and the first class scout has relatively modest qualities – he is able to read and write, he has sixpence in the savings bank and he has taken an oath to honour God and the King. The Scouts' laws enjoin him to be honourable, loyal, useful, friendly, courteous in his dealings, kind to animals, to obey orders with a smile and to look after his money in a thrifty fashion. Throughout the book great emphasis is placed on individual self-discipline and improvement with a hostility to rote learning and drill. The fully equipped Scout is sketched as a fine upstanding young man striding purposefuly towards adult life with an easy self-confident gait in contrast to the streetcorner loafer, visibly depressed and round-shouldered, idling his time away with fags and football matches.[5] This early and most famous version of Baden-Powell's manly character has a number of distinctive emphases, all of which are developed further in his writings for young men. There is, firstly, the strongly stated value of training in the outdoors, even if this has to be the street or alley and scout games all involve spooring, tracking and stalking designed to improve the basic sensory skills of sight, sound and touch. Ideally, these qualities are best acquired in camp and the virtues of Zulu and Swazi initiations are extolled as showing 'how necessary it is that boys should be trained to manliness and not allowed to drift into being poor spirited wasters who can only look on at man's work.[6] A British boy who as had to rough it in camp 'finds that when he comes back to civilization he is more easily able to obtain employment because he is ready to turn his hand to whatever kind of work may turn up.[7] Secondly, there is an emphasis on practical skills and learning by doing and little space is devoted to book learning. Baden-Powell remained a persistent critic of the limitations of both the public school and the elementary school curriculum with its emphasis on either the classics or basic literacy.[8] Thirdly, there is a concern for personal health as well as individual and national fitness. This took a variety of forms; personal cleanliness, a balanced diet, regular exercise and sensible clothing all feature prominently. Baden-Powell shared many of the Edwardian anxieties about self-abuse and was also energetically hostile to juvenile smoking while at the same time encouraging the adopting of the innovative Swedish exercises against the more traditional physical drill. Despite fads about clean blood and regular bowel movements, most of the advice is commonsensical.[9] The fourth feature of a Scout's training is its highly individualistic bias with little emphasis on team games. Athleticism was thought to have gone too far and sports like hiking, climbing and canoeing were seen as equally valuable. Solitary pursuits were not excluded either, drawing, photography and nature-study being recommended. Baden-Powell was himself a skilled water-colourist and also a keen photographer later in life and it is perhaps significant that his own schooldays at Charterhouse were not marked by the all pervasive cult of games.[10] The final distinctive quality of the training scheme was that it lacked any specific Christian content. Boys were encouraged to become good citizens first and not necessarily more committed believers. What was needed was a practical working religion and this was presented as a new chivalry in which the knights appeared as the patrol leaders of the nation devoted to public service and honour. Although the tone is certainly moralistic, the figure of Christ remains in the shadows neither appearing as personal saviour nor as the exemplar of all the manly virtues.[11]

Scouting for Boys was a great popular success and the appeal of the movement quickly extended beyond the intended age range of twelve to sixteen. By the end of the First World War it was clear that some provision would have to be made for those over eighteen and for whom *Rovering to Success* was written in 1922. Sub-titled 'A Book of Life Sport for Young Men', it developed many of the themes in the author's earlier writings. In it Rovering is presented as an approach to life, essentially purposive and requiring 'concentrated attention, pluck and activity'. The young man is encouraged to 'paddle his own canoe', for which he needs proper training, given that urban living has made men 'soft and feckless beings'.

'God made men to be men... We badly need some training for our lads if we are to keep up manliness in our race instead of lapsing into a nation of soft, sloppy, cigarette suckers'.[12]

After such a brisk opening Baden-Powell goes on to discuss the dangers facing the young man as he paddles his way on the river of life. The first is entitled 'Horses' and it enables him to expand on true sportmanship which is 'the active playing the game by the individual in place of being merely one of the crowd looking on or having the sport done for you or even helped by a paid hand'. Active participation is therefore the crucial test and, of all sports, mountaineering is recommended, combining as it does cheapness, physical fitness and spirituality. 'When you come down to earth again you will find yourself another man in body, mind and spirit'. The reader is also encouraged to take up useful and worthwhile hobbies which will help him avoid dead-end employments and equip him to climb the ladder of life.[13] The second danger facing the Rover is 'Wine' and in this section are outlined the familiar dangers of excess and the virtues of manly self-control, which are an object lesson in how to avoid dependence on alcohol, smoking ('false manliness'), bad language, superfluous food and an unhealthy balance between work and leisure.[14]. Women constitute the third hazard and in this chapter on sexual relations Baden-Powell alters the tone and content of the advice given in *Scouting for Boys*, reassuring the young man that sexual instincts are perfectly natural and that earlier fears about self-abuse had proved largely groundless. For those anxious about adolescent sexuality, Rovering is the answer. 'Instead of aimless loafing and smutty talk you will find lots to do in the way of hiking and the enjoyment of the out-of-door manly activities'. For those tempted to have sexual relations outside marriage, the spectre of venereal disease is raised and personal self-control advised: 'For this he must use his self-control to switch off all that is impure from his mind and ensure that his own ideas are clean and honourable, that his sense of duty is so high that ridicule and chaff will mean nothing to him.[15] In the fourth section dealing with the dangers facing the Rover, the reader comes directly upon the elements in manly character hostile to the political, intellectual and artistic worlds in about equal measure. Headed 'Cuckoos and Highbrows', the chapter vigorously ridicules the opinionated, 'such as cranks, political tub-thumpers, intellectual highbrows, and social snobs and other extremists', and urges the Rover to seek out the balance between the extremes. This robust anti-intellectualism is linked to an attack on snobbery in all forms as being ultimately ungentlemanly and as undermining an ideal of social harmony and co-operation and the

204 MANLINESS AND MORALITY

chapter finishes with the advice to the Rover that he should inform himself about national and international institutions so as to avoid a narrow chauvinism.[16] The final barrier to true manliness is 'Irreligion' and here Baden-Powell shows how far he is from the Christian emphases of Kingsley and Hughes. Not that he is in any doubt that the Rover needs a religious basis for life, which comes from an acceptance of God and a desire to help other people. To help him he not only has the Bible but also the Book of Nature, for there is 'a mystic power in Nature with which you are concerned – remotely not individually'. Such feelings lead onto a rhapsodic praise of hiking and the outdoor life, concluding that the person without religion will learn more from nature than from any book.[17] Reviewing the whole book, Baden-Powell returns to the value of Rovering itself and how he sees it as an antidote to the evils of town life: 'For my own part I feel that living in towns has a great deal to say to the want of manliness'. What was needed was a renewal of the spirit of the pioneer and the backwoodsman: 'Though self-sufficing, the backwoodsman is not self-sufficient. He is a rough diamond but a gentleman, as chivalrous as a knight of olden times'. The Rover Scout is to be this new urban backwoodsman, this twentieth century pioneer: 'He is a hefty Rover Scout, about eighteen years of age, that is a fellow training to be a man. He has tramped from a distance with his pack. . . . In addition to this load he carries a more important thing. . . a happy smile on his weather-tanned face. . . Altogether a healthy, cheery young backwoodsman. Yet this chap is a "Townie", but one who has made himself a Man'.[18]

The Rover Scout Section 1918-66:
The attempt to make a reality out of an ideal[19]

From 1916 onwards it became clear that a Scout scheme for young men had to be devised and it was hoped that Baden-Powell would lay down a practical basis for this in *Rovering to Success*. In this expectation, the Headquarters of the Association were to be disappointed when the book appeared in 1922 in that it was more about an approach to life than a clearly articulated structure of organisation and training. As a result, the years that followed saw a whole series of attempts to give the local reality and variety of Rovering a national definition acceptable to the adult leadership and the young men themselves. In fact the Rover Scouts were a continuing difficulty for the Headquarters, posing specific problems never satisfactorily resolved, which in turn highlighted a more profound lack of understanding of the reasons which led the young men to use so much of their leisure time in this way.

Turning to the practical consequences of this failure of perception, the first problem was to whom was the section to apply? What was its age range to be? During the whole history of the Rovers until their final abolition in 1966, there was continuing and inconclusive debate on this subject. At first it was thought that the 'Senior Scout' plan would be for the boy aged between fourteen and seventeen, whereby a new range of activities would help to retain his interest. But as the war progressed, the balance of the discussion shifted. Increasingly, as the adult leaders were called up, boy patrol leaders took over the running of Scout troops and often added to this responsibility some pre-military training for themselves through the newly established Scout Defence Corps. In their turn, these sixteen and seventeen year old boys began holding patrol leader conferences to discuss scout topics and it was clear that some provision would have to be made for them post-war. It was also widely assumed that demobilised soldiers would resume their local scouting connections in peace time. Almost inevitably, therefore, the Rover Scout scheme emerged to meet the needs of this older age range.[20] This raised the more profound question, however, of what was this section to be? Was it a third training scheme whereby young men would become more useful citizens as a result or was it more a philosophy of life, which it was hoped would ultimately transform society? If the former, then clearly an upper age limit would be sensible, if the latter, then presumably one might be a Rover Scout throughout life. As early as 1921 one critic was asking for a clear-cut decision on this question because, as he saw it: 'The Rover movement cannot at one and the same time be a mens' and a senior boys' movement.[21] Ten years later the problem remained unresolved as Charles Dymoke Green, Secretary to the Association commented, 'We should never have attempted to organise a movement for men but been content to remain a Boys movement retaining elder Scouts only so far as they could or might become useful to the Boys' movement. This alone would have done much to obviate the difficulties we have now encountered'.[22] Diagnosing the problem was relatively easy, finding an effective solution much more difficult. Baden-Powell did not help much either, his writing very much suggesting a life-long Toc H type organisation rather than a training section preparatory to adult membership like the YMCA. In any case, the number of Rover Scouts nationally before 1939 made it impossible to impose locally any policy on the age range, particularly if it involved the expulsion of older members. Even in 1955 when numbers nationally had fallen to eight thousand the decision to limit membership to those under 24 provoked the protest that such a move went against the whole spirit of a 'lay brotherhood'.[23]

The second difficulty centred on who should control Rovering. Initially assimilating much of the anarchic libertarianism of the woodcraft cult, little thought had been given to questions of authority and responsibility in the enthusiasm for the regenerative power of nature and the brotherhood of the 'open road'.[24] Baden-Powell shared many of these feelings and had made no provision for structure or organisation, groups of Rovers being only loosely attached to local associations which were often themselves fragile collections of volunteers widely scattered. Local difficulties were bound to arise but it was not until the late 1920s that Rover Crews were made the responsibility of the newly established post of Group Scoutmaster. At the same time an energetic attempt was started to appoint Rover leaders who would point the Crew in the right direction of training and service. These reforms were only partly effective and half of the registered Crews remained without leaders.[25] At a more symbolic level, these tensions between freedom and control focused on disputes over details of uniform, often heightened by strong feelings of local autonomy. From the late 1920s there was a long-running battle between the national headquarters and the west of Scotland over the 'bonnet question' and whether Glasgow Rovers should be allowed to wear the bonnet instead of the official pointed hat. So strong were the feelings generated and such the intransigence of Baden-Powell in particular, that fears were expressed about a possible break-away section and eventually he was persuaded to back down. The constant delays in introducing new rules for Rovers after 1945 shows how aware the headquarters were of the limits of their own authority and it was with some nervousness that the decision to abolish the section was taken in 1966.[26]

The third difficulty and the most profound related to the programme. What were Rovers expected to do week by week? The inter-war years saw a confusion on this question also. At first (and before 1914) a Scouts Friendly Society was established which was thought to meet the basic need and encouraged thrift at the same time. The outbreak of war prevented anything more than a modest growth in the society and by 1917 the perspective was different. Fears of compulsory military training for the young and the challenge of new educational provisions created an emphasis on a preparation for future work through a badge scheme in which practical skills were taught. Only slowly was it appreciated that scouting was part of these young men's leisure time and if they were to use it constructively then a change of tack was needed. Influenced by the current woodcraft fad, a new training programme was put together which replicated the younger scouts' activities with the emphasis on camping and backwoodsmanship and in 1921 a new Rambler badge was introduced involving a hundred mile hike. The hike excepted, such a boy orientated plan was unpopular and not widely adopted. Through the decade this concern about the programme continued. Churchmen in particular expressed anxiety that an open-air cult was an insufficiently spiritual basis for the senior training section of the movement. *Rovering to Success* did not give much help either, given its back-to-nature bias and its lack of suggestions of what to do on a weekly basis. The winter months were often the real problem for although talks on current affairs or first aid instruction had their appeal they did not rival the attractions of the camping season and the interest of members could wane between November and May. Similarly, ideals of service could pall denuded of their chivalric glow in the grey reality of provincial life, challenged by the gaudy colour of the picture house or the sexual anticipations of the dance hall. In the same way, the advent of a girl friend (called 'girlitis') could quickly disrupt a small Crew.[27]

These worries led the headquarters to make a concerted effort to give some clear definition to Rovering at two large national gatherings (called 'Moots') in 1926 and 1928. At the first of these, Baden-Powell and his Rover commissioner, P. B. Nevill constructed a large tableau vivant entitled 'The Vigil' in which Rovers acted out an imaginary chivalric investiture and dedication ceremony as a kind of living icon before the young Rover knights. This theme was extended in a later tableau called 'The Quest for Service' in which the young 'squire' made a life-long commitment to a specific form of republic service. The new Rover commissioner, F. W. W. Griffin, was particularly keen on the chivalric ideal and had been much impressed by the eccentric foundation of a self-made businessman near Tintagel called the Knights of the Round Table. The result was a new set of rules which included a vigil in a church or a place of awesome beauty where the intending Rover could reflect on his investiture and its significance. How the theme of specific quests was to be worked out in practice was left rather vague, although Baden-Powell came out with his own variant which he called 'Brenting' which seemed to involve a minstrel gang of Rovers rambling through the English countryside providing a wayside entertainment. Nor surprisingly, such a bizarre concoction was variously adopted and adapted around the country. A formal Rover investiture, sometimes preceded by a vigil, was widely accepted and particularly by Crews with a close church connection. 'Questing' did not feature much after the early 1930s although it may have concentrated Crews' attention on service for a short period. 'Brenting' seems to have disappeared without trace. It must be concluded that the attempts to give Rovering a greater definition met with only partial success and Baden-Powell felt himself that too much was being made of the spiritual aspect at the expense of a straightforward open-air fellowship. As a result, it was acknowledged in 1936 that a formal training scheme could not be imposed and that the content of the programme would have to be left as a matter for local discretion. There the matter was left for twenty years and it was not until 1956, when Rover numbers were much reduced, that a final attempt was made to institute a formal training scheme confined to those aged between 18 and 24. Such plans had never captured the imagination of the age group before and were even less likely to do so in the changed conditions of the post-war years. Not surprisingly, in a major review of the Association's activities in 1966 it was finally concluded that the twin objectives of a training section and a life-long service ideal were incompatible and that the Rovers should be abolished.[28]

The Rover Crew in action: the local reality

From what has already been described it could be too readily concluded that there was an almost total disjuncture between the ideals of manly character as expressed in *Rovering to Success* and the reality on the ground. But that would be a mistake or at least it should not be assumed until that local dimension is examined. Clearly the idea of Rovering, however defined, prompted a popular response in the 1930s when membership peaked at just under forty thousand. Many Crews remained small and the average size was between eight and nine with an often intermittent existence as particular peer groups of young men passed out into the wider world of work, marriage or removal from a home locality. Most of the members were aged between 18 and 23 in fact, nearly all had been members of a local Scout troop and many also held a leader appointment in a troop or Wolf Cub pack. Membership of a Rover Crew represented therefore an extension of pattern of leisure time already firmly established, the vitality of which would very much depend on local circumstances. Even so, a common pattern does emerge through the calendar of annual activity. During the autumn and winter the Crew would meet weekly at the 'Den' either for training or merely socially. In all the literature great importance is attached to the place of the Den as somewhere devoted exclusively to Rover use and often built and maintained by them and for which they were responsible. In many cases this ideal was not realised and members met in a church room or in the Scouts' hut. But in many it was and so provided a focal point for young men; somewhere between the street and the parish hall, neither rough nor respectable. It was here that the instruction in life-saving and first aid was given along with the debates or talks on civic themes, the Den also being the place to meet and talk away from the custodial eye of parent, schoolmaster or boss. During these winter months Crews were often involved in the increasingly popular troop or 'Gang' shows, which had their inspiration from the entertainments staged by Ralph Reader and the Holborn Rovers. In some areas a sporting bias predominated, which in the thirties usually meant athletics, given the current enthusiasm for fitness and the fact that most Crews were too small to field a team on a regular basis. But what predominated was an enthusiasm for hiking, camping and all the outdoor activities. These could be variously adventurous from merely helping at the camps for younger Scouts to separately organised camps and rambling or climbing expeditions at home or abroad. Throughout the summer months all other events had to be fitted around the camping programme.

The service component of Rovering was also interpreted in various ways. About a quarter of all Rovers also held leader appointments as well. Many Crews were closely linked to a sponsoring church or religious body so that service was carried out through its involvement in the local community. Rover Crew meetings were much patronised by civic leaders and this led them into being asked to assist in local self-help efforts, which ranged from selling coronation souvenir programmes to litter campaigns and, during the war, collecting metal and being part of the civil defence team. *The Rover World*, published between 1934 and 1938, gives the flavour and variety of what the more active Crews did. In early 1934 the Newcastle-upon-Tyne Rovers are reported as having adopted the blood transfusion service while the Birkenhead members had been running a club for the unemployed for the previous two years. In Oxford a Toc H Rover branch was formed and in the University of Wales there was a Crew in each of the constituent colleges. At the Manchester 'get-together' there was a talk on 'citizen Rover Scouts' and 'on the creative use of leisure', while the Chester Rovers debated whether there should be a standard training scheme and those at Bury listened to talks on hiking, mountaineering and welfare work. Meanwhile, London Rovers held a cross-country championship and the Beckenham Crews a twenty-four hour hiking competition. On the other hand, those in Sandown on the Isle of Wight were members of the local life-saving team while those at West Hatch in Somerset had become bell ringers.[29]

But perhaps the best way to get the flavour of the local reality is to look at two Crews in particular and where records are especially full. The first is the 23rd Cambridge (St Matthew's), which had a successful Crew from 1923 until 1945. At first beginning as three or four older boys meeting separately and helping at other Scout functions, the Crew started offici-ally in 1926 and then met continously until 1939 when civil defence duties meant that such a regular programme became impossible. Institutional support was provided by the local church and membership overlapped considerably with that of the Church of England Mens' Society, with the Crew regularly attending the monthly corporate communion in the parish. The relationship had its difficult moments as well. Weekend camp-ing in the summer months denuded the Bible class and the Sunday School and the rector on occasion complained that the Scouts were of little use as far as the church was concerned, since they rarely attended its services while continuing to use its property without contributing anything in return. But for most of the time church and crew tolerated one another, recognising their mutual dependence. During the winter months the weekly meetings very much centred on discussions and debates. In 1928 a prohibition motion was carried, in 1930 in succeeding weeks discussions were held on the debilitating effects of civilisation and on whether Eng-land was becoming a c3 nation and a year later a protection resolution was endorsed. Into this programme of informal education was blended a pattern of social events largely centred on the church and Scout troop – concerts, harvest suppers, Ranger Guide/Rover socials and joint meetings with Cambridge College Crews – all feature prominently. Most members also helped in local Scout troops around the town. During the summer months this pattern of activities was very much disrupted by the demands of the camping season and by the fact that many Rovers were also mem-bers of one of the rowing clubs, each of which had its own training schedule in the weeks leading up to competitions. As a result, the autumn was often the most lively time of the year with old members returning from their summer camps being joined by new recruits from the Scout troop who had now become eighteen. At its strongest the Crew con-tained about twenty members and the impression left, after reading the Crew's log-book, is of an active, educational, social and service pro-gramme directly arising out of the life of the church and the Scout troop. What was lacking was any desire to be involved in any sort of formal training or badge scheme. Similarly, although closely linked to the church, there was considerable resistance to raising the level of spiritual or moral commitment. For some individuals the investiture and the vigil were important occasions but the attempt by the leader to change the balance away from constructive leisure towards a more formalised 'Questing' largely failed.[30]

The second example can be described more quickly and shows how varied the local experience could be. The 5th Bromley (St Luke's) Scout group was also long and well established, having been set up in 1912, and similarly was linked to the nearby church although the working connection was much less close. Continuity was maintained during the Second World War when most of the leaders were called up through a strong sense of corporate loyalty developed out of a regular tradition of troop camping in the years before the war and which is reflected in the troop log-book with its entries from leaders serving in the forces. Despite these strengths the group never had much success with Rover Scouts. An attempt was made to run a Crew between 1937 and 1940 with membership reaching a peak as Rovers waited to be called up. But in terms of a programme, Rovering was never more than an acceptable way to socialise and meetings quickly moved on to the chip shop and the pub or became the focus for establishing contact with the local Ranger Guides. At an Easter camp in 1940 a large number of the Crew got drunk after a day felling trees and were suspended for a month. Along with the regular attritions through call-up and the rather sour atmosphere after this incident there was little enthusiasm for the Rovers during the war. In 1948 a new attempt was made with the Group Scoutmaster attending all the meetings but again the programme was largely made up of social events and helping stage the group's annual show. There was none of the range of activities which had marked the life of the Cambridge Crew before the war and numbers never rose above six or seven. A final effort was made in 1956 after a new set of headquarters regulations had been promulgated and briefly there was a Crew of sixteen members but enthusiasm seems to have quickly evaporated and it became defunct later in the same year. In the 5th Bromley's case being a Rover never became anything more than a temporary rite of passage for a few young men as they made their way out into a wider adult world.[31]

Conclusion

After an inevitably brief look at the local reality, what conclusions can be drawn about the relationship between the ideals of a popular manly culture and the ways in which the Rover section worked in practice? The previous section outlined how important was the local context in determining the vitality and character of Rovering; something the headquarters never fully understood and which explains their own frustrations. As a result, the Rovers never became the manly ideal they had hoped and this is hardly surprising given that so many potentially conflicting qualities were gathered under the umbrella of manliness: health, the simple life, a suspicion of sophisticated thinking and a firm belief in straightforward dealing and in revived chivalric code. It would have been remarkable if a single organisation for young men had encompassed and impressed such diverse aspirations.

The question perhaps needs to be put another way. The second section of this essay tried to assess the distinctive gloss that Baden-Powell had put upon the concept of manliness in his writings and the most useful question the historian can ask is how far the Rover Scouts matched those particular qualities. In this context it is worth noting that *Rovering to Success* had considerable popular sales. By 1930 some 171,000 copies had been sold and it remained in print until the early 1960s. It also had a directly personal impact as the individual letters to the author show. Most of these contain requests for reassurance about sexual anxieties or for guidance on 'how to get on in life' or how to acquire greater self-confidence. In a single case the writer rather movingly thanks Baden-Powell for the help the book has given him in overcoming the disability of being both blind and deaf. Most of the correspondents seem to have been clerks or apprentices in their late teens or early twenties and so broadly reflected the membership as a whole.[32]

Turning to the distinctive gloss that Baden-Powell put upon manly character, it is clear that at least some of his enthusiasms were shared at local level. Firstly, a belief in the outdoors as a training ground for character was clearly widely accepted and it provided the bedrock of sentiment on which the section was founded. Similarly, the association between the healing and regenerative power of nature and the development of the whole personality, while often wildly naïve and romanticised, evoked a response and contributed significantly to the cult of camping and rambling in the 1920s and 1930s. Secondly, the emphasis on practical as distinct from literate skills was something which touched a nerve-end, especially when combined with a philosophy of active doing rather than reflection, idle or otherwise. Where successful the whole tone of Rovering was towards purposeful activity in the Den, in camp or through acts of public service with the reflective and aesthetic pursuits often ignored. Thirdly, the concern for improved health in its many guises prompted a reaction which in its turn contributed if only marginally to the increase in the fitness of some sections of the population. A greater candour in sexual matters, a more rational approach to dress, the wisdom of a balanced diet with the avoiding of excess and finally the value of exercise all featured prominently in Baden-Powell's writings during the thirties and was evidenced in the interest in fitness among Rover Crews. Fourthly, the balance between individual freedom and corporate involvement expressed in Rovering to Success did roughly and perhaps unconsciously reflect the young Rover's situation, poised between the home-based dependence of family life and the world of adult work, courtship and home-making. At a minimum, the Rover Crew was a relatively brief rite of passage into that wider world. At most it provided a framework of purposive leisure, often outdoors, combined with a pattern of civic training and community service which could profoundly influence the young man's future life. Finally, the numerical success of the Rover Scouts between the wars and perhaps that of the Scout movement more generally shows that there was scope for the emergence of a non-Christian manliness along the lines laid down by Baden-Powell in his writings. Essentially worldly and humanistic, an ideal was presented of personal development and fulfilment through constructive citizenship and community service. Linked to this was the belief that such an aim would not be achieved in a wholly urban environment and that the world of nature and the outdoors provided an essential training ground and simultaneously a basis for spiritual renewal. As such it contained moral and spiritual elements, in addition to the cult of the merely physical and athletic, which in their turn allowed those whose hopes were more directly Christian to reconcile themselves to the inherent contradictions of local practice. Shorn of its more exotic embellishments, there remained a core of sentiment which elicited a continuing response.

Nevertheless by the late 1930s the cultural climate in which manliness had had its origins was changing with the result that the general concept had less and less credibility. This was due in part to longer-term changes in society. The decline in religious practice, the reaction against a team ethic in some sports, a more individualistic attitude to the outdoors, a retreat from the previously fashionable eugenic thinking and a cynicism about straightforward values in the years following the Great War all contributed to a sense that manliness had become outdated by the later 1930s. Moreover, for those who wanted a concept comprehensive enough to incorporate many of the individual elements that had constituted the ideal, it was readily at hand in the Fitness campaign which for many of its supporters included a powerful moral and spiritual dimension as well as the desire to improve physical health. Turning to the local rality, it is clear that the world that had encouraged the evolution and growth of the Rover Scouts was dissolving during the decade. Improvements in nutrition and health were leading to earlier maturation in the young and a changing chronology of youthful development. Interest in the opposite sex and courtship now began at an earlier age and C. E. B. Russell's view expressed early in the century that the years between fifteen and seventeen were ones in which boys lived almost exclusively in male company was becoming less and less true.[33] Secondly, the social dislocation brought about by the housing boom of the thirties and by the spread of suburbia increasingly broke the pattern of communal continuity which had enabled Rover Scouting to grow out of the established lineaments of social life in any particular area. Finally, and by far the most importantly, the introduction of conscription in 1939 and its continuance for nearly twenty years broke into the young man's experience at the exact point that he was expected to join the Rover Scouts. Two years of military service with all its contrasts in terms of training, location and a new life meant that a later return to the Crew's activities centred on the Den seemed indissolubly associated with childhood. For those wanting to re-establish links with the Scout movement there were opportunities for service as an adult leader or a non-uniformed helper. For most, however, it marked the end of an association with the Scouts which in many cases had already lasted ten years. Its logical foundations were now weak and, in the self-critical atmosphere of the 1960s, its abolition provoked only the occasional ripple. Some of the sentiments and aspirations which had made up the ideal of manly character were doubtless carried over into the new training section for boys (and later girls) between the ages of sixteen and twenty, the Venture Scouts, but the old language and ideology were dead.

Notes

1 I should like to thank the Economic and Social Research Council for its support, which enabled the initial research for this essay to be undertaken. The Scout Association

has kindly allowed me to consult material in its keeping and its archivist, Mr Graham Coombe, has been extremely helpful. I am also most grateful to the Librarian, Cambridge City Library, for allowing me to consult the local collection and to Mr W. Lucas for making available the records of the 5th Bromley (St. Luke's) Scout Group. Finally Mr John Welshman of Corpus Christi College, Oxford allowed me to read his unpublished paper, 'Images of youth: the problem of juvenile smoking, 1900 to 1939', read at the conference of the British Sociology Association at York University on 28 September 1985.

2 J. A. Mangan, *Athleticism in the Victorian and Edwardian Public School: The Emergence and Consolidation of an Educational Ideology,* 1981; Norman Vance, 'The ideal of manliness', *The Victorian Public School: Studies in the Development of an Educational Institution, a Symposium,* Brian Simon and Ian Bradley (eds.), Dublin, 1975, pp. 115-28, R. N. C. Vance, 'The ideal of Christian manliness in the novels of Charles Kingsley and Thomas Hughes, in relation to the mid-Victorian religious, intellectual and literary background', University of Oxford PH.D. 1975.

3 R.S.S. Baden-Powell, *Scouting for Boys: A Handbook for Instruction in Good Citizenship, a Facsimile Edition of the Original Parts,* 1957, *Rovering to Success, A Book of Life Sport for Young Men,* 1922.

4 For Baden-Powell's career, E. E. Reynolds, *Baden-Powell: A Biography of Lord Baden-Powell of Gilwell,* OM, GCMG, GCVO, KCB, 2nd ed., 1957; William Hillcourt with Olave, Lady Baden-Powell, *Baden-Powell, Two Lives of a Hero,* 1964.

5 Baden-Powell, *Scouting for Boys,* pp. 13-18, 20-1, 36-40, 49-51, 217, 223.

6 Baden-Powell, *Scouting for Boys,* 4th ed., 1911, p. 56.

7 Baden-Powell, *Scouting for Boys, p.* 175.

8 For one example of his critical view of the current state of education, see Baden-Powell to Alex. Devine, 12 October 1910, Scout Association Archives TC/23, Devine, one of the founders of the Boys' Club movement, was the headmaster of Clayesmore School. See also Alex Devine, *A crisis in the Education of the Governing Classes of England,* 1910, *A Sympathetic Boyhood: The Public Schools and Social Questions,* Frank Whitbourn, *Lex, being the Biography of Alexander Devine, Founder of Clayesmore School,* 1937.

9 Baden-Powell, *Scouting for Boys,* pp. 221-38.

10 Baden-Powell, *ibid,* pps. 73-142, 173-97. For school life at Charterhouse in the 1870s see Harold Haig Brown (ed.), *William Haig Brown of Charterhouse: A Short Biographical memoir,* 1908; W. H. Holden (ed.), *The Charterhouse we knew,* 1950.

11 Baden-Powell, *Scouting for Boys,* pp. 239-64.

12 Baden-Powell, *Rovering to Success,* pp. 11-28.

13 *Ibid.,* pp. 31-63.

14 *Ibid.,* pp. 67-98.

15 *Ibid.,* pp. 101-31.

16 *Ibid.,* pp. 135-71.

17 *Ibid.,* pp. 175-99.

18 *Ibid.,* pp. 205-47.

19 The bulk of the material used in this section is to be found in The Scout Association Archives (subsequently referred to as SAA). This consists of the surviving office papers of Baden-Powell and the official journals of the Association – *The Headquarters Gazette* (later retitled *The Scouter*), *The Trail* and *The Rover World* as well as the regularly published *Policy, Organisation and Rules.*

20 For these discussions, see, *The Headquarters Gazette,* March 1911, May 1912, January 1913, March 1913, November 1913, November 1914, January 1915, November 1916, December 1916, April 1917, August 1917, September 1918.

21 R. S. Wood, 'The Rover movement in London: the need for a clear-cut policy', *The Trail*, May 1921. Wood was the commissioner for Shoreditch and later a prominent official at the Board of Education.

22 SAA TC/27.

23 For statistics on membership see, *The Scouter*, February 1934, March 1936, September 1954, also Henry Collis, Fred Hurll and Rex Hazlewood, *B-P's Scouts: An Official History of The Boy Scouts Association*, 1961, pp. 257-304. The reference to a 'lay brotherhood' is to be found in *The Scouter*, September 1955.

24 For the woodcraft cult and Rovering see, *The Trail*, November 1919. The emancipationist and pantheistic tone of the woodcraft movement is well illustrated in John Hargrave, *The Great War brings it Home: The Natural Reconstruction of an Unnatural Existence*, 1919.

25 For these administrative changes, see *The Headquarters Gazette* (and later *The Scouter*) December 1921, December 1924, June 1925, February 1926, January 1927, September 1927, February 1929.

26 Not surprisingly these disputes did not surface in the columns of *The Headquarters Gazette*. For the details see the minutes of the Committee of the Council, 12 June 1925, 11 July 1930, 11 December 1931, 14 October 1932, 9 December 1932, 7 April 1933, 10 May 1935, 13 September 1935. For the recommendation to abolish the Rover section see *The Report of the Chief Scout's advanced Party*, 1966 – all to be found in the SAA.

27 For these discussions on programme and training see *The Headquarters Gazette* (and later *The Scouter*), November 1913, November 1914, February 1915, April 1917, August 1917, November 1919, December 1921, December 1924, June 1926, June 1927, January 1928, July 1930.

28 For the origins of these two moots and the connections with the Arthurian movement, see file headed 'Rover Scout Presentation Ceremony, 1925-1939', SAA TC/34. For the Vigil and the Quest as well as Brenting, see *The Scouter*, July 1928, September 1928, July 1930, November 1931. The failure of any training scheme was acknowledged in *The Scouter*, March 1936, and the details of the last attempt to establish such a structure are to be found in *The Scouter* March 1956 and May 1956. The tone of F. W. W. Griffin's mixture of spiritual renewal and physical fitness is best seen in F.W.W. Griffin, *Rover Scouting: Chats with Rover Scouts and their Mates*, 1930; F. W. W. Griffin and J. K. McConnel, *Health and Muscular Habits*, 1937.

29 *The Rover World* 1934-8; a good early description of Rover Scouting is to be found in the *Headquarters Gazette* April 1921 and the details of the number of warrant holders in *The Scouter* May 1929.

30 Material on the 23rd Cambridge (St. Matthew's) Scout Group has been deposited in the City Library, Cambridge.

31 Material on the 5th Bromley (St Luke's) was made available by Mr W. Lucas.

32 These private letters to Baden-Powell are contained in SAA TC/40.

33 CEB Russell and Lilian Rigby, *Working Lads Clubs*, 1908, p. 26.

34 Initially the outbreak of hostilities in 1939 gave a stimulus to overall numbers in the Rover section through Crews being set up on service establishments but in the longer term the effect of conscription was clearly very damaging. For a local example of this, see Howard Peters, *The History of Scouting in Darwen 1909-1979*, Darwen, 1979. A copy is held in the Scout Association Archives.

EASTER, 1926

The

Rover Moot

Official Programme
Price One Shilling

"SERVICE"

THE BOY SCOUTS ASSOCIATION
IMPERIAL HEADQUARTERS
25, BUCKINGHAM PALACE ROAD, LONDON, S.W.1

The theme of service was expressed as a renewed chivalry with Rover Scouts as the nation's young knights.

Boys' Brigade in Enfield, Middlesex, early 1900s

WILL YOU HELP US TO TURN **THESE**

INTO

THIS?

IF SO

PLEASE FILL UP AND RETURN THE FORM ON OPPOSITE PAGE.

Church Lads' Brigade leaflet of the 1890s which depicts the movement as an agency of social control to attract the middle-class subscriber

(Top left) Cleanliness, if not next to godliness, was certainly close to manliness

(Left) How the Boy Scouts have helped the Homeland in the hours of peril

chapter eleven DONALD J. MROZEK

The habit of victory: the American military and the cult of manliness

The concept of 'manliness' is an elusive one and the role of United States military officers in advancing it in the Army and Navy and throughout society during the Victorian period was as subtle in motive as it was often blunt in method. The elusiveness came, in part, because the idea of 'manliness' required some sense of what it meant to possess 'manly vigour' and also because, apart from being a quality in itself, 'manliness' could consist of a cluster of 'virtues characteristic of a man'.[1] But the determination of what qualities were distinctly male and manly varied greatly from one culture to another and from one era to the next. At the same time, it has been argued, the need for defence exaggerated behavioural differences between men and women, thus according special importance to military institutions in preserving the notion of a distinctive sphere of male virtues.[2] At the same time, the military institutions' seeming descent from the ancient roles of hunter and defender made them a relatively easy place in which to identify with masculinity and manliness.[3] Similarly, it was easy to define success in both of these primal tasks and the military cult of manliness, while aping primitive traditions, came to serve the habit of victory in the modern era.

Victorian manliness and the American military ethos:
A matter of complexity

The Victorian age lent special approval to courage and valour among 'the qualities eminently becoming a man', virtues in which military officers traditionally prided themselves, and both identified 'manhood' as a temporal state as well, something not only different from womanhood but also from childhood and adolescence.⁴ As Joseph F. Kett has noted, however, the distinctive contribution of the Victorian era to the understanding of manliness lay less in the distinction between childhood and maturity (in which guise it supported the development of the concept and institutions of adolescence) than in the difference between masculinity and feminity (in which form it added all the more to the sexual freight of male adolescence).⁵ In a time increasingly alive to the issues of developmental psychology, then, the striving for 'manliness' constituted a search for passage into some discernible social, personal and sexual identity in the midst of significant personal and social change.

Despite the development of corporate institutions at the turn of the century, the psychological impulse sharpened the place of the individual. Pre-existing familial and communitarian associations declined in power and the individual faced what Emile Durkheim called *anomie* – a deep loss of the sense of identity. It was up to the individual to create associations anew or to transform the vestiges of past patterns into something applicable to present needs. The military stood as one rare institution which at once enjoyed long standing and also sufficient ability to adapt. Although most men in post-hunting cultures did not actually engage in war themselves, the military became a model of male association and bonding and of manly values; and it remained so into the modern era. Great institutions such as the organised churches which had traditionally met men's needs for renewal and regeneration were losing sway for many Americans, while the very character of modern life ate away at the more personal need for intimacy and friendship.⁶

In yet another way, military institutions differed from civilian ones – in the fact that their substantial separation from the swift turns of civilian fashion and custom allowed them a much greater potential for continuity. As J. A. Mangan has pointed out, significant change in Victorian culture often showed itself as a matter of 'ambience' and this matter of tone and custom – conveyed through such words as commitment, piety, dedication and compassion – proved comparatively stable in the military. Thus, as the idealistic pursuit of a 'golden mean' in the civilian realm was transformed into materialistic and sensory gratification, the Victorian tension which linked sacrifice and duty to fulfilment and gain remained strong within the military, largely because its military origins pre-dated its Victorian manifestation.[7] In this way, Victorian manliness actually reaffirmed a pre-existing military code of manliness, adding a supportive 'encrusting' set of rhetoric, ritual and symbol.[8]

The American military ethos had always been stiffened by the air of duty and, even apart from the special rituals which the armed forces gradually acquired, service itself had often been seen as a rite of passage. As a male preserve, it also simplified the matter of identity – perhaps overly so – by institutionalised distancing not only from women but from 'feminine traits.' The hardihood of military life further protected male friendship from insinuations of homosexuality. Since the disorder which resulted from change was widely seen as a central problem confronting society, it is no wonder that an insistence upon strong and strict codes of behaviour appeared providing a device for reaffirming discipline and orderliness.[9] Yet, at the same time, the 'logistical mothering' of the Army surrounded the men's assertiveness, producing what Rupert Wilkinson has called 'aggressive expressions of oral dependency', such as flamboyant bouts of drinking and carousing.[10] In a sense, the principle of order was verified by – indeed, even expressed by – periodic resort to excess. For military officers, commitment to a moral code was a comfortable proposition, much like their own commitment to the intrinsic worth and practical benefits of hierarchy and authority. The military's inner sense of certitude paralleled the moral absolutism which was central to American Victorianism.[11]

Manliness as a matter of style

The inner realities and instincts of Victorian manliness may be best grasped through manner as much as action, through a rhetoric of adjectives and adverbs more than nouns and verbs and through matters of style which suggested underlying disposition. Victorian concern for proper dress, playing potential for activity against a penchant for restraint and constriction, affected men as well as women.[12] Display appealed deeply to men, whether the flamboyance of Theodore Roosevelt's buckskins or the spectacle of the athletic uniform, but this was display bounded within conventions asserted by dominant groups in the culture. Military heroes such as Nelson Miles and George Dewey, prominent athletes such as college football's Poe brothers and frontier personalities such as 'Buffalo Bill' Cody represented different facets of this exuberance. A critical distinction, however, was that military display had its own history and justification which remained separate from those in civilian society, no matter how often they paralleled them. In civilian life, the tense balance between display and restraint came under increasing assault from the image of the 'dude' and, at the lower end of the social scale, from that of the 'masher'. The 'masher's' stylish clothes and swaggering manner reflected what Theodore Dreiser called his 'insatiable love of variable pleasure'. As Lois Banner rightly observed, the appeal of the 'masher' signified the beginning of the end for Victorian culture. The military however, could exempt themselves from these extremes of fashion, maintaining the tension and balance between exuberance and order and, in that way, seeming to carry forward the Victorian manner of manliness, despite its decline in the civilian world.[13]

The manners permissible within the military sometimes differed from those of the society as a whole. The habit of spitting in public, for example, waxed and waned in the civilian world, as did cigar-chomping and tobacco chewing – not unrelated to the spitting. Such behaviour, though common, was widely detested by women and it seems to have been used partly for the sake of firming up gender distinctions.[14] Again, the insulation which the armed forces enjoyed from significant challenge by women or by the civilian society as a whole allowed the Army and Navy to retain such habits as harmless customs, even while they less consciously used them for the strengthening of identity and self-image. The difference in frame of mind which marked Victorianism off from what preceded and what followed it permitted such tension between high idealism as the military enshrined and such petty vulgarities as it exploited. Indeed, even when such customs as smoking and spitting roused disgust in some quarters, they formed a vocabulary of behaviour which acted out a military dialect of manliness. Within this special set of circumstances, they even aped gentlemanliness.

Even at the end of World War I, when interest ran high in the practical role of sport in preserving discipline and order among the troops, the high and congenial rhetorical tone persisted. In advocating a 'Military Olympics' to be held in France after 'the strenuous game of beating the Hun' had been won, Elwood S. Brown of the Paris YMCA assured US Army officials that it would 'be a great factor in cementing on the field of sport those friendly ties between the men of the Allied Armies that have sprung up on the common field of battle'. Such an international meet would, in Brown's view, develop 'mutual respect and understanding'.[15] The exaggerated praise of egalitarianism on the playing field, so much a part of the Victorian manly tradition, returned. 'When dressed for the game,' the promoters observed, 'all ranks met on a universal plane where "a man's a man for a' that."'[16] As the official commemorative volume for the Games noted, 'Mr Brown saw multitudes of men bound together by strong ties of sympathy in the common ideals for which they were fighting, yet often knowing each other not at all.' Engaging in sport after the war, the men would meet in a manner 'most revealing, most harmonizing, most natural'. Such men, 'animated in advance by interest in and admiration for one another', could be of 'fundamental importance to the future welfare of the world.'[17] It was not mere distraction which Brown advocated for the Army, nor was it mere physical preparedness and toughness, but rather the continuing service of broader ideals. Surely, Paul Fussell is right in saying that World War I laid waste the 'high diction' and idealism of the pre-war years; yet this was particularly true for Europe.[18] In America much of it survived and so did a considerable residue of manly gentleness.

It is crucial to note that US military officers were a least as likely to need cultivation of the gentler skills than of aggressive attitudes and physical prowess and they were similarly diligent to see that their men followed the same pattern. Since Victorian manliness was not mere brute strength and unrestricted will, it was equally important to develop the sense of restraint, to instil an instinct for balance and to cultivate the habit of grace under pressure. Military courage and manliness thus inspired a rhetoric of 'softening' as much as 'toughening', especially since the armed forces tended to draw so much of their manpower from outside the middle and upper classes.[19]

For US Army officers promoting physical training within the armed forces, brute strength lacked the appeal of style and skill. Writing in the important *Journal of the Military Service Institution of the United States* in 1891, Major John Brooke of the Army Medical Department noted his preference for the 'Belvedere Apollo' over the 'Farnese Hercules' and, the next year, Lieutenant Colonel A. A. Woodhull favoured the lithe and skilful boxer James J. Corbett over his opponent the great John L. Sullivan. Primal strength was crucial but its style had to be simple and unboastful.

Theodore Roosevelt expressed this same underlying sentiment when he endorsed the 'lift toward lofty things', emoted over the 'infinite woe and suffering' of the Civil War but deplored the bully as a kind of moral pervert and social degenerate.[20] Such language helps to explain Roosevelt's displeasure with many of his own military officers – those who seemed to abuse their rank and to exploit privilege without performing well enough to merit sincere deference. A frontier fighter and manly hero such as General George Crook painted an ugly picture of such men. When he first entered the Army, Crook later confessed, his first impressions were 'not favourable'. He continued: 'Most of the customs and habits that I witnessed were not calculated to impress one's morals or usefulness. Most of the commanding officers were petty tyrants, styled by some Martinets. They lost no opportunities to snub those under them, and prided themselves in saying disagreeable things'.[21]

They were guilty of bad form. In his own foreign and military policy, appropriately enough, Roosevelt insisted that the United States 'carry a big stick' but he just as strongly called for 'speaking softly'. In this he captured much that was central to the military manly spirit, even as he achieved compact expression of his personal way of dealing with the world.

The instinct towards wholeness

Daniel Walker Howe has observed that 'Victorianism may be thought of as that culture which characterized the climactic era of modernization for the English-speakers'[22] but the modernisation was complex and the 'English-speakers' were a heterogeneous lot – both rural and urban, largely bourgeois but sometimes genteel, beneficial to capitalists yet often complementary with the interests of the proletariat. Among the underlying common threads of Victorianism, however, were the Victorians' own remarkable degree of consciousness about themselves and their culture and also their intense interest in national identity.[23] These threads had long been woven into the web of military ideology in America. Moreover, the military retained their own traditional concern over possible vulnerability to attack by foreign enemies, a fear which inspired in them a sense that the present moment – indeed, *every* present moment – was heavy with danger. This strain closely matched the deeply rooted 'demand for a sense of cosmic momentousness' which D. H. Meyer has astutely identified as a crucial element for American Victorians trying to make metaphysical sense out of existence. Seeing man as inherently a creature of morals, the Victorians matched the military officers' customary exaltation of behavioural routine and deferential relationships.[24] The military officers were hardly clones of civilian exponents of American

Victorianism but the practical intersection of their interests and attitudes often made determining the differences between them relatively unimportant.

Notwithstanding the actual pluralism of American culture, at virtually any time in its history, the US military have been more likely than civilians to envision a unitary culture and society – or, at least, to set narrower parameters for variations from the culture's norms. Yet, as Howe has also noted, it is more proper to speak of 'Victorian culture in America' than of the 'culture of Victorian America'. That is, the passionate dedication to discipline and order, the biblical rhetoric, the relish for technology and much else that typified American Victorianism remained first the enthusiasm of only a segment of the population, even if admittedly an influential one, which was finally able to impose its stamp most visibly on what remained a largely pluralistic society.[25] Such qualities as flourished in the climate of American Victorianism closely suited both the taste and the culture of US military officers. The spirit of professionalism quickened among them and it accepted the mantle of science while taking up the instruments of advanced technology. A religious disposition and rhetoric thrived among them, even when their moral fervour was turned to the secular faith of the civil state. Discipline, order and predictability – always important to military institutions – surpassed their status as tenets in a military creed and became the template of daily experience.[26]

Although this predisposition towards unity spread widely in the culture, one of its most engaging manifestations appeared in the role of the western frontier as a testing ground for manly vigour and as a crucible of military and Victorian idealism. The 'wilds', even along the eastern seaboard, had long been taken as a special preserve for men, in which they might at least briefly escape the complexities of relationships with women.[27] By the late nineteenth century, however, many Americans, including notable ones such as Theodore Roosevelt, had developed the dual thesis that character was formed in frontier challenge and conquest and that the character was unified and distinctively American.[28] The latter thesis and the role which it ascribed to the frontier did not displace the earlier notion, however, and male character-formation thus retained a sex-related undercurrent. Added to this was the special association of the US military with the vast 'internal empire' which the western territories constituted.[29] In a sense, what better symbol could one have wished for American Victorian culture's quest for wholeness than the whole process of settling the West and bringing it into the national society and economy?

Some officers, such as General George Crook, came to be regarded as 'friends of the Indians', who saw the natives as sharing in the basic virtues which distinguished the manly civilised Victorian. Despite the convenience of this resuscitation of the myth of the 'noble savage', it sharpened the focus on character rather than trappings and it underscored the special tie between the American West and the shaping of moral values.[30] In turn, the distinctive importance of the Army in the development of the frontier made it the last major element in a trinity of value-shaping circumstances. Aggressiveness, order, pathos and wholeness all merged in a single experience. 'Winning' the West and 'winning' the wars against Indian tribes meant not only the defeat of armed hostile forces, it meant the achievement of the sense as well as some substance of unity. So, too, on the specific level, the actual inner workings of the American military were surely as complicated and disorderly as those of any other major component in the social system of that time but its public face was strong and simple, a mask of Victorian commitment and wholeness, shielding a maze of competing emotions.

Playing at admiration for the noble savage, lavishing attention on the white-skinned warrior heroes, pining for the challenge of the frontier – these did more than extend historic themes in the development of the American West. They formed a readily accessible part of the late-nineteenth-century love of the primitive, the ease with 'primal irrationality' and an anti-modernism in psychology and spirit which paradoxically aided accommodation with the mechanism, the logic and the corporatism of some of the most forceful social developments in contemporary America.[31] The ascription of nobility to the savage depended in large measure on his simplicity and calling him 'childlike' was a form of praise, somewhat like calling Teddy Roosevelt 'boyish' even as late as his presidency, and not merely a pretext for mistreatment.[32] 'Innocent sincerity' and a 'primitivist veneration for vitality', twin objects of fascination and yearning for turn-of-the-century Americans,[33] were credible values in the mythologised West, especially so for the military men in whom these qualities seemed to take on practical benefit. Rather than strands of a lost tapestry, such values and personal qualities thus become meaningful threads in a web of challenge and experience – whole, purposeful, beautiful.

Heroic officers as symbols of ideology

Heroes may be thought of as imaginary constructs, freely based on the life experiences of actual human persona, re-enforced by the steel of an ideology.[34] American military men included such heroes among their number – mere mortals turned into emblems of the prevailing military ethos and of the conjunction with societal values that it was temporarily enjoying. Among the most widely touted was General Leonard Wood, a Harvard graduate and medical doctor who rose to Chief of Staff of the Army during the presidency of William Howard Taft. Wood rose to prominence in part because of his enthusiastic service with General Nelson A. Miles during the campaign against the Apache and a key to Wood's success were those qualities which typified the tradition of manliness. According to historian Jack C. Lane, Miles 'undoubtedly saw in the officer much of his own personality: cockiness, self-assurance, a consuming ambition, and particularly, an almost zealous devotion to physical fitness'. Miles' own words for Wood, as in praising Wood's will to 'endure' whatever the Apache would endure, underscored the imagery of ritualised duty.[35]

To be sure, Wood was a lively and engaging man. He became fast friends with Theodore Roosevelt, acting rough and rowdy as schoolboys with him even during the latter's presidency. Wood played at singlestick with Roosevelt, a variant of the mediaeval sport which became part of West Point's regimen at much the same time as the Academy's architecture was transformed in the manner of the Gothic revival. So vigorously did they engage in combat that General Wood came to work with red welts visible at the neck, while the President occasionally lost the use of his hand from his own injuries and once suffered a black eye that served as fodder for popular journalists for days.[36]

But Wood was ultimately much more useful as the stuff of legend – a bit like Teddy Roosevelt himself.[37] In a contemporary biography published in 1920 writer John G. Holme observed similarities in the two leaders' experiences and character: 'Both had succumbed to the Western fever early in their youth, and both had reached middle age with a remarkable similarity of views, retaining a clean, boyish enthusiasm for sports and athletic games, and all keen physical exercise, and a boyish admiration for feats of physical strength and prowess'.[38]

This set of attitudes – especially this ability to preserve boyish enthusiasm and optimism in the face of life's day-to-day struggles – struck

Holme as a 'gift of the gods', a disposition which was the secret to the popularity which both men enjoyed.[39]

What Holme wrote was true, or at least it was based on actual occurrences. The two men did practise sport, whether alone or together. They skied on the slopes and along the ravines of Washington's Rock Creek Park and they boxed and wrestled[40] but the fact that the proportion of Holme's biography devoted to the quasi-missionary enthusiasms of the age and to manly rites such as athletics was so very large took on a significance of its own. To a degree difficult to define precisely, the manly enthusiasm was itself an important theme of Holme's work and his work left strong implications of how one might follow, in the path of the legendary Wood. Holme described those who enlisted in the First US Volunteer Cavalry Regiment, the 'Rough Riders', in ways that linked sport, egalitarianism, personal distinction and manly commitment:

> Among the recruits were star football and tennis players and other college athletes, such as Dudley Dean, Harvard quarterback; Robert Wrenn, another quarter, and at that time the champion tennis player of the country; Hamilton Fish, captain of the Columbia crew; and Woodbury Kane, a famous yachtsman and society leader. . . Young Wall Street bankers and brokers, who measured up to the high physical standard set, abandoned their offices and their luxurious homes, just as did their sons and nephews [in World War I], and enlisted, neither seeking nor obtaining preferential treatment.[41]

Wood contributed to his own legend by actually being so much of what was attributed to him and by genuinely valuing the qualities ascribed to him. His love of athletics and his conviction that competitive sport built the manly spirit made him every bit as conscious of the sporting backgrounds of the 'Rough Riders' as were writers such as Holme. The convenience, in the end, was that individuals such as Leonard Wood encapsulated so many drives, interests and motivations, enabling them to serve as heroic symbols of individual aspiration at the same time as they acted as 'archetypal symbols' of a shared manly ideology.[42] Wood's watchword coupled the Victorian mix of inspiration and practicality with a measure of the male bonding which demanded total reliability from one's 'buddies'. ('We want to stand with our feet squarely on the earth,' he remarked bravely, 'our eyes on God, our ideals high, but steady'.)[43] Pronouncing judgment on Wood's life, Teddy Roosevelt succinctly gave voice to the heroic archetype: 'He combined in a very high degree the qualities of entire manliness with entire uprightness and cleanliness of character.'[44]

The presentation of a renowned soldier, John J. 'Black Jack' Pershing, again revealed discrepancies between the reality of an individual's life and the reality of his image. An accomplished counter-guerrilla fighter in the Philippines after the Spanish-American War and Commander of the American Expeditionary Force in World War 1, Pershing came to be wrapped in a hagiography rich with the rhetoric of Victorian manliness. For all the coolness of a description offered by Charles Walcutt, Pershing's room-mate at West Point, 'Black Jack' seemed to meet the stereotyped demands. 'He was conscientious', Walcutt reported, 'took the requirements of the Academy very seriously and gave his best in every element going to make up the sum total of life at that institution. He was a strict disciplinarian,' Walcutt added, 'and one who observed very closely his own precepts'.[45] Pershing's actual conduct at West Point may have been rigorous and disciplined but it also smacked of less noble instincts. He was remembered as 'a champion at deviling plebes', so much so that he was particularly dreaded by the new cadets. He was recalled as saying, 'I hope the day will never come when hazing is abolished'.[46] This, too, could be assigned to his belief in discipline, yet hazing sufficiently resembled the action of a mere bully, especially when one proved so distinguished in its execution, that a less admirable or at least less heroic interpretation was also possible. Biographer Donald Smythe has written of Pershing's life at posts in the desert west after leaving West Point, seeing the real man as human and likeable – but far from the image which was to overtake him in later years. 'He was no tin soldier,' Smythe has noted, 'and certainly no figurine saint.' He enjoyed himself, letting himself 'become a poker fanatic, note good places for making love, and drink himself full as eighteen goats.'[47] But even in much later decades, one of Pershing's biographers still drew on the sort of rhetoric that shrouded him as a manly model by the time of World War 1. Pershing, it was said, assumed 'the yoke of manhood.'[48] The relevant reality was the societal rather than the individual one.

The high moral time set by such writings about military leaders was institutionalised at the US Military Academy at West Point which was charged with taking mere men and turning them into officers with heroic potential. The general vision set for the Academy by General Douglas MacArthur, in the era of Word War 1, encompassed the 'wholeness' to which American Victorianism aspired.[49] MacArthur thought that true reform at West Point required that the Academy shun the corporatist, bureaucratic tendencies of the age. Although specialised knowledge and technological skills had value, MacArthur worried that they led to narrow, uninspired and uninspiring officers unworthy of leadership. As one historian of West Point has put it, MacArthur sought an all-round development and 'military bearing, leadership and personality, military efficiency, athletic performance, and cadet participation in such activities as choir or the YMCA all counted.'[50] These were not 'extras' added on; choir, personality development, YMCA activities – all were elements of duty for the whole man.

But perhaps the most striking single vehicle through which the Academy furthered the military ideal in Victorian dress remained its 'honor code.' The honour system at West Point was absolute, requiring complete truthfulness in every regard. A cadet must himself be honest in all things. If he should break that trust, he must report that he had done so. If he observed breaches of the code by others, he must report that. The insistence upon absolute truthfulness paralleled the military's need for total reliability – surely, one must be able to believe absolutely what one's comrades in arms said, to trust in their faithfulness and to enjoy a shared respect for motivations held in common.[51]

At the same time, however, something less conscious was at work. The need for absolute reliability appears to have been a common element in male bonding. One might walk side by side with one's wife but a man's buddy fought back-to-back when the going was especially tough. A little wandering afield by one's wife might be tolerated – not in superficial liaisons but in an elementally gripping loss of certainty in one's relationship with her. When psychologically side by side, after all, one could still keep the woman within one's field of vision but the loyal male friend was the one you could have at your back, never flinching and never doubting.[52] Since the turn-of-the-century notions of manliness heightened attention to distinction between male and female as well as that between baseness and nobility of spirit, the practice of male bonding took on heightened importance in the pursuit of manliness itself. At times, the rigorous quest for such absolute truthfulness had comic overtones. In the Army-Navy football game of 1890, for example, a major controversy ensued after the Navy team 'faked' a pass.[53] The action was derided as 'ungentlemanly', since it seemed to violate the bond that one was as good as one's word or one's professions of intent but the humour of the situation, such as it was, was lost upon the officers who worshipped at the shrines of civic virtue, proudly wearing 'the uniform' as the vestments of a special morality. Victory was central but so was the manner of its attainment. Gentlemen officers did not 'fake it', nor did those few who were promoted to the ranks of heroes.

The military ethos and Victorian survivals

Among the ways we may grasp what Victorian culture meant *for* Americans – as distinct from what it may have have meant *to* them – are various assessments made largely after its passing by the President's Research Committee on Social Trends, established by Herbert Hoover to provide a basis on which private citizens and private enterprise might forecast their respective futures.[54] The key to such forward planning, however, was an appreciation of the comparatively recent past and, central to appreciating that past, was understanding the values from which Americans appeared to be departing. In essence, the Research Committee on Social Trends summarised the general elements of American Victorianism, noting limited survivals. They included 'the lingering Puritan tradition of abstinence which makes play idleness and free spending sin', 'the tradition that rigorous saving and paying cash are the marks of sound family economy and personal self-respect', 'the deep rooted philosophy of hardship viewing this stern discipline as the inevitable lot of men,' and the tradition of cutting expenses to fit one's income which suggested an underlying apprehension of limits and depletion.[55]

One cannot overestimate the influence which Americans' fears of depletion and exhaustion had had in shaping their manners and morals – their culture as a whole – during the nineteenth century. Despite the objective potential for abundance which America's vast resources offered, the actuality was immeasurably less expansive. The world, the nation and the individual human life were all a kind of 'zero-sum game,' in which every chosen action and expenditure of energy reduced the reserves available to pursue other options.[56] This sense of constraint – of 'tightness' and stricture – was at the foundation of American Victorian morality and it was the basis for the American conception of manliness during the Victorian era – that cluster of character traits which suggested power and potential by preserving them in a cocoon of rules and manners.

Similarly, one cannot overestimate the extent to which the growing sense of abundance in America tore at the fabric of Victorianism and eventually left the US military, once again, turned in upon its own values and resources. The military may have seemed to many the keeper of the vestiges of Victorian codes, while in fact they were sustaining their own relatively constant and persistent values. For their part, the military live in a culture of perpetual perceived scarcity in which limited resources can never match the grandeur of fears for the security of one's nation. In this sense, the kinds of circumstances which helped civilian Victorians to flourish were immutable conditions for the American military.

The material conditions mattered, in part, because they served as stimuli for moral responses and as potential re-enforcement for prevailing manners. For what mattered was, in a sense, less what a man did than how he comported himself and what tone he projected. '"Character" in the Victorian sense,' Stanley Coben has written, 'bore only the slightest relationship to the faceless efficiency of the interchangeable headquarters executives, sales engineers, and research scientists at most huge industrial corporations.'[57] It is significant, in this regard, that some of the highest ranking US Army officers – those raised up and tempered at the height of American Victorianism – resisted the introduction of corporatist organisational structures and methods in their own service, even though they might have expanded their authority if those structures had been established.

Parallels did exist between the civilian and the military spheres. The military did incorporate aspects of the new bureaucratic, organisational impulse[58] and they did draw on the same pool of rhetoric and values[59] but there was always a genuine divide between the military professional and the Victorian enthusiast. In the end, the Victorian civilian lived in a world filled with change – one in which the very basis upon which social and moral values were built could shift. The military officer's convictions as a professional man were narrowly founded, narrowly framed but thus narrowly defensible.

It is possible that some of what has been attributed to manliness within the military may apply more fully in years when the professionals shared service with conscripts and short-term volunteers, as during World War I. For example, it has been argued that the actual experience of the war may have provided a means through which many males coped with their tangled feelings about women and about their own sexuality. At the time of World War I, the inherited belief in the importance of sexual restraint lingered, as did the notion that women were at once sexually extreme but natively asexual. At the same time, new habits and customs favouring social interaction among men and women were emerging. Against this jumble of thoughts and feelings, the war created a strong, though temporary, male preserve which radically simplified the definition of manliness by radically reducing its association with sexual activity and cross-gender relationships.[60]

The seeming similarity of sensuality and sexuality permitted the rough-and-tumble imagery of the military life to serve as a symbolism of masculinity, while at the same time compensating for the irregularity with which heterosexual liaisons might be consummated. Boldly physical as sexual expression was, the stress and pain of hard military training, of althetics used in preparing the men and of actual combat provided an alternative bodily commitment, meanwhile bolstering the equation of masculinity with roughness; and they served as forerunners to the elevation of 'toughness' over 'fitness' as the emotional contribution to manliness to be sought from physical training.[61] The risk that manliness could degenerate into mere brutality was real.[62] At the same time, the sensual immediacy of the physical side of military life and military manliness contributed to a stereotype of American masculinity emerging through mid-century and after. However, military manliness after the Victorian and Edwardian age once again set out substantially on its own course, carrying the military ethos forward into the century yet shorn of many links it had enjoyed with civilian institutions at the turn of the century.

The ultimate meaning of 'manliness' for the military – or of the concept altogether – may remain elusive, largely because its supposed attributes closely resemble those customarily related to the more general notion of 'character.' As Warren Susman has shown, suggesting the critical role of the idea of 'personality' in shaping twentieth-century culture, the emphasis in describing 'character' has typically shown itself in such words as *'citizenship, duty, democracy, work, building, golden deeds, outdoor life, conquest, honour, reputation, morals, manners, integrity,* and above all, *manhood.'* As Susman observes, 'the stress was clearly moral and the interest was almost always in some sort of higher moral law.'[63] Still, each culture and each era give special concrete meanings to these words and the special meanings given them by the American military subculture may be sensed in how the words took flesh.

Curiously, the American military ethos matched Victorian values both in detail and in general – in the specifics of disposition and belief and also in the much broader fact that each was only a subculture in America as a whole, no matter how important. One may infer that American military officers appreciated as a badge of elitism those same Victorian values which they consciously pursued to serve as a basis for national moral strength and military professionalism.[64] This compatibility is critical in understandng the special place of the US military in developing the cult of manliness in America during Victorian and post-Victorian times. At once, each appealed to the enterprising spirit of organisational change and technological advancement and also to a deceptive self-image as conservator of traditional values against the onslaught of degenerate forces.

The US military sought victory and implicitly pledged it in return for support and manliness gave that quest for victory a special face, a distinctive tone of voice and a nuance of rhetoric which endured for decades.

Notes

1   See *Oxford English Dictionary,* Oxford, Clarendon Press, 1933, Vol. VI 'L-M,' p. 127.

2   See, for example, Peter N. Stearns, *Be a Man! Males in Modern Society,* New York, Holmes & Meier Publishers, Inc., 1979, p. 20.

3   See Stearns, *Be a Man!,* pp. 98-9. Stearns also suggests, however, that this positive association of manliness and war suffered deeply with the experience of World War I.

4   *Ibid.,* p. 120.

5   See Joseph F. Kett, *Rites of Passage, Adolescence in America, 1790 to the Present,* New York, Basic Books, 1977, p. 173.

6   The matter of male friendship has become a subject of considerable contemporary attention as men's studies have risen to complement the efforts of researchers in women's studies. On the fears of male friendship and the constraints against intimacy, see Stuart Miller, *Men and Friendship,* Boston, Houghton Mifflin Company, 1983.

7   See, for example, J. A. Mangan, *Athleticism in the Victorian and Edwardian Public School, The Emergence and Consolidation of an Educational Ideology,* Cambridge, Cambridge University Press, 1981, especially pp. 43-9, 53.

8   Mangan, *Athleticism in the Victorian and Edwardian Public School,* especially p. 140ff, details the development of such 'encrustation' in the educational system in Britain and within its ideology. Parallel developments may be seen within the US military as an overlay upon existing systems of symbols and rites.

9   Kett notes that American psychologists and 'boy workers' such as G. Stanley Hall believed that military training and service provided an excellent means for imposing needed discipline upon the young, thus helping them achieve passage through the dangerous years of adolescence. See Kett, *Rites of Passage,* pp. 197-8, 219-21.

10   Rupert Wilkinson, *American Tough, The Tough-Guy Tradition and American Character,* Westport CT, Greenwood Press, 1984, p. 63.

11   On the matter of Victorian certitude, see the various essays in Howe, *Victorian America,* especially Stanley Coben, 'The Assault on Victorianism in the Twentieth Century,' pp. 160-81. Coben observes that the key to destroying Victorianism as a dominant force in America, notwithstanding its local survivals, lay in the rise of cultural relativism typified by the work of such scholars as Franz Boas and Ruth Benedict. Also see Henry May, *The End of American Innocence,* New York, Knopf, 1959.

12   It has been most common to discuss the issue of nineteenth-century dress as a matter of discriminatory restriction of women, at least until the emergence of dress reform, represented by the advocacy of Amelia Bloomer. See, for example, Dexter C. Bloomer, *The Life and Writings of Amelia Bloomer,* Boston, Arena, 1895. Dress reform was also ardently supported by certain male physical educators and others, including Dudley A. Sargent. But, as Lois Banner has recently pointed out, men's dress – a matter of social choice and fashion – was also hotly contested during the nineteenth century, especially in later years when as 'assertive' style emerged which threatened to strip away some of the restraints and restrictiveness that were hallmarks of style in the Victorian era. See Lois W. Banner, *American Beauty,* New York, Alfred A. Knopf, 1983, especially pp. 226-48.

13   Dreiser is quoted in Banner, *American Beauty,* p. 240. Banner does not deal with the autonomous dress styles of the US military but it is clear that several of the ideas which she applies to civilian trends could be played off against developments in the military.

14   *Ibid.,* pp. 228-9.

15   Joseph Mills Hanson, ed., *The Inter-Allied Games, Paris, 22nd June to 6th July,* 1919, Paris, The Games Committee, 1919, pp. 19-20.

16   *Ibid.,* p. 38.

17   *Ibid.,* p. 14.

18   Paul Fussell, *The Great War and Modern Memory,* London, Oxford University Press, 1975. It is significant that some participants in the Military Olympics actually delayed their return to their home countries in order to participate in the gathering. For such men, the Games were more than a means to pass the time; they offered the positive goals of bonding with one's 'brothers in arms,' thus suggesting that the disillusionment so often attributed to survivors of the war was, at the very least, far from a universal phenomenon. Concerning the delays in departing France, see Hanson, ed., *The Inter-Allied Games,* p. 84 f.

19   For those entering the officer corps from relatively humble origins, military service constituted a form of upward mobility and possession of officer rank sufficed as a badge of admission into middle and upper-class civilian institutions, such as urban clubs, which were themselves partly populated by civilians themselves only recently risen from simpler beginnings.

20   See Theodore Roosevelt, 'Manhood and statehood,' 'Manly virtues and practical politics,' and 'The American boy,' in Theodore Roosevelt, *The Works of Theodore Roosevelt,* New York, Collier's, 1905.

21   See Martin F. Schmitt, ed., *General George Crook, His Autobiography,* Norman, OK, University of Oklahoma Press, 1960, p. 10.

22   Daniel Walker Howe, 'Victorian culture in America,' in *Victorian America,* ed. Howe, Philadelphia, University of Pennsylvania Press, p. 8·

23   *Ibid.,* pp. 7-11.

24   See D. H. Meyer, 'The Victorian Crisis of Faith,' in *Victorian America,* pp. 68-73.

25   Daniel Walker Howe, 'Victorian Culture in America,' in Howe, ed., *Victorian America,* Philadelphia, University of Pennsylvania Press, 1976, pp. 3-7.

26   The literature on the US military is enormous, even on the matter of modernising its institutions, improving its hardware and many other specific aspects. See, however, Walter Millis, *Arms and Men: A Study in American Military History,* New York, Putnam, 1956; Russell F. Weigley, *The American Way of War: A History of United States Military Strategy and Policy,* New York, Macmillan, 1973; Graham Cosmas, *An Army for Empire: The United States Army in the Spanish-American War,* Columbia MO, University of Missouri Press, 1971. Although the US military has often been a bastion of traditionalist manners and customs, it has also been a frequent exponent of technological innovation since before the American Civil War, and it served as one of the most diligent 'point' forces in the 'modernisation' of America, especially in the years after the Civil War and through World War I.

27   See, for example, comments concerning Rev John Todd, the prolific writer of anti-masturbation literature, in G. J. Barker-Benfield, *The Horrors of the Half-Known Life, Male Attitudes toward Women and Sexuality in Nineteenth-century America,* New York, Harper, 1976, pp. 156-7.

28   See, for example, Theodore Roosevelt, *The Winning of the West,* 1, New York, Putnam's, 1889. It is useful to recall that such relatively popular writings as Roosevelt's appeared at the same time as the professionally heralded 'frontier thesis' of Frederick Jackson Turner and sometimes even earlier.

29   Studies of the special role of the Army in the West include: William H. Goetzmann, *Army Exploration in the American West*, 1803-1863, New Haven CT, Yale University Press, 1959, Francis P. Prucha, *Broadax and Bayonet: The Role of the United States Army in the Development of the Northwest*, 1815-1860, Madison WI, State Historical Society of Wisconsin, 1953, and *Sword of the Republic: The United States Army on the Frontier*, 1783-1846, New York, Macmillan, 1969, Robert M. Utley, *Frontier Regulars: The United States Army and the Indian*, 1886-1891, New York, Macmillan, 1974.

30   See, for example, John Bourke, *On the Border with Crook*, New York, Scribner's 1891.

31   See T. J. Jackson Lears, *No Place of Grace, Antimodernism and the Transformation of American Culture*, 1880-1920, New York, Pantheon Books, 1981, especially pp. 142-9, 164-5.

32   Lears, *No Place of Grace*, deals with the notion of childhood and the 'childhood of the race,' especially pp. 144-9.

33   These terms come from Lears, *No Place of Grace*, p. 146. Also see his specific discussion of the US military and antimodernism, pp. 112-3, 116-7, 138.

34   Useful to this notion is seeing heroes as 'human value filters' as suggested in Mangan, *Athleticism in the Victorian and Edwardian Public Schools*, p. 156.

35   See Jack C. Lane, *Armed Progressive: General Leonard Wood*, San Rafael CA, Presidio Press, 1978, p. 17. Also see Virginia W. Johnson, *The Unregimented General: A Biography of Nelson A. Miles*, Boston, Houghton Mifflin, 1962.

36   Lane, *Armed Progressive*, pp. 117-8.

37   A fine example of writing that helped to fabricate the Roosevelt legend is Herrmann Hagedorn, *The Boys' Life of Theodore Roosevelt*, New York, Harper, 1918.

38   John G. Holme, *The Life of Leonard Wood*, Garden City NY, Doubleday, Page & Company, 1920, pp. 37-8.

39   Holme, *The Life of Leonard Wood*, p. 38.

40   Holme, *The Life of Leonard Wood*, pp. 40-1.

41   Holme, *The Life of Leonard Wood*, p. 47. Concerning the later recruiting pattern for the voluntary military training camps of the Plattsburgh Movement, another largely elitist manly enterprise, see John Garry Clifford, *The Citizen Soldiers, The Plattsburgh Training Camp Movement*, 1913-1920, Lexington KY, University Press of Kentucky, 1972, pp. 58, 94.

42   The term in quotation marks is from J. A. Mangan, *Athleticism in the Victorian and Edwardian Public School*, p. 156.

43   Quoted in Holme, *The Life of Leonard Wood*, p. 227.

44   Quoted in Holme, *The Life of Leonard Wood*, pp. 227-8.

45   Walcutt is quoted in Donald Smythe, *Guerrilla Warrior, The Early Life of John J. Pershing*, New York, Charles Scribner's Sons, 1973, pp. 7-8.

46   Smythe, *Guerrilla Warrior*, p. 13.

47   Smythe, *Guerrilla Warrior*, pp. 25-6.

48   Frank E. Vandiver, *Black Jack, The Life and Times of John J. Pershing*, I, College Station TX, Texas A & M University Press, 1977, p. 11.

49   See Stephen E. Ambrose, *Duty, Honor, Country, A History of West Point*, Baltimore, John Hopkins University Press, 1966; Thomas J. Fleming, *West Point, The Men and Times of the United States Military Academy*, New York, William Morrow & Company, Inc., 1969. Also see scenes of sporting life, fencing, drawing maps in rooms adorned with copies of classical statuary, singlestick and the like in Jeffrey Simpson, *Soldiers and Statesmen, Historic West Point in Photographs*, Tarrytown NY, Sleepy Hollow Press, 1982.

50   Ambrose, *Duty, Honor, Country*, pp. 280-1.

51   See Ambrose, *Duty, Honor, Country*, pp. 279-80.

52   On this matter see Peter N. Stearns, *Be A Man! Males in Modern Society*, New York,

Holmes & Meier, 1979, *passim*.

53   Ambrose, *Duty, Honor, Country*, p. 259.

54   The point of the rhetorical distinction between 'for' and 'to' here is to emphasise the diversity which remained strong among America's many subcultures, even in those times when Victorian values held centre stage. Moreover, it is to reaffirm that intention often differs from impact – a fact which is critical in appreciating, for example, how the US military had the effect of encouraging the eventual growth of a mass leisure culture in America, despite their having no intention of doing so.

55   President's Research Committee on Social Trends, *Recent Social Trends*, New York, McGraw-Hill Book Company, Inc., 1933, p. 867.

56   On the level of national and international affairs, a good illustration of this 'zero-sum sensibility' is Brooks Adams, *The Law of Civilization and Decay, An Essay on History*, New York, Macmillan, 1896. On the most personal level, the notion of 'spermatic economy' – that males were endowed with only a finite reserve of energy, which might be applied to physical tasks from work through sport through sexual expression – is explored in G. J. Barker-Benfield, *The Horrors of the Half-Known Life, Male Attitudes Toward Women and Sexuality in Nineteenth-Century America*, New York, Harper, 1976. Also see Peter N. Stearns, *Be a Man! Males in Modern Society*, New York, Holmes & Meier, 1979.

It is worth recalling that the United States was rather a 'have not' nation in the nineteenth century, at least in those terms which meant most to Americans themselves. In a sense, the maintenance of Victorian values depended on that 'have not' status, even though some of the sharpest articulations of Victorian thinking came when America was achieving economic eminence. In America, the imposition of a guiding ideology or rationale, as in the Victorian structure of values, could not rely on the strength of a dominant social class, since class in America remained largely contingent on relative wealth and on the relative power of different posts such as doctor, minister or educator. Even such power as might be attached to a position, however, was relative to wealth and its trappings. In short, as wealth in America increased sharply and fell into different patterns, the most crucial underlying instinct for Victorian values – the sense of scarcity – was savaged at the same time as the key exponents of those values were stripped of their greatest social power.

57   See Stanley Coben, 'The assault on Victorianism,' p. 176.

58   See, for example, Elting E. Morison, *Men, Machines, and Modern Times*, Cambridge MA, MIT Press, 1900.

59   See Donald J. Mrozek, *Sport and American Mentality, 1880-1910*, Knoxville TN, The University of Tennessee Press, 1983, especially 'Social efficiency and the spirit of victory', pp. 28-66.

60   See Peter Filene, 'Men and manliness before World War I' (paper delivered at the annual conference of the Organisation of American Historians, April 1972).

61   On manliness and its relationship to sexuality, as well as on the interplay between pain and aspirations towards sexual expression, see J. A. Mangan, *Athleticism in the Victorian and Edwardian Public School*, p. 176ff and p. 186ff. Although the specific object of study is different, Mangan's ideas are substantially applicable to US military institutions at about the same time.

62   The confusion over manliness and toughness later in the century is suggested in Donald J. Mrozek, 'The cult and ritual of toughness in cold war America' in Ray Browne, ed., *Rituals and Ceremonies in Popular Culture*, Bowling Green OH, Bowling Green University Popular Press, 1980, pp. 178-91.

63   See Warren I. Susman, 'Personality and the Making of Twentieth-Century Culture' in John Higham and Paul K. Conkin, *New Directions in American Intellectual History*, Balti-

more, John Hopkins University Press, 1979, p. 214.

64   Although it does not deal with the period after the American Civil War, Marcus
Cunliffe, *Soldiers and Civilians: The Martial Spirit in America*, 1775-1865, Boston, Little,
Brown, 1968, does suggest the underlying elitist instincts among American officers,
instincts which paralleled other professionalising groups in America before the Civil War
and which became even stronger in later decades.

'Frank did not hesitate to tackle the giant of the gridiron'.

Admiral Robley D. Evans became one of the great early promoters of sport and athletic competition within the US Navy while commanding the North Atlantic Squadron. Admiral Evans accepted the argument that sport strengthened character. By putting sport on to the schedule of activities in the sailor's 'duty day', he officially sanctioned sport – but not as 'fun' or 'self-expression'

Troopers of the 4th Cavalry, probably 'C' Troop, stage a boxing match at Fort Riley, Kansas, *c.* 1910. Boxing emerged as one of the most highly-regarded sports among the military, despite unsavoury association throughout the nineteenth century. The military services were clearly attracted by the one-to-one confrontation which boxing demanded, yet they also loved the restraint and self-control without which victory was likely to be elusive

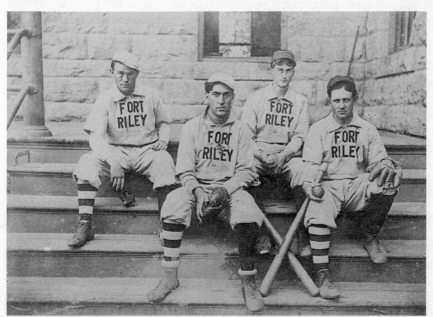

Members of a Fort Riley, Kansas, unit baseball team, *c.* 1910

Symbols of moral superiority: slavery, sport and the changing world order, 1800-1950

Writing in 1888, a commentator on football remarked: 'Health, endurance, courage, judgement, and above all a sense of fair play, are gained upon the football field. A footballer must learn, and does learn, to play fairly in the thick and heat of a struggle. Such qualities are those which make a nation brave and great. The game is manly and fit for Englishmen; it puts a courage into their hearts to meet any enemy in the face.'[1]

It was commonly assumed that the English were, without question, a brave nation, whose bravery could be recited through the annals of their history and more especially through the story of their expansion and adventures abroad. Patriotism was a virtue widely promoted not only through the obvious and familiar agencies of, for example, the public schools, but no less potently through printed material which permeated through all social classes. In a pamphlet published by the Religious Tract Society, the author described a debate between children. In discussing the Empire, one child said, 'We must be proper patriots, and love our mother country like nothing else, and fight for her and die for her.'[2]

There were, by the late nineteenth century, plenty of opportunities for young men to die for their country in that host of little wars and overseas adventures which slowly but effectively aggregated to Britain the largest Empire the world had seen. Although the Crimean War remained the only major conflict which punctuated the eighty plus years between the ending of the Napoleonic wars and the South African conflict, that myriad of imperial and colonial wars and skirmishes (and their attendant diseases) consumed British manpower. Moreover, they provided further evidence, and proof, for those keen to discuss the matter at home that Britain's unique role in the world – her apparently irresistible rise to global pre-eminence – was shaped by the distinctive qualities of her menfolk.

It is possible to trace the origins of this belief to the evangelical campaign, particularly against slavery, in the early nineteenth century. The course – and motives – for that campaign are unusually complex[3] but the consequences of emancipation (after 1838) had far-reaching effects on the way the British talked about themselves and their 'national character'. Ignoring the fact that for almost two centuries the British had been the western world's pre-eminent slave trader, emancipation allowed the British to congratulate themselves on their moral superiority in having ended slavery. Not only that, but the survival of slavery – in the USA, in South America, Africa and elsewhere – provided the British with a perfect illustration of their own moral superiority. What made the British feel superior was not merely the military facts of empire or the undeniable evidence of industrial and economic power, but that superior morality which, in the case of slavery, provided so distinguishing a difference between Britain and the rest of the world. The evangelical drive against slavery, firstly in British possessions, later against foreign slaveries, itself became a form of cultural imperialism, enabling Britian to hawk its moral superiority around the world and to insist that others – Europeans as well as 'native peoples' – should accord to the standards of the new found morality. Anti-slavery became in effect a cultural talisman which distinguished the good (the British) from the bad (the others).

While it may be felt that anti-slavery was a limited phenomenon, restricted to a passionate and articulate minority, this was far from the case. Indeed what gave the anti-slavery crusade so irresistible a dynamic was the extraordinary support it accumulated from all classes – and both sexes. By the time British slavery was fully terminated in 1838, the anti-slavery movement had become *the* most popular of all contemporary political campaigns. In large part this was a result of astute and effective tactics by the abolitionists but their success was to a degree rooted in forces beyond their control: in the changing face of Britain itself. As Britain became an increasingly urbanised – and to some degree industrialised – society, literacy and the printed word became the distinguishing feature of this new society. Anti-slavery succeeded in part because of the avalanche of propaganda unleashed upon an increasingly literate nation. Moreover, in the urbanising world of the early nineteenth century, there were few prominent institutions which refused to join the cause or place their facilities at the cause's disposal. This was spectacularly so in the case of organised religion, more especially that mosaic of non-conformist chapels which dotted plebeian communities. Through their preachers, Sunday Schools, printed texts and spoken words, the non-conformists (and even, though belatedly, members of the Established Church) acquired a fierce hostility – rooted in their particular religion – to slavery. Despite the evidence of the previous two centuries, Christianity – in Britain at least – had begun to present itself, by the mid-nineteenth century, as the aggressive opponent of slavery and of any society which was based on slavery or dabbled with it. By the end of British slavery, that crusading zeal against slavery which had begun life as a minority sensibility among a small band of evangelicals had become a national and pervasive obsession which had captured the imagination and the energies of millions.

Throughout the subsequent history of British imperialism, the British gave themselves the task of stamping out slavery and slave-trading among those indigenous peoples they governed or came into contact with. Slavery, along with 'heathenism', was henceforth regarded as the major vice of uncivilised peoples, to be purged and destroyed and to be replaced by labour systems, cultural values and religion transplanted by the conquering and superior British. This is not to deny however that until 1919 the British themselves remained addicted to a form of bondage – indentured labour – which seemed to many like a variant of slavery and which involved an international maritime trade in humanity not totally dissimilar to the old slave trade.[4]

It is also important to stress that the ending of slavery took place within the context of major economic change as British economic priorities began to shift from a commitment to the protection of the old imperial system to the freer market – in labour, goods and materials – of the new industrial order. Yet the basic point which needs to be stressed is that the unquestioned commitment to the culture of slavery which had been so important a feature of mid-eighteenth century British life had, a century later, been utterly replaced by an assertive culture of anti-slavery.

By that time, and for a complexity of reasons, Britain was also becoming perceptibly more refined, more 'civilised', both in the way people conducted their social and leisure lives and in the way they viewed the world at large. The 'peaceable kingdom' of the late nineteenth century – so sharp a contrast to that 'ungovernable people' of the late eighteenth century and earlier – was a nation which took great pride not only in its obvious material achievements – exemplified by the 1851 Exhibition – but, more fundamentally, in the power, the irresistible power, of its own civilisation. Wilberforce and other evangelicals had set out in the late eighteenth century to encourage a 'refinement of manners' among the British people but by the mid-nineteenth century – and for reasons not always connected to evangelical activity – this had become a striking feature of British life. Indeed, the key point here is that the British – but especially the English – had come to view themselves as a civilised people, qualitatively superior to all others (including white Europeans and North Americans). Henceforth, they set themselves the task of civilising the world (to which end, of course, the ending of slavery had been a major contribution).

For much of the second half of the nineteenth century slavery continued to attract British attention. Foreign Office treaties – many with subservient or client states in no position to refuse or resist – were supported by the considerable power of the Royal Navy operating in the Atlantic and Indian Oceans but as long as slavery continued in the Americas (as it did until the 1880s in Brazil and Cuba) Africa remained prey to predatory traders willing to risk the obvious dangers in return for the possible profits. Slavery and slave trading were, then, major issues of international diplomacy and, as such, continued to attract attention but the culture of anti-slavery went much deeper than mere diplomacy. In churches, schools and in an abundance of popular literature the moral lessons of slavery were paraded before the reading pulbic. Moreover, the reading public was also expanding, itself a function of formal and informal educational changes. The highly-literate British people were regaled with stories of slavery – and of British virtue in combating it – on all hands. This was especially striking in children's literature, in books, magazines, comics and a host of ephemeral literature. Boys' literature in particular abounded with tales of British heroism and Christian zeal in confronting and suppressing slavery in hostile regions of the world. A child's board game, for instance – a type of noughts and crosses – concluded with the King of England granting freedom to a kneeling slave.[5]

Throughout much of the nineteenth century, anti-slavery was a potent symbol of British superiority. It was an ideal flaunted around the world; a standard to which the rest of mankind was expected to conform. It was however undermined by its own success, for as slavery withered so too did the potency of the appeal to anti-slavery. Yet the insistence on British moral superiority remained – indeed grew more insistent – with the remarkable expansion of British imperialism and commerical strength. By the late nineteenth century the most striking, influential – and abiding – form of this urge to impress British superiority was the new-fangled cult of sporting manliness and the arena for displays of such manliness was, increasingly, the expanding world of empire and overseas expansion.

There was a broad literary *genre* of military and overseas adventure and warfare which proved influential among the young well into the twentieth century. Factual accounts, fictional stories, historical episodes – even the lessons of geography – were proffered to young readers as proof of their country's superiority over all other peoples. In seeking to explain why the British came to view themselves to be superior to the rest of mankind – white as well as black – historians have rarely turned to that most potent and abiding influence – the lessons of childhood. It is perfectly true, as John MacKenzie has shown, that the commitment to and the propaganda of empire (which itself subsumed distinct concepts of superiority) was purveyed by a host of formal and informal agencies[6] but it is also important to stress the degree to which boys and girls, of all social classes, were exposed to powerful lessons of cultural superiority throughout the nineteenth century.[7] Moreover, this process began long before the apogee of formal empire in the late century for it was given its initial impetus and direction, from the 1820s onwards, by the crusade against slavery. Whatever the cause, British children were accustomed to learn of their own superiority – though often this was described as an *English* phenomenon. 'The English are a grave, sober people, fond of their houses and families; they are kind to each other and to people in distress; industrious and active; fond of liberty themselves and willing to allow it to others'.[8]

Such qualities were often described as historically-determined but they were, more importantly, God given; blessings from a Deity which favoured the British Isles:

> How happy is our lot
> Who live on Britain's isle!
> Which is of heaven the favour'd spot,
> Where countless blessings smile.

The prayer, 'The English Child', intoned in a similar vein:

> I was not born as thousands are,
> Where God was never known;

And taught to pray a useless pray'r
To blocks of wood and stone.[9]

Britain's civilising mission was, in large part, portrayed as a drive to purge the 'uncivilised' world of its pagan habits, of worshipping wood and stone, persuading them instead of the one and only true religion – Christianity. Conversely, English children were urged to count their blessings, to thank their good fortune in being born in England.

I thank the Goodness and the Grace
That on my birth have smiled,
And made me, in these Christian Days
A happy English child.[10]

Of course, children's literature was extraordinary rich and varied and changed a great deal in the course of the nineteenth century but a number of themes remained relatively constant and unchanging; the British – but especially the English – were elevated to the position of chosen people, while the great bulk of the world's indigenous peoples were relegated and denigrated. Sometimes the impression was adequately conveyed by a book's title. *Funny Foreigners* and *Odd People, or Singular Races of Man* were two such titles.[11] Even for children unable to read, a similar message was conveyed in graphic, cariacatured form. Blacks were normally warlike – or lazy:

Sun so hot – O!
Take it easy!
That's the motto
In Zambesi![12]

Exotic peoples – even those with unquestionably ancient cultures of a kind admitted and admired by Europeans – were ridiculed:

So there are the Chinese! O what comical creatures!
At least they appear so to me:
How dreadful his nails and how funny her features!
I suppose they are going to tea.[13]

Africa and Africans were readily dismissed: 'Most of the inhabitants have black skins and are very rude and uneducated.' The same was true for Australia: 'a very uncivilised place, except that part of it which has been peopled from England.'[14] Even European neighbours were subjected to critical scrutiny and invariably found wanting. Whatever their own distinctive qualities, they lacked the main ingredients which, it was felt, elevated the English to the pre-eminent position among people of the world:

> Beautiful England – on her island throne –
> Grandly she rules, with half the world her own.
> From her vast empire, the sun ne'er departs.
> She reigns a Queen, Victoria, Queen of hearts.[15]

This view of a benign British imperialism motivated by good will towards less fortunate mankind took hold of most forms of learning, informal and formal, directed towards the nation's young. The most obvious place for rehearsing such ideals was, of course, the schools; private ('public schools') in the case of the propertied and well-to-do, board and elementary schools from 1880 onwards for the great mass of the nation's young, now caught in the web of compulsory education. The public schools have been a favourite topic for historians of the period and it seems clear that they were the seed-bed for many of the most influential ideas which were disseminated in late Victorian and Edwardian Britain. Empire and foreign adventure were carefully cultivated among public school men – for a variety of reasons. Firstly, the outposts of empire were occupied by public school men. The empire employed 20,000 men as colonial administrators, 146,000 as soldiers – of whom 8,000 were officers – and many more as clerks, doctors, advisers and the like.[16] The upper reaches of these colonial cadres were drawn primarily from the public schools, who saw it as a prime task to produce manpower for the empire's growing elite.

In retrospect it is easy to minimise the physical dangers and hardships of life on the imperial frontiers. Contemporary travel and hygiene, the infancy of tropical medicine and the simple newness of so many colonial and overseas Europeans settlements determined that a life of 'duty', in the imperial or trading cause, would be arduous and difficult. And how were young men to be trained and conditioned for the physical rigours of such a life? Fortunately, British schools had developed the perfect tool for perfecting and honing the physical and collective qualities needed in such a venture – school games. The playing field – later the playground in the state schools – was as important as the class room in inculcating a number of attitudes and in encouraging the physical fitness which imperial life demanded. Moreover, it was at games that the British excelled like no other poeple, not surprisingly perhaps since they were the pioneers and originators of many of the games which, though new at the time, have subsequently come to dominate modern mass leisure pursuits.

The ideal of public school athleticism began earlier in the century in the idealised world of Thomas Hughes. Although historians have commonly referred to that athleticism as 'muscular Christianity', J. A. Mangan has reminded us that by late century the reality within the schools was quite different. The playing fields were the place where public schools put into practice their own distinctive brand of Social Darwinism; in games, only the fittest survived or triumphed. One public school man argued that the rigours of the school system forced its pupils to be 'broken in to many things, and hardened simply by a process of friction to endure, to suffer, to be patient, to bide his time. . , to take care of himself, to hold his own, to fight his way, to trust to his best, his own determination, and coolness, and pluck. . .'.

And all this was preparation for 'the great world of business and society'.[17] It was, however, in the more dangerous world of colonial adventure and government that such lessons were thought most valuable. One Head claimed, 'we desire our games to foster the spirit that faces danger. . . cricket, football, hockey, fives can all be painful enough; often victory is only to be won by a clenching of the teeth and the sternest of resolve to "stick to it" in the face of exhaustion'.[18] Time and again, public school men were encouraged, through games, to acquire 'a grounding in those qualities so dear to men of his station – Fortitude and Endurance.'[19] Games demanded physical exertion and bravery. The outcome was undisputable.

> Brave boys make brave men. Good soldiers, dauntless hunters, adventurous explorers, and good volunteers, all owe a great deal to the pastimes they enjoyed between school hours and in vacations. Indeed much of the greatness of our nation is to be attributed to the training which takes place in the playground. For summer we have a capital game in cricket; for winter. . . we have football.[20]

Edward Thring, the reforming Head of Uppingham, was no less certain of the importance of games, in the context of the broader public school education, in fostering England's uniqueness: 'with all their faults. . . the public schools are the cause of the "manliness".'[21]

The history of modern team games is the history of the nineteenth century public school. There, the games were codified, rationalised and disciplined. The natural instinct for play among the young was given a new focus and purpose. Games became an agency for disciplining the young and addicting them to a number of important individual and collective qualities: obedience, physical commitment, accepting rules and authority and to give one's all for the good of the team (or house, or school, or country). They also of course involved the universal lessons of endurance and fortitude, and give and take and striving to win, but team sports in particular also encapsulated a number of important ideals about rank, social role, class and race – all of which had important ramifications for Britain's role in the wider world. Endurance and toughness – finely tuned in the Social Darwinism of public school games – were clearly important (as contemporary boys' magazines regularly told) in the world of imperial conquest and administration.

The two games which dominated the lives of public school athleticism (and later the board schools) – football and cricket – were highly structured and disciplined. If their pre-modern folk roots were indisciplined and informal, by the late nineteenth century they were formal and disciplined, with their own codes of behaviour and governing bodies and impartial officials (on and off the field). Both were subjected to the determining regulation of the clock and both demanded of their players an acceptance of a given role within the team. A player's role and value was subsumed to the greater needs of the team itself (notwithstanding the fact that the games' best-remembered players are men whose distinctive athletic genius allowed them to flaunt team play). As teams, cricket and football had a chain of command which reached from the playing field into a higher structure of authority (house or school captain). Playing these games, like working in many of the newer industrial occupations, was a means of accepting that structure of authority; obedience to betters/ superiors, obeying orders and a commitment to pursuing the interests of the team – all of these had abiding importance in the broader conduct of British life at home and abroad. Games were, in some key respects, an illustration of contemporary Social Darwinism but they were equally instrumental in establishing a broadly-based discipline whose consequences transcended the mere playing of games.

The key issue however is not that the British simply played games but that they were *better* than others at those games. British athleticism – original, manly and pioneering – was but another illustration of the superiority of the British. Sports and games seemed to confirm the abundant evidence which was available on all hands – economic ascendancy, imperial prime, diplomatic assertiveness – that Britain was the world's pre-eminent power. Moreover, that global pre-eminence was to be found in the personal and collective qualities of her people. If Britain was the world's leading power, it was because her people were superior. There is again a welter of evidence to illustrate the fact that the British *believed* themselves to be superior.

Much of that belief was a function of contemporary racial thought. What made the British superior, selected by natural qualities, was their racial superiority. By the late century, at the time of imperial expansion, the commitment to a racial view of mankind was all-pervasive. In part, this was a direct function of a eugenics movement whose influence rapidly disseminated key concepts of race, but schools – notably the public schools – were, once more, crucial in establishing a belief in race as the key categories of mankind, among successive generations of pupils. It was an article of faith that the white races of the world were superior to the non-white races in all worthwhile human endeavours. From the mid-century onwards there was a growing commitment to the concept of race as the key determining category of mankind. Two major imperial revolts – the Indian Mutiny of 1857 and the Jamaican revolt of 1865 – served to alienate much of the surviving sympathy for native peoples and to reinforce the growing commitments to the idea that their inferiority was racially-determined (as too was the British right to govern them). Robert Knox, the Scottish anatomist, put the point starkly: 'that race is in human affairs everything is simply a fact, the most remarkable, the most comprehensive, which philosophy had ever announced. Race is everything: literature, science, art – in a word civilisation – depends on it.'[22]

The public schools took up the challenge of spreading this racial view of mankind. The Head of Marlborough, Frederick William Farrar, who was also a popular novelist, argued in 1861 that 'the savage races are without a past and without a future, doomed as races infinitely nobler have been before them, to a rapid and entire and perhaps for the highest destinies of mankind, an enviable extinction.'[23]

There were, however, distinctly worrying dimensions to this interpretation, especially when, from the 1860s, it came to be applied to *domestic* British life; when sociologists and anthropologists in analysing Britsh life began to speak of the lower order as a race apart. While it was possible to claim that the upper and middle orders held sway because of their racial superiority over the poorer classes, what did these racial fissures do to the alleged claim of an *overall* British racial superiority? How could the British be so superior if, by the same criteria of natural selection and racial categorisation, a substantial part (perhaps a majority) of British life itself consisted of racially-inferior beings? In 1864, the *Saturday Review* wrote: 'The Bethnal Green poor, as compared with the comfortable inhabitants of western London, are a caste apart, a race of whom we know nothing, whose lives are of a quite different complexion from ours. . .'[24]

Lazy, stupid, ignorant, unwilling to work unless compelled; the urban poor shared a racially-determined category remarkably like colonial blacks, and few British people were so frequently denounced in racial terms as the Irish, hundreds of thousands of whom lived the lives of helots in major English and Scottish cities.[25]

Notwithstanding the difficulties of using racial categories to describe British and native peoples – a usage which severely dinted the racially-determined claims of superiority abroad – the British continued to divide the world into the inferior races, fit only to be governed, and themselves (and a few others), the naturally (because racially) determined governors of mankind. The degree to which this view was basic to public school education is amply documented but it needs to be stressed that similar views spread widely among even the poorest of children, notably through the teaching at the elementary schools and, less formally, through the popular culture of comics, magazines, penny dreadfuls and popular song. Textbooks – and the lessons based on them – commonly portrayed British achievements as triumphs for the race: 'the bold, frank, sturdy character which so marks the Anglo-Saxon race'. Lord Palmerston, typically, was described as 'cheery, high-spirited and worthily representing the race to which he belonged.'[26] Subject peoples fell into an altogether inferior category. Hindus, it was claimed, were 'an innocent race of men, whose only food is rice, and are maintained for three half pence a day per man'. As late as 1911 a school text book claimed that black West Indians were 'lazy, vicious and incapable of serious improvement or of work unless under compulsion. In such a climate a few bananas will sustain the life of the negro quite sufficiently; why should he work to get more than this?'[27] It is scarcely surprising that well into the twentieth century so many Britons should grow up with a commitment to the racially-determined view of mankind. Indeed, as late as the 1950s when the British Cabinet began to consider restricting West Indian and Indian immigration into Britain, older ministers (themselves Victorians and Edwardians in upbringing and education) expressed views remarkably like those referred to here. 'Coloured' immigration, it was feared, would harmfully change the 'racial stock' of the British people.[28]

At the turn of the century, however, the 'Anglo-Saxon' race seemed to reign supreme: 'so proud-reaching, self-confident and determined, this race which neither climate nor change can degenerate, which will infallibly be the predominant force of future history and universal civilisation.'[29]

Similar views recurred time and again in the literary and political debate about Britain and Britain's role in the world in the years up to 1914. It would be wrong, however, to imagine that this debate was merely abstract or theoretical. It was firmly rooted in the undeniable progress and dominance of a British economy and empire which seemed irresistible. Those educationalists and politicians who needed support for their claim of British superiority needed only to point to the map to clinch their arguments. Imperial advancement in the years before 1914 did not create the racial thought to justify itself, but found, in existing views of race, an ideology which was congruent with the needs of empire. And what better evidence could there be that the British *were* the ascendant 'race' than looking at the course of empire.

The statistics of the British empire were impressive in themselves. By 1907 the empire embraced one-fifth of the world's land surface – some twelve million square miles – home to 400 million people. A nation of forty-one million inhabitants controlled an empire ten times as populous. Although one-eighth of them were white,[30] the rest were the 'beneficiaries' of the urge by the British to transplant their superior civilisation around the world and it was widely assumed, by politicians and colonists, that the course of empire was good for domestic economic well-being – that trade followed the flag. An expansive imperialism was supported from the belief that its attendant commercial impact was vital to the mother country. However, the statistics of overseas trade and even of imported foodstuffs clearly contradicted this view. The lion's share of trade between colonies and metropolis passed between Britain and the old established white colonies,[31] and much of the political debate about the empire consisted of arguments about the nature of the links between Britain and its white colonies – Canada, Australasia and South Africa. That debate was, again, often couched in racial terms; a federation of countries held together by the shared experience of common blood and kinship. When in 1897 white colonial troops paraded in London to celebrate the Queen's Jubilee, the *Daily Mail* remarked that every man was 'such a splendid specimen and testimony to the Greatness of the British Race. . .'.[32]

That self-confidence and assertive commitment to imperial expansion was shaken and checked by the reverses of the Boer War. Not least, alarm was spread by the discoveries of the appalling physical condition of large numbers of volunteers for the British army. In 1900, of 20,292 volunteers, only 14,068 were considered fit to join.[33] Yet here was a war which enabled the British to claim 'that her people were still the finest race on earth'.[34] The domestic consequences of that war compounded some of the uncertainties about the racially-based view of British superiority. Moreover, there was an accumulation of evidence, from other sources, that all was not well with the domestic – particularly the *urban* – heart of the British empire. The publication of Rowntree's study, *Poverty*, in 1901 was but the latest in a series of withering empirical studies about the extent and depth of urban British poverty. The young Winston Churchill was one such deeply impressed by Rowntree's book and its implications: 'For my own part, I see little glory in an Empire which can rule the waves and is unable to flush its own sewers. The difficulty has been so far that the people who have looked abroad have paid no attention to domestic matters, and those who are centred on domestic matters regard the Empire merely as an encumbrance.'[35]

Churchill, an archetypal late-Victorian imperialist who had enjoyed formative youthful experiences in the empire, was but one who came to see the centrality of domestic issues to the well-being and future course of empire.

Rowntree was in a long and well-established tradition of empirical studies of urban poverty; from Henry Mayhew in the mid-century through to Charles Booth in London in the late century, the accumulation of evidence pointed irresistibly to the existence of staggering levels of poverty in British cities. Moreover, Britain was an increasingly urban society; by 1901 eighty per cent of people in England and Wales lived in towns and cities. With levels of urban poverty standing at between one-third to one-fifth, Britain presented an extraordinarily contradictory image, both to itself and to its external critics. The world's leading empire and economy could govern a substantial part of mankind (in the name of superiority: of race, achievement and civilisation) and yet could not guarantee a modicum of material decency to its own people. This contradiction was not new (and had been highlighted by various critics of empire at earlier periods) but by the early years of the twentieth century it was accentuated by the parallel debates about empire (sponsored by the Boer War) and by the debate about domestic social welfare initiated by Rowntree and, after 1906, by the new Liberal government's welfare legislation.

Awareness of material deprivation among the urban poor had been one inspiration behind the urge to encourage athleticism and manliness among the young. The reasons for the development of manliness among public school boys is clear enough. More bemusing is why this concept – specific to a particular educational and social *milieu* – should be extended among working class boys. As we have seen, from the mid-nineteenth century, there was mounting concern about the 'condition of England' as evidence came to hand, from diverse sources, of the human wretchedness in urban life. Moreover, it was equally clear that the young suffered from many of the physical ailments and afflictions worse than adults. Indeed, lingering and fatal illness among the young was an inescapable fact of Victorian society.[36] An increasingly professional medical world steadily accumulated – and published – a mass of ghastly evidence about the physical weaknesses and shortcomings of urban children. Moreover, that data was added to by evidence more broadly available after all the urban young began to attend schools in the last quarter of the century. In 1870 medical observers began to call for physical exercises – drill – among school children as an antidote to a number of widespread ailments.[37] In the last twenty years of the century, physical education made great progress throughout English elementary schools.[38] Of course, these were the years of the extraordinary explosion in mass leisure pursuits in Britain when the British turned to organised games and commerical pleasures to a degree, and in numbers, which amazed contemporaries. With a little more spare cash available and with entrepreneurs actively creating varied commerical entertainments, millions of people now spent their free time at organised leisure – at football, music hall, seaside and the like.

There was, in effect, a congruence of forces propelling people, especially the young, towards a number of leisure forms which had the virtues of being enjoyable and apparently healthy. Games were actively encouraged among working class children by those public school men whose calling – in the churches, schools or simply as voluntary workers drew them into working class life. Ministers and curates, keen to help their flock to lead a better, fuller life and committed to the view that 'the laws of physical well-being are the laws of God',[39] established games, teams, leagues and competitions. Indeed, a substantial number of modern soccer teams began life as church or Sunday school teams. This was a development paralleled in the new school system. Again, the public schools led by example as their ex-pupils – now teachers, heads and administrators – actively promoted their old schools' games in working class communities. There followed a pattern which had been noticeable in public schools a generation earlier. Competitions proliferated among plebeian boys' teams, between schools, leagues and later even between different towns and cities. By the end of the century thousands of spectators paid to watch the finals of schoolboy football matches. How many of those tens of thousands of committed spectators and players knew that the games, the competitions, the trophies and the very enthusiasm were, like the FA Cup itself, inspired and founded by the public schools?

By the turn of the century, the commitment to manly pursuits among working class boys had begun to worry some observers who appreciated its obvious risks: 'Our school competitions in football and other sports have now become a severe tax on the strength of any boy and particularly on the poorly-clad and ill-fed.'[40]

What made football so abidingly popular with young working class boys was, however, its basic attraction: the ease with which it could be organised and played, in most urban areas, with indeterminate numbers. This was, in a sense, a return to the popularity of the game as a *folk* custom though, by the late nineteenth century, overlaid with a new structure and meaning. Boys playing football in the street was a common complaint and a cause of regular and numerous non-indictable juvenile offences.[41] This basic enthusiasm was tapped by energetic and enthusiastic teachers, anxious to direct their pupils' energies into useful channels and to put youthful zest to good ends. When football established itself in schools it often became an attraction, luring boys to, or keeping them at, school. Gradually this enthusiasm persuaded even the most resistant of educationalists that vigorous team games were of great educational and social importance. By 1900, members of staff were instructed to 'teach the most skilful method of play, and should encourage orderly behaviour.' In 1904 the New Code of Regulations for Elementary Schools – prefaced by Robert Moran, himself an ex-Winchester pupil – stated: 'The corporate life of the school, especially in the playground, should develop the instinct for fair play and for loyalty to one another which is the germ of a wider sense of honour in later life.'[42] The physical facilities available remained, in general, poor but could occasionally be supplemented by neighbouring municipal facilities and open spaces, encouraged by associations devoted to acquiring and maintaining public playing fields.

However ill or well-endowed, the playing field or playground was the place where new plebeian footballers were expected to acquire those qualities long familiar to the public school player, and time and again the late century working class game was extolled for the same virtues. In 1893, the headmaster of Loretto thought football and rugby a 'means of testing the manly prowess of representative teams of schools, colleges, clubs, villages or other communities. . .'. A letter in the *Glasgow Herald* a year later claimed that football developed 'physical strength and agility, swiftness of foot, self-control, courage and manliness.' Lord Rosebery, presenting the FA Cup in 1897 claimed that the game encouraged those 'splendid characteristics of the British race – stamina and indomitable pluck.'[43] By the end of the century, major football matches attracted leaders of the main political parties; in a democracy, elected teachers needed to associate themselves with the games of the people. Furthermore, it was even argued that the game healed political divides: 'all Englishmen meet upon common ground for the furtherance of every pursuit which can add to the manliness of the people, or to the available strength and resources of the country.'[44] On the eve of World War I, proponents of football in particular (and of competitive sports in general) imputed to the game a host of extra-ordinary personal and collective qualities. It was viewed as the elixir of personal and social ills – regular doses from an early age would work magical cures – and, in the process, the national good was greatly enhanced; national unity, physical well-being, social harmony and cohesion would be furthered.

It is easy to poke holes in these arguments advanced by sporting enthusiasts in late Victorian and Edwardian Britain but it is important to penetrate behind the smoke-screen of their claims and justifications and to explore the problems for which sport and its associated manliness were claimed as a cure or antidote. Despite the extraordinary power and ascendancy of Britain in the years 1880-1914, there were obvious flaws in the nation's position. At a purely economic level, there was mounting concern at the industrial and commercial threat from Germany and the USA. The initial advantages, acquired by being the first industrial nation, were being eroded in a number of key areas and, while the problem was not widely appreciated, those concerned were anxious to head off the economic challenge by major educational and industrial initiatives. Similarly, and despite Britain's imperial grandeur, there were serious problems posed by the imperial network – a number of them thrown into stark relief by the disasters of the Boer War. The relationship with the white dominions, the economic utility of many recent colonial acquisitions, the sheer burden and complexity of governing so vast a mosaic of peoples and cultures – all this and more posed serious questions about empire, which transcended the pomp and obvious glories of the empire. Furthermore, the difficulties of empire and of British economic performance converged to illustrate a more immediate domestic problem: the nature and

258 MANLINESS AND MORALITY

extent of British poverty and urban destitution. Awareness of the wretchedness of much of working class life was, by the turn of the century,
widespread and raised serious and nagging doubts about the future direction of British domestic and even imperial policy. How could a nation
hope to maintain its economic pre-eminence or its imperial ascendancy in
the teeth of such ubiquitous poverty? How could the challenge from Germany and the USA in particular be repelled when upwards of a third of
the domestic population was trapped in a quagmire of poverty which
diminished their physical activities and stunted their intellectual
ambitions and attainments? And how could the physical challenges of
global ascendancy be met by a nation whose physical well-being was so
corroded? Moreover, these obvious physical problems were in addition
to the separate but related issues of self-confidence, or national ideology.
How could the claims and myths of empire and of industrialism – that
British superiority was rooted in racially-determined national qualities –
be reconciled with the known facts about British poverty and misery?

Sport offered the comforting illusion of continuing effortless superiority and of the means of restoring the nation to good health and mental
security. It was reassuring to believe that the cult of manliness which
underpinned the development of public-school and popular games was a
key agency in this process. There is no doubt that it was a quite remarkably powerful force – an inspiration and belief among successive generations of public school men, who took their proselytising commitment to
games and manliness throughout Britain and around the world – but this
is not to concede that manliness and its attendant games had the effects,
in Britain or overseas, expected of them. Indeed, it is possible to claim
that while the cult of manliness was an unquestionable driving force
behind a veritable army of public school 'missionaries', its attractions
were less obviously appealing to the tens of thousands of players around
the world who quickly adopted the games of their colonial governors or
social betters. Australian cricketers, black South African footballers,
Indian cricketers or British footballers (and the armies of spectators who
watched them) turned to their particular games and sports for a myriad
of reasons. Nor were these reasons necessarily those which inspired the
pioneers and missionaries of the game.

Paradoxical as it may sound, the games and gaming cults of the colonial
masters were themselves to be colonised by indigenous or local peoples
and, at a later date, to be used as a means of asserting national, ethnic or
local identity against the former colonial power. The games which at the
turn of the century were viewed as an indication and a tool of British

superiority, were, within two generations, to become the agency for asserting colonial independence or cultural autonomy against the British themselves. Of course, this belongs to a different phase of modern history, to the world of post-colonial, independent nationhood. But it is worth considering the point that those games and the manly cult which had been viewed as an example of British superiority – an illustration of the power of the British 'race' – were, ultimately, to be used to illustrate the equality of peoples (and sometimes the inferiority of the British). By then, however there could no longer be any doubt that Britain had slipped from its position of global pre-eminence. The nation which, before 1914, seemed to lead the world in most important activities and which gave its sports to great tracts of the world, declined as a successful sporting nation in proportion to its material and international slide from power.

Notes

1 Montague Shearman, *Athletics and Football*, The Badminton Library, London, 1888, pp. 369-70.
2 *Us and our Empire*, London, n.d., Religious Tract Society, p. II.
3 James Walvin, *England, Slaves and Freedom, 1776-1838*, London, 1986.
4 Hugh Tinker, *A New System of Slavery*, London, 1974.
5 J. Campbell, *Hottentot Children*, London, c. 1840; M. A. Hedge, *Sambo; or the African Boy*, London, 1823; *British Sovereigns. A Game*, London, 1836.
6 J. M. MacKenzie, *Propaganda and Empire*, Manchester, 1984.
7 J. A. Mangan, *The Games Ethic and Imperialism*, London, 1986, Ch. I.
8 I. Bowring, *The First Book of Geography for Children*, 1838, p. 46.
9 T. Bilby, *A Course of Lessons*, London, 1823, pp. 94, 85.
10 J. and A. Taylor, *Hymns for Infant Minds*, London, 1812, p. 1.
11 C. Merton, *Funny Foreigners. . .*, London, 1878; M. Read, *Odd People. Or Singular Races of Man*, London, 1860.
12 C. Merton, *Ibid.*, Letter 'Z'.
13 *The Costumes, Manners and Peculiarities of Different Inhabitants of the Globe*, London, 1831.
14 *The World and its Inhabitants*, London, c. 1845.
15 *Geographical Fun*, London, 1868-9.
16 Bernard Porter, *The Lion's Share*, London, 1975, p. 199.
17 See J. A. Mangan, 'Darwinism and English Upper-Class Education, chapter seven, p. 146.
18 *Ibid.*, p. 108.
19 G. Avery, *Childhood's Patterns*, London, 1975, pp. 117-8.
20 *The Boys' Journal*, 1865, II, p. 17.
21 Quoted in D. Newsome, *Godliness and Good Learning*, London, 1961, p. 222.
22 R. Knox, *The Races of Man*, London, 1850, p. v.
23 Quoted in James Walvin, *Passage to Britain*, London, 1884, p. 42.

24   Quoted in Douglas A. Lorimer, *Colour, Class and the Victorians,* Leicester, 1978, p. 101.

25   S. Gilley, 'English Attitudes to the Irish, 1789-1900', in C. Holmes ed., *Immigrants and Minorities in British Society,* London, 1978; L. H. Lees, *Exiles of Erin,* Manchester, 1979.

26   Quoted in James Walvin, 'Recurring themes: white images of black life during and after slavery', *Slavery and Abolition,* V, 2, September 1984, p. 136.

27   Quoted in V. E. Chancellor, *History for their Masters,* Bath, 1970, pp. 118, 122, 124.

28   *The Times,* 2 January 1986.

29   Quoted in V. E. Chancellor *op. cit.,* p. 115.

30   Donald Read, *England, 1868-1914,* London, 1979, p. 360.

31   *Ibid.,* p. 362.

32   Quoted in *Ibid.,* p. 363.

33   R. Price, *An Imperial War and the British Working Class,* London, 1972, p. 196, n. 66.

34   *Ibid.,* p. 1.

35   R. S. Churchill, *Winston Spencer Churchill; Young Statesman,* London, 1967, p. 32.

36   James Walvin, *A Child's World,* London, 1982, Chapters 1-2.

37   F. B. Smith, *The People's Health,* London, 1979, p. 184.

38   J. Lawson and H. Silver, *A Social History of Education in England,* London, 1973, p. 331.

39   Quoted in James Walvin, *The People's Game,* London, 1975, p. 56.

40   Quoted in *Ibid.,* p. 59.

41   Tony Mason, *Association Football and English Society, 1863-1915,* Brighton, 1980, p. 82.

42   Quoted in *Ibid.,* p. 86.

43   Quoted in *Ibid.,* pp. 224-5.

44   Quoted in *Ibid.,* p. 229.

Select bibliography

Chapter one

Bruce Haley, *The Healthy Body and Victorian Culture,* Cambridge, Mass., 1978.

John A. Lucas and Ronald A. Smith, *Saga of American Sport,* Philadelphia, 1978.

James A, Mangan, *Athleticism in the Victorian and Edwardian Public School: The Emergence and Consolidation of an Educational Ideology,* Cambridge, 1981.

John J. MacAloon, *This Great Symbol: Pierre de Coubertin and the Origins of the Modern Olympic Games,* Chicago, 1981.

Donald J. Mrozek, *Sport and American Mentality,* 1880-1910, Knoxville, TN, 1983.

Elizabeth H. Pleck and Joseph H. Pleck, *The American Man,* Englewood Cliffs, NJ, 1980.

Peter Stearns, *Be A Man! Males in Modern Society,* New York, 1979.

James C. Whorton, *Crusaders for Fitness: The History of American Health Reformers,* Princeton, 1982.

Chapter two

Ronald P. Byars, 'The making of the self-made man: the development of masculine roles and images in ante-bellum America', unpublished PH.D. dissertation, Michigan State University, 1979.

Mark Carnes, 'A pilgrimage for light: fraternal ritualism in America', unpublished PH.D. dissertation, Columbia University, 1982.

Peter Filene, *Him/Her/Self: Sex Roles in Modern America,* New York, 1975.

Jeffrey Hantover, 'The Boy Scouts and the validation of masculinity,' in Elizabeth Pleck and Joseph H. Pleck, eds., *The American Man,* Englewood Cliffs, NJ, 1979.

Charles Rosenberg, 'Sexuality, Class, and Role in 19th Century America,' in Elizabeth Pleck and Joseph H. Pleck, eds., *The American Man,* Englewood Cliffs, NJ, 1979.

E. Anthony Rotundo, 'Manhood in America: The Northern Middle Class, 1770-1920,' unpublished Ph.D. dissertation, Brandeis University, 1982.

Mary P. Ryan, *Cradle of the Middle Class: The Family in Oneida County, New York*, 1780-1865, New York, 1981.

Carroll Smith-Rosenberg, 'Sex as symbol in Victorian purity: an ethnohistorical analysis of Jacksonian America,' in John Demos and Sarane Spence Boocock, (eds.), *Turning Points: Historical and Sociological Essays on the Family*, Chicago, 1978.

Chapter three

Norman Vance, *The Sinews of the Spirit: The Ideal of Christian Manliness in Victorian Literature and Religious Thought*, Cambridge, 1985.

David Newsome, *Godliness and Good Learning: Four Studies on a Victorian Ideal*, London, 1961.

Bruce Haley, *The Healthy Body and Victorian Culture*, Cambridge Mass, 1978.

Mark Girouard, *The Return to Camelot: Chivalry and the English Gentleman*, New Haven and London, 1981.

J. A. Mangan, *Athleticism in the Victorian and Edwardian Public School: The Emergence and Consolidation of an Educational Ideology*, Cambridge, 1981.

John Springhall (Ed.), *Sure and Stedfast: A History of the Boys' Brigade*, 1883-1983, Collins, 1983.

Patrick Dunae, 'Boy's Own Paper: origins and editorial policies', *The Private Library*, IX, 4, Winter 1976, pp. 123-58.

Patrick Dunae, 'British juvenile literature in an age of Empire, 1880-1914', Ph.D. 1975, University of Manchester.

Chapter four

Peter N. and Carol Z. Stearns, *Anger: The Struggle for Emotional Control in America's History*, Chicago, 1986.

Peter Filene, *Him/Her/Self: Sex Roles in Modern America*, New York, 1975.

Joseph Kett, *Rites of Passage: Adolescence in America from 1790 to the Present*, New York, 1977.

Jean Baker Miller, *The Construction of Anger in Men and Women*, Wellesley, 1983.

Bernard Wishy, *The Child and the Republic*, New York, 1968.

Philip J. Greven, Jr, *The Protestant Temperament*, New York, 1977.

A. de Swaan, 'The politics of agoraphobia: on changes in emotional and relational management', *Theory and Society*, 10, 1981, pp. 359-85.

Peter N. Stearns with Carol Z. Stearns, 'Emotionology: claryifying the study of the history of emotion,' *American Historical Review*, 90, 1985, pp. 813-36.

Chapter five

Richard Jenkyns, *The Victorians and Ancient Greece*, Oxford, 1981.

Mark Girouard, *The Return to Camelot: Chivalry and the English Gentleman*, New Haven and London, 1981.

David Newsome, *Godliness and Good Learning*, London, 1961.

David Newsome, *On the Edge of Paradise*, London, 1980.

J. R. de S. Honey, *Tom Brown's Universe*, London, 1977.

Jonathan Gathorne-Hardy, *The Public School Phenomenon*, Harmondsworth, 1979.

Martin Green, *Dreams of Adventure, Deeds of Empire*, London, 1980.

Alec Waugh, *Public School Life*, London, 1922.

Chapter six

Paul Boyer, *Urban Masses and Moral Order in America*, 1820-1920, Cambridge, MA, 1978.

Dominick J. Cavallo, *Muscles and Morals: Organized Playgrounds and Urban Reform*, 1880-1920, Philadelphia, 1981.

G. Stanley Hall, *Adolescence*, 2 vols., New York, 1905.

Joseph F. Kett, *Rites of Passage: Adolescence in America*, 1790 to the Present, New York, 1977.

Benjamin G. Rader, *American Sports: From the Age of Folk Games to the Age of Spectators*, Englewood Cliffs, NJ, 1983.

Clarence Rainwater, *They Play Movement in the United States: The Study of Community Recreation*, Chicago, 1922.

Chapter seven

J. A. Mangan, *Athleticism in the Victorian and Edwardian Public School: the Emergence and Consolidation of an Educational Ideology*, Cambridge, 1981.

D. Newsome. *Godliness and Good Learning*, London, 1961.

Gertude Himmelfarb, *Victorian Minds*, London, 1968.

Robert C. Barrister, *Social Darwinism: Science and Myth in Anglo-American Social Thought*, Philadelphia, 1980.

Alec Waugh, *The Loom of Youth*, London, 1917.

T. C. Worsley, *Barbarians and Phillistines*, London, 1940.

F. P. Crozier, *Five Years Hard*, London, 1932.

Chapter eight

A Turning Point in Higher Education: The Inaugural Address of Charles William Eliot as President of Harvard College, Oct. 19, 1869. Cambridge, Mass., 1969.

Anson Phelps Stokes, *Memorials of Eminent Yale Men*, New Haven, Conn., 1915.

James Ballowe, *George Santayana's America: Essays on Literature and Culture,* Urbana, III, 1967.

Clarence Wilkins, *Clarence King: A Biography,* New York, 1958.

G. Edward White, *The Eastern Establishment and the Western Experience: The West of Frederic Remington, Theodore Roosevelt, and Owen Wister,* New Haven 1968.

Peter H. Hassrick, *Frederic Remington: Paintings, Drawings, and Sculpture in the Amon Carter Museum and the Sid W. Richardson Foundation Collections,* New York, 1973.

Harriet Hinsdale and Tony London, *Frank Merriwell's 'Father': An Autobiography, Norman, Oklahoma,* 1964.

Owen Johnson, *Stover at Yale,* New York, 1968.

Chapter nine

R. S. S. Baden-Powell, *Scouting for Boys,* London, 1908.

Theodore Roosevelt, *Ranch Life and the Hunting Trail,* Gloucester, 1985. (reprint of the 1896 edition).

Willie Orr, *Deer Forests, Landlords, and Crofters, the Western Highlands in Victorian and Edwardian Times,* Edinburgh, 1982.

John Ross, *The Book of the Red Deer and Empire Big Game,* London, 1925.

R. S. S. Baden-Powell, *Pig Sticking or Hog Hunting,* London, 1924.

F. C. Selous, *African Nature Notes and Reminiscences,* London, 1908.

Sir Frederick Jackson, *Early Days in East Africa,* London, 1969, first 1930.

Patrick A. Dunae, 'British juvenile literature in an age of Empire, 1880-1914', unpublished ph.·. thesis, University of Manchester, 1975.

Chapter ten

John Springhall, *Youth, Empire and Society, British Youth Movements,* 1883-1940, London 1977.

William Hillcourt with Olave, Lady Baden-Powell, *Baden-Powell, The Two Lives of a Hero,* London, 1964.

Henry Collis, Fred Hurll and Rex Hazlewood, *B-P's Scouts: An Official History of The Boy Scouts Association,* London, 1961.

R. S. S. Baden-Powell, *Scouting for Boys: A Handbook for Instruction in Good Citizenship,* London, 1908. There are many later and often heavily revised editions of Baden-Powell's original, of which the best is the facsimile of the original published in 1957 to celebrate the centenary of his birth with a forward by Lord Rowallan.

R. S. S. Baden-Powell, *Rovering to Success: A Book of Life-Sport for Young Men,* London, 1922. There are again many later and revised editions.

Allen Warren, 'Sir Robert Baden-Powell, the Scout movement and citizen training in Great Britain, 1900-1920', *English Historical Review,* CI, April 1986, pp. 56-78; 'Citizens of the Empire: Baden-Powell,Scouts and Guides and an imperial ideal', in John M. MacKenzie (ed.), *Imperialism and Popular Culture,* Manchester 1986.

Chapter eleven

Lawrence W. Fielding, 'Sport as a Training Technique in the Union Army.' *The Physical Educator,* 34, October 1977, pp. 145-52.

Joseph F. Kett, *Rites of Passage, Adolescence in America,* 1790 to the Present, New York, 1977.

T. J. Jackson Lears, *No Place of Grace, Antimodernism and the Transformation of American Culture,* 1800-1920, New York 1981, especially concerning militarism as a form of 'bourgeois self-reformation.'

Guy Lewis, 'The military Olympics at Paris, France, 1919, *The Physical Educator,* 31, December 1974, pp. 172-5.

Guy Lewis, 'World War 1 and the emergence of sport for the masses, *The Maryland Historian* 4, Fall 1973, pp. 109-22.

Donald J. Mrozek, 'Sport and the American military: diversion and duty', *Research Quarterly for Exercise and Sport, Centennial Issue,* April 1985, pp. 38-45.

Peter N. Stearns, *Be a Man! Males in Modern Society,* New York 1977.

Russell F. Weigley, *The American Way of War,* New York 1973.

Chapter twelve

C. Bolt, *Victorian Attitudes to Race,* London, 1971.

V. E. Chancellor, *History for their Masters,* Bath, 1970.

Douglas A. Lorimer, *Colour, Class and the Victorians,* Leicester, 1978.

J. M. MacKenzie, *Propaganda and Empire,* Manchester, 1984.

J. A. Mangan, *The Games Ethic and Imperialism,* London, 1986.

Index

action, 10, 36, 38
Acton, Lord, 93
Adams, Henry, 162-5
adolescence, 105-7, 125
Adolescence, 27-8, 127
Aelred of Rievaulx, 96-7, 102, 112
Africa, 176-8, 184-6, 193, 243, 245, 247
'African Lion', 192
agnosticism, 145
aggression, 84-5, 87
Aids to Scouting, 201
Alcott, Bionson, 16
Alcott, William A., 16
Alexander, 93
Alger, Horatio, 81
Allan Quatermain, 181, 191
Almond, Hely Hutchinson, 144
Amazon, 192
Ambrose, 96
American Annals of Education, 14, 16
American Association for the Advancement
   of Physical Education, 8, 12, 25-7
American Campfire Girls, 125
American Expeditionary Force, 230
American Historical Association, 130
American Institute of Child Life, 81
American Journal of Education, 14, 25
American Quarterly Review, 13
Amherst College, 28
anger, 77-88; channelling of, 82-6; and child
   rearing, 79-88; concealment of, 87; con-
   trol, 77-9; and gender, 78-80, 83, 85-7;

and moral indignation, 82, 86-7; posi-
   tive, 81-2
Anglican Church, 62
anomie, 221
Anstey, F., 106
anthropometry, 19, 22, 26, 28-9, 40-1
anti-intellectualism, 203
Apache, the, 228
Archer, Geoffrey, 187
Aristotle, 95-6, 102
Arnoldianism, 140
Arnold, Matthew, 145, 162
Arnold, Thomas, 4, 54, 61, 63, 102-3, 112
athleticism, 61-3, 66-7, 103, 105, 141, 189, 202,
   248-50, 258
athletics, 9-12, 18-22, 127, 129 *see also* games,
   sport
Atlantic Ocean, 245
Austen, Jane, 109
Australasia, 178, 193, 253
Australia, 247
Avon County Reference Library, 61

Baden-Powell, R. S. S., 53, 68, 102, 107, 176-
   8, 186-8, 192-3, 200-3, 205-7, 212-13
Badminton Library, 178
Baffin Land, 192
Balestier, Wolcott, 108
Ballantyne, R. M., 62-3, 65, 190-1
Balliet, T. M., 25
Bancroft, George, 15
Banner, Lois, 223